THE COMPLETE PATIENCE BOOK

Also available in Pan Books

Bridge for Beginners
Victor Mollo and Nico Gardener

How to Play a Good Game of Bridge
Terence Rees and Albert Dormer

Commonsense Bridge
Rixi Markus

The Pan Book of Card Games
Hubert Phillips

Waddingtons Family Card Games
Robert Harbin

THE COMPLETE
PATIENCE BOOK

BASIL DALTON

Pan Books London and Sydney

First published 1948 by John Baker Publishers Ltd
This edition published 1967 by
Pan Books Ltd, Cavaye Place, London SW10 9PG
8th printing 1975
© John Baker Publishers Ltd, 1964
ISBN 0 330 30041 5

Printed and bound in Great Britain by
Cox & Wyman Ltd, London, Reading and Fakenham

CONTENTS

PAGE

Part One:

Single Pack Patience . . . 17

Part Two:

Double Pack Patience . . . 63

Part Three:

Patience Problems and Puzzles . 167

FOREWORD

IN round numbers some three hundred and fifty varieties of Patience were examined before this selection (with its sequel: *Double Pack Patience*) was made.

These range from the ingenuously inane to the ingeniously irritating, so here should be food for every taste; but, one and all, if approached in the spirit of the real Patience player, they demand that rarest form of honesty – mental honesty with oneself. Herein, if anywhere, lies the moral value of Patience. Whether it be a mental sedative may well be questioned. It can certainly be made to pass time. The great majority of us do not want to think hard, especially in our relaxations – which is why more people enjoy Nap than Chess! – but many of us like to *think* we are thinking, and so find a mental titillation in bringing a Patience to a successful conclusion.

Those who recall H. M. Bateman's little drawing called 'The Colonel's Patience' will recognize therein one familiar type of player. The Colonel WILL NOT cheat, we know. We know he WILL NOT swear; but we also know from the frigid terror on the face of his wife as she sits on an adjacent ottoman that the game had much better do as it is told and 'come out' or the fish at dinner will be denounced as 'a disgrace to a Bloomsbury boarding-house!'

And who has not met the dear lady in one of Mr E. F. Benson's novels, who, playing Miss Milligan every night after dinner, if faced with obstinate cards, begins with unfailing regularity to cheat ten minutes before Evening Family Prayers are timed to take place; so that her triumphant solution and sweeping up of the pack may synchronize with the servants' entrance?

It is hoped that those who use this book will find the descriptions clear – which is more than the author can say for some of the books he has consulted.

CONTENTS: PART ONE

	PAGE
Some Patience Terms Defined	16
Agnes	19
Alternate	19
Bisley	20
Block Eleven	21
Brigade	22
Burleigh	22
The Carpet	23
Clock	23
Contending Knights	24
Corner	25
Court Puzzle	25
Cribbage	26
Czarina	27
The Demon	28
{ Superior Demon	29
{ Demon Fan	30
Divorce	31
Doublets	31
Florentine	31
The Flower Garden	32
Following	33
Fours	33
Golf	35
King Albert	36
Ladies' Battle	37
Lady Betty	37
Martha	38
The Missing Link	38
Monte Carlo	39
Nines	39
Ninety-one	40
Number Eleven	40
Oracle	41
Pairs	42

Poker   42
Puss in the Corner   43
Quadrille   43
Queen and Her Lad   44
Reverse Puzzle   44
Rosamund's Bower   45
Seventh Wonder   45
Sir Tommy   46
Spanish   46
Sprint   47
Stone-wall   47
Ten to Five Puzzle   48
Tower of Hanoy   48
Travellers   49
Triple Alliance or Triplets   49
Vanbrugh   50
York and Lancaster   51

APPENDICES

APPENDIX

   I.   Agnes (Specimen Game)   52
  II.   Bisley (Specimen Game)   53
 III.   Brigade (Specimen Game)   54
  IV.   Court Puzzle (Solution)   54
   V.   The Flower Garden (Specimen Game) 55
  VI.   King Albert (Specimen Game)   55
 VII.   Ninety-one (Specimen Game)   57
VIII.   Puss in the Corner (Specimen Game) 58
  IX.   Reverse Puzzle (Solution)   59
   X.   Stone-wall (Specimen Game)   60
  XI.   Ten to Five Puzzle (Solution)   61
 XII.   Tower of Hanoy (Arrangement)   61

CONTENTS: PART TWO

	PAGE
Above and Below	67
Backbone	69
Battalion	71
Bezique (*see* Persian)	
Blockade (British)	73
Cock o' the North	76
Corona, The, or Round Dozen	77
Diamond	79
Display	80
Double Fan, The	81
Double Pyramid, The	83
Emperor, The	84
Four Corner	87
Four Marriages, The	88
Gemini	88
General's, The	89
Giant (*see* Miss Milligan)	
Grandfather's	91
Grandmamma's	91
Grandfather's Clock	92
Grand Round	95
Haden	96
Harp, The	97
Hat, The	98
Heads and Tails	101
Heap	102
Herring Bone	103
Intrigue or Picture Gallery	105
King's Patience	106
K C	107
King's Way	108
Limited	109
Mathematics (*see* Senior Wrangler)	
Milton	110
Miss Milligan	112

Number Fourteen	114
Octave	114
Odds and Evens	115
Persian (Bezique)	116
Picture Gallery (*see* Intrigue)	
Right and Left	118
Round Dozen (*see* The Corona)	
Rovers	119
Royal Parade or Procession	121
Russian	123
'S'	124
St Helena	125
Senior Wrangler	127
Snake, The	129
Spider, The	130
Squaring the Circle	132
Sultan, The	133
Three Up (*see* Royal Parade)	
Wheat-ear	134
Wheel of Fortune	135
Windmill, The	136

APPENDICES

APPENDIX		PAGE
I.	Above and Below (Game and Solution)	138
II.	Backbone (Solution)	140
III.	Battalion (Solution)	141
IV.	British Blockade (Solution and Game)	142
V.	Corona (Solution)	143
VI.	Double Fan (Solution)	144
VII.	Double Pyramid (Solution)	145
VIII.	Emperor, The (Solution and Game)	146
IX.	General's, The (Solution)	148
X.	Grandfather's Clock (Solution)	150
XI.	Harp, The (Solution)	151
XII.	Hat, The (Solution)	152

XIII.	Heap (Solution)	154
XIV.	KC (Solution)	155
XV.	Limited (Solution)	157
XVI.	Miss Milligan (Solution and Game)	158
XVII.	Persian (Solution)	159
XVIII.	Right and Left (Solution)	159
XIX.	Russian (Solution)	161
XX.	Snake, The (Solution)	162
XXI.	Spider, The (Solution)	163
XXII.	Sultan, The (Solution)	164

CONTENTS: PART THREE

PROBLEMS	PAGE
Battalion I	169
Battalion II	169
Bisley I (Single Pack)	170
Bisley II	170
The British Blockade I	170
The British Blockade II	170
The Emperor I	171
The Emperor II	172
The General I	173
The General II	174
Grandfather's Clock	174
Grandmamma's	175
The Harp	176
The Hat I	176
The Hat II	177
Heads and Tails	178
Heap	178
King Albert I (Single Pack)	179
King Albert II	179
Limited I	180
Limited II	180
Milton	181
Miss Milligan I	181
Miss Milligan II	182
Persian I	183
Persian II	183
Russian I	184
Russian II	184
'S'	185
Senior Wrangler I	185
Senior Wrangler II	186
The Spider I	188
The Spider II	189
Squaring the Circle	190

Superior Demon I (Single Pack)   191
Superior Demon II   191

SOLUTIONS

Battalion I   192
Battalion II   193
Bisley I   193
Bisley II   194
The British Blockade I   194
The British Blockade II   196
The Emperor I   197
The Emperor II   198
The General I   199
The General II   201
Grandfather's Clock   202
Grandmamma's   203
The Harp   204
The Hat I   205
The Hat II   206
Heads and Tails   207
Heap   208
King Albert I   209
King Albert II   209
Limited I   210
Limited II   212
Milton   213
Miss Milligan I   214
Miss Milligan II   215
Persian I   215
Persian II   216
Russian I   216
Russian II   217
'S'   218
Senior Wrangler I   219
Senior Wrangler II   220
Spider I   221
Spider II   222

Squaring the Circle   222
Superior Demon I   224
Superior Demon II   224

TRICK AND PUZZLE PATIENCES

Patience Squares
   The Sixteen Square (Two Variations)   225
   The Thirty-six Square   225
   The Sixty-four Square   226
   Pips   226
   The Mysterious Deal   227
Sequences
   The Alternate Sequence   228
   The Ohio Cut   229
   The Spelling Sequence   229
   The French Spelling Sequence   230
   The Piquet Point   230
Ten to Five Puzzle   231
Solutions to the Squares   231

SOME PATIENCE TERMS DEFINED

BASE-CARD. – The card which forms the foundation of a packet.

BUILDING. – Placing cards on the base-packets in different varieties of sequence.

COLUMN. – Cards placed perpendicularly – one immediately below the other.

CHOCKERED. – Cards are said to be 'chockered' when they are blocked by any cards that by the laws of the particular game they cannot be used for packing or building.

EXPOSED CARDS. – Cards at the bottom of columns, such as have no cards below them.

FAMILY. – All the cards of the same suit.

FAN. – Cards arranged in open formation like a fan; the right-hand one is the exposed card.

LAY-OUT. – The original order in which the cards are laid on the table in any particular game.

MARRIAGE. – Two cards of consecutive value placed together.

PACKING. – Placing cards on the exposed ones in the lay-out.

ROW. – Cards placed horizontally; side by side.

RUBBISH-HEAP. – A packet made up of cards which cannot be placed either on base-packets or exposed cards in the lay-out.

SEQUENCE. – Cards following one another in proper rotation, but not necessarily of the same suit.

STOCK. – A number of cards counted out at the beginning of a game, packed apart to be used as directed by the particular laws of that game.

VACANCY. – An empty space made in the top row of the lay-out.

WAIVING*. – Lifting a card, and using the one beneath it.

WORRYING-BACK*. – Returning cards from base-packets to the lay-out (generally to make possible further building on the exposed cards of the lay-out).

* Special privileges limited to a few games.

Part One

SINGLE PACK PATIENCE

AGNES

DEAL out twenty-eight cards from the pack in seven rows,
seven cards in the top-row, six in second, five in third, down
to a single card at the bottom of the inverted triangle. The
twenty-ninth card is the first of the bases, and it and its three
fellows are to be built up in ascending suit-sequence. The other
three base-cards are put out as soon as available; immediately,
if they happen to be exposed in the lay-out.

'Exposed' cards are the bottom-cards of each column (which,
of course, change whenever a card is built or packed). These
can either be built on a foundation packet or packed on each
other in descending sequence, red suit on either red suit, black
suit on either black suit. Sequences can be shifted *en bloc*,
if they consist of the same suit. After doing all the packing and
building possible deal *seven* more cards, one at the foot of
each column, starting from the bottom row and filling vacant
rows, if any have been made. These new cards must all come
into play and be placed before any card is moved. If you make
a vacant column it can, but *need not*, be filled by an exposed
card before dealing again.

No second deal is allowed, and the odds against success
are estimated at 6 or 7 to 1.

(A game is worked out in Appendix I.)

ALTERNATE

TAKE out the Ace of Hearts, the King of Clubs, the Ace of
Diamonds and the King of Spades, arranging them from left
to right in that order to form foundations for columns to be
built on in alternate colours, but from the Aces in ascending,
from the Kings in descending sequence. Thus success implies
the Ace-columns ending in red Kings, the King-columns in
black Aces. Deal the cards into four rubbish-heaps, keeping a
wary eye not to miss chances of building.

When the pack is exhausted gather up the rubbish-heaps

without shuffling and re-form them. Much can be done by the
way in which you play on the rubbish-heaps, especially the
second round. Remember that the black Aces, Queens and
Threes, the red Kings, Deuces and Jacks won't be wanted till
the end, but of course without a friendly run of the cards
you're done.

You will probably find the opposite sequences very con-
fusing, and must keep very alert.

BISLEY

ONE of the better games. Lay out the whole pack in four rows,
each of thirteen cards. In the first four places of the top-row
put the four Aces. After completing the board you can only
play at first from the bottom-row. If there are any Deuces
there, take them out and place on their proper Aces; if any
Kings, take out and form a row beneath.

The Aces are to be built up in ascending sequence, the
Kings in descending, each in their proper suit.

On the board itself you may pack in either upward or
downward suit-sequence only with 'exposed' cards (i.e. cards
with none below them), but this packing may be altered at
pleasure; e.g. suppose you have an 8 with a 6 underneath it,
while somewhere else on the board is an exposed 5. On this 5
the 6 may be packed, and if a 7 afterwards turns up, it can be
placed on the 8, and the 6 and 5 transferred to the eight-packet.
Thus:

Move (2) under (3), (4) under (1), (2) back again under (4),
(3) under (2). Never miss an opportunity of building on the

Aces upwards, downwards on the Kings, and when the two sequences meet, put them together as a finished packet.

Some care is required in packing to avoid a 'cross-block', i.e. a high card blocking a considerably lower one in one column, and a low card blocking a higher one in another column, all in the same suit. Such a combination occurring in the lay-out, success may be seen to be impossible from the outset; for in this game you have not the privilege of moving a card into a vacancy made in the top row. Inspect, therefore, the lay-out carefully before beginning to pack, anticipating as far as you can the results of your proposed moves; for, although every card moved sets free the one above it, a card packed on blocks its column until unloaded.

Novices will find it useful

(1) to free Kings as soon as possible if there are none to start with in the bottom line.

(2) taking the special lie of the cards into consideration, to build upwards (roughly) from the 8, downwards from the 7.

(*See* Appendix II for two games worked out in full.)

BLOCK ELEVEN

LAY out nine cards in three rows of three. If any two cards among these nine make eleven, by 'pips', e.g. a 10 and an Ace, a 9 and a 2, a 4 and a 7, deal a card on each. Court cards don't come in; but if a King, a Queen and a Knave are on the board together, deal a card on all three.

If at any time no two of the nine top-cards make eleven, neither are there the three court cards on the board, you are blocked, but there remains the privilege of putting one card on the centre packet. This may, and often does, open fresh combinations and start you again. If it doesn't, the Patience has failed, and all you can do is to shuffle and start again.

The nine cards in the lay-out below could all be covered:

9 of Diamonds.	J. of Spades.	3 Clubs.
K of Hearts.	8 of Spades.	5 Diamonds.
2 of Clubs.	6 of Hearts.	Q of Hearts.

(cp. Number Eleven Patience.)

BRIGADE

LAY out five rows of seven cards, making seven columns of
five cards, placing the Aces below, as they occur, to form
foundations. These foundations to be built upwards in suit-
sequence. The thirteen cards that remain ($52 - 35 - 4 = 13$) are
called the 'Reserve', and may be laid out above the columns,
or simply held in the hand.

Next pack as much as possible by moving 'Exposed' cards
(for 'exposed' *see* Definitions) from column to column, regardless of suit but in descending order only. You may move
exposed cards backwards and forwards, pack and unpack at
will, and use the Reserve whenever it suits your packing and
building. You may also place any exposed card in the vacancy
formed if you can dispose of an entire column; and, as a last
hope, should both packing and building come to an end you
may place *one* exposed card in the Reserve, provided that the
Reserve contains the card next higher to the one you move.
A card once placed on the Ace-foundations cannot be taken
back for sequence convenience in the lay-out, i.e. there is no
'worrying-back' (*see* Definitions).

Clearly the higher card you get at the head of your lay-out
sequences the better.

(*See* Appendix III for a game fully worked out.)

BURLEIGH

LAY out two rows of six cards each: Aces, as they turn up, to
be placed apart to form foundations and be built up in ascending suit-sequence to their respective Kings. On the twelve
cards of the lay-out form suit-sequences either ascending or
descending. If any of the first twelve cards can do this, arrange
them so before turning up the top-card of the pack. Place
this, if available, in its sequence. Go on like this till a card
comes along which won't go anywhere on the board. This you
lay face-upwards, and take the next card from the *bottom* of

the pack. Go on from the bottom till a vacancy is made on the board where the rejected card can go, then take the top-card again. If both top- and bottom-card are failures, you're done; but two or more cards may be transferred from one packet to another packet if in sequence with *either its top- or bottom-card*.

But here comes in the distinctive feature of this Patience: you are assumed to be on honour not to look at the covered cards in any packet to see if a transference is possible. You must trust entirely to memory; and, naturally, if you have made a mistake, it will appear when you start building up.

THE CARPET

LAY out twenty cards face-upwards in four rows of five cards each – these are the 'Carpet'. Place the four Aces below, as they appear, for foundations to be built in upward suit-sequence to their Kings. Should any Deuces appear in the Carpet, place them on their proper Aces and the same with threes, etc., in their due sequence, filling their places in the carpet by the cards from stock.

After this deal the cards from stock face-upwards to a waste-heap. The top-card of the waste-heap may always be played if suitable to one of the sequences; and as long as there are any cards in the waste-heap they are to be used for filling up vacancies in the Carpet in preference to cards from the stock. No second deal is allowed as the chances of success and failure are about 'evens'.

CLOCK

LAY out face-upwards a dozen cards dealt from the shuffled pack in the form of the diagram on p. 24. When court-cards occur place them underneath the pack in your hand. Proceed by placing cards from the top of the pack on any two cards which added together make eleven (as 7 and 4, 10 and Ace) until the pack is finished.

If successful, you will have a court-card left to cover each packet in the original clock-face.

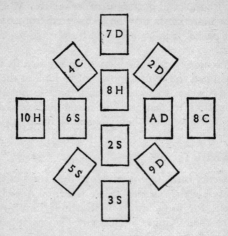

CONTENDING KNIGHTS

ARRANGE the four Knaves in a row in the following order: Heart, Club, Diamond, Spade.

Deal four cards from the rest of the pack; the red Knaves take the even cards, the black Knaves the odd cards (Queens count as odd, Kings as even).

The Knave of Hearts has first shot, he takes the 'evens' out of the first four cards dealt, and they are placed below him. More cards are dealt to make the line up to four, and the Club Knave's turn comes next; and so on with evens for the Diamond Knave, odds for the Spade. If a Knave cannot take any cards when his turn comes (e.g. all odds in the line for the Diamond Knave) his turn passes to the next. If he sweeps the lot (e.g. four odd cards in the line when the Knave of Spades' turn comes), he receives one each from the other Knaves' piles. (Of course this penalty can't be exacted on the first deal of all.)

When the pack is played out, reckon up each Knave's pile, and score all over twelve to the respective owner.

Shuffle the pack well and repeat the game twice. The Knave with the highest score at the end of the third round wins.

An inane game!

CORNER

LAY out three rows of cards, three in each row. The first card laid out is placed in the left-hand top corner, and determines the four base-cards, i.e. if an 8 be the first card, the other three corners of the oblong to be eventually formed remain vacant till the other 8's turn up. These bases are to be built up in *ascending* suit-sequences.

You need not fill the other five spaces all at once. Upon the other five cards you pack *downwards* without attention to suit or colour; and, if in sequence, cards may be moved about from one of these five packs to another to make vacancies or get at buried cards.

Vacancies can be filled from the rubbish-heap. By the strict rule you may not have a second turn at the rubbish-heap, so to win success care is required in packing.

Naturally in the five free places you will not want cards immediately lower than the bases, e.g. if your corner-cards be 8's you will not want 7's on the board, for they will be the last to work off.

COURT PUZZLE

TAKE the Aces, Kings, Queens and Knaves from a pack. Place them in four rows each of four cards in such a way that the sequence King, Queen, Knave, Ace or Ace, Knave, Queen, King shall make up each side of your quadrilateral (horizontally and perpendicularly), and one of each denomination be found in the two middle rows.

(For solution *see* Appendix IV.)

CRIBBAGE

THE game stands to Cribbage much as Poker Patience*
stands to Poker. Sixteen cards are dealt face-upwards, one at
a time, the pack, of course, being kept face-downwards. Each
card is placed face-upwards on the table, and each subsequent
card must be placed next to the one already on the table,
directly above or below, or by the side or touching at the
corner (in fact, the King's move at Chess). Eventually you get
an Oblong with four cards a side. The seventeenth card from
the pack becomes the 'turn-up card', and the score of the four
rows from left to right *plus* the four columns from top to
bottom is reckoned according to the rules of six-card
Cribbage.†

If the turn-up, or seventeenth card, happens to be of the
same suit, a flush counting 4 in either row or column becomes
worth 5. If the turn-up card is a Knave, he does not score
'one for his heels'; but in the lay-out a Knave of the same suit
as the turn-up scores 'one for his nob', both in his row and in
his column. A maximum score of 172 could be made thus:

				Horizontal Score
H 6	: D 6	: S 4	: C 4	=24
H 4	: D 4	: S 6	: C 6	=24
H 5	: D 5	: S 5	: C 10	=28
H Jack	: D Jack	: S Jack	: C Jack	=21

Turn-up Card C5

$$97 + 75 = 172.$$

Vertical Score
20   20   20   15

Rows I and II score 8 for four fifteens, 12 for four runs of
three and 4 for two pairs.

Row III. 8 for the four fifteens with the 10 of Clubs, 8 for
four fifteens of fives only and 12 for six pairs.

Row IV. 8 for four fifteens, 12 for six pairs, and 1 for his
nob.

* *See* Poker Patience, *infra.*
† *See* my book, *Ten Best Card Games for Two.*

Cols. I, II, and III. 8 for four fifteens, 6 for two runs of three, 4 for the flush, 2 for the pair.

Col. IV. 6 for three fifteens, 3 for a run of three, 5 for a flush, 1 for his nob.*

The game can be adapted for two or more players, each having his own pack of cards, though whether any two Cribbage players will prefer the shadow to the substance is – at least – doubtful.

CZARINA

THE first card turned up from the pack is a base-card and placed in, say, the top left-hand corner of the board. The other three of the same denomination fill the other corners as they appear.

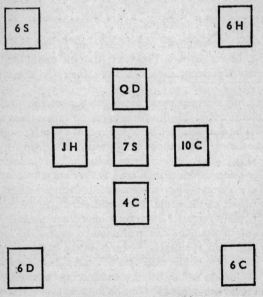

* Mr W. T. Quine has shown this.

Form the lay-out by placing five cards as in the diagram (*see* p. 27).

Base-cards are built up in ascending suit-sequence, lay-out cards packed downwards without regard to suit. Cards may be moved from one board-packet to another if value allows: all vacancies to be filled from the pack.

Success implies that when all the pack is played the cards on the board will all have been absorbed in suits by the base-cards at the corners. But failing this you have one privilege, and gathering up the rubbish-heap may turn and lay down the first and second card. If either can be placed, play can be continued; if neither, 'finis Poloniae'. Skill has nothing to do with the game: it is merely a matter of the lie of the cards, but it possesses the saving grace of irritation.

THE DEMON

THIS game is generally considered one of the best, if not *the* best, of single-pack Patiences, though undoubtedly the comparatively recent *King Albert* is a finer and more skilful game.

Count off thirteen cards from the top of the pack, and place them on the table in a packet face-upwards: these are the 'stock'. The next four cards are laid out in a row face-upwards to be heads of columns. The eighteenth card forms the first base and is placed above the first column. The three cards of the same denomination are placed as they come to hand over the other columns. The remaining cards form the reserve.

The object of the game is to build sequences up from the bases in their proper suits, the columns are packed downwards also in sequence, but in alternate colours. The top-card of the stock can, if suitable, be built on the bases or columns at any time. One of the essentials of success is to get through the stock as soon as may be. One column can be transferred to another if the top-card of the one be the next lower in sequence but of alternate colour to the bottom-card of the other.

The top-card of stock fills the vacant place to start another column.*

After the lay-out and the immediate arrangements possible, take the three top-cards of the reserve in a packet and turn over the packet so that the third card comes first face-upwards. It may be able to go on one of the bases or columns, and then the second of the packet is treated similarly and the third. But if the first can be placed nowhere, take another packet of three cards from the reserve, and so on, till you have exhausted it.

Then gather up all the cards you have not been able to play, and, without shuffling, turn over three at a time as before. When the reserve is reduced to two cards you may play either.

If you have a choice between playing a card on base or column, choose the base; but not always.

One 'grace', and one only, is allowed – once only you may transfer the top-card of any one of the bases to the bottom of one of the columns ('worry-back' in fact); and this will sometimes get you out of a block.

Success comes with the completion of the bases, or is implied when the columns and bases have absorbed between them both stock and reserve.

SUPERIOR DEMON

Faute de mieux let the title stand. The differences between this and the older form (see last game) are that –

(1) The 'stock' is *not* placed in a complete packet with only the top-card for the time being exposed, but all thirteen cards are shown in column. Sometimes this will help your play, sometimes you will be able to see from the beginning that you can't succeed.

(2) A vacancy in the four columns need not be filled up at

---

* This must be done at once, i.e. a column may not be left vacant. When for this purpose stock is exhausted, the top card of the Reserve is taken to head the new column. Cp. the greater freedom of Superior Demon.

once from stock, but can remain open for a suitable card coming along.

(3) Whole or *part* of a sequence can be moved from one column to another.

Some authorities regard these changes as 'improvements on the original game, which allowed no power of choice and gave, therefore, no scope for the exercise of judgement'.

They certainly make it easier to circumvent the Demon: whether this is an improvement is a matter of opinion.

DEMON FAN

LAY out the whole pack in sixteen 'fans' (*see* 'Patience Terms Defined') of three cards each, two face-downwards, the third face-upwards, and two fans of two cards each, one card concealed, the other exposed. Lay out in four rows of the three-card fans, the fifth row taking the two smaller fans. The game consists in releasing the Aces and building up from them in suit-sequence to the Kings.

From the exposed cards remove any Aces and sequence-cards, each card removed causing the one beneath it in the fan to become exposed. Build on the remainder in downward-sequence but alternate colour. It is wiser not to do this to any great extent until you get to the bottom card of the fan; for, though the cards may be moved from one fan to another, they may only be moved singly, and if a whole fan be got rid of on one of the bases you gain nothing in the way of being allowed to fill up the vacancy.

When all possible packing and building is done, gather up the exposed cards, and deal again in fans starting from the lowest line, so also with the concealed cards, but in both cases without shuffling.

Any two cards over are treated as in the first deal, a single card being left face-upward. Pack and build as before. By this time, if you are likely to succeed, all the Aces should be out.

Seven deals are allowed, but even so failure is frequent.

An intriguing game!

DIVORCE

BEGIN by forming four rubbish-heaps, placing the Aces in a row above and their respective Deuces in a row below, as they turn up. Each of these eight foundations is built up in alternate numbers and alternate colours, e.g. a red Ace is followed by a black 3, then a red 5; a black Deuce by a red 4, then a black 6. Thus the Ace-bases will end in Kings, the Deuce-bases in Queens, and in the event of success the Kings and Queens will be found wrongly mated. (Hence the game's title.)

You may only go through the pack once, so care must be taken with the packing of the rubbish-heaps. Keep one for Kings and Queens, and avoid as far as you can putting higher even cards over lower even ones, higher odd over lower odd.

DOUBLETS

LAY out twelve packets of three cards face-downwards, followed by one exposed card on each packet. Lay aside the remaining four cards face-downwards.

Search through the exposed cards for pairs (doublets). These you throw out, turning up the under ones. If a vacancy occurs through the whole of a packet having been thrown out turn up one of the reserve cards to fill it.

You will fail unless by the time the fourth (and last) card of the reserve is turned up you have arranged all the pack into doublets.

FLORENTINE

LAY out five cards in the form of a cross, the sixth card and the three others of the same denomination form the bases to be placed in the corners as they turn up, and are built on in ascending suit-sequence. The four outer cards of the cross are to be packed in downward-sequence without regarding suit.

If one of these cards be removed either on a base or for packing on another heap, (1) the vacancy can be filled from the rubbish-heap, or (2) if preferred, the centre card of the cross may be moved into the space and the card from the rubbish-heap into the middle. But this centre card may not at any time be packed on.

You may turn the rubbish-heap once.

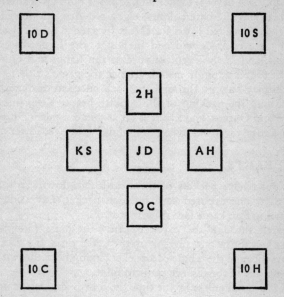

THE FLOWER GARDEN

ONE of the better games. Lay out six 'fans' (*see* Terms Defined) of six cards each, face-upwards. These are the flower-beds and the card at the right-hand end of each bed is exposed. The remaining sixteen cards are kept in hand and are called the 'bouquet', which may conveniently be sorted into suits. Your aim is to get out the Aces as foundations and to build on them in ascending suit-sequences to their Kings.

Any card can be taken from the bouquet, but only the for-the-time outer card from each bed. After taking out any Aces and subsequent cards that may be immediately available, build on the exposed cards in downward sequence *not regarding suits*. Exposed sequences may be moved bodily whenever they fit from one bed to another; cards from the bouquet may at any time be taken to help in forming sequences.

If a flower-bed be completely cleared you can fill the space either from the bouquet, or by an exposed card or sequence from another bed.

(*See* Appendix V for game fully worked out.)

FOLLOWING

A GOOD exercise in concentration, for the cards can only be placed, packed or built in one rotation of the suits, viz. Hearts, Clubs, Diamonds, Spades. On a Heart only a Club can be placed, on a Diamond a Spade, on a Spade a Heart. One mistake in this and success is out of the question.

Lay out six cards on the board: if any can be packed in a downward sequence do so, filling vacant spaces from the pack. As the Aces turn up either now, or when you commence the rubbish-heap, place them above the board in the order Hearts, Clubs, Diamonds, Spades from left to right. Build on these in upward sequence (though you pack on the board in downward), but *still in the same rotation*. Thus the Ace of Diamonds can only be covered by the Deuce of Spades, the Deuce of Spades by the 3 of Hearts. You may build either from exposed cards on the board or the top of the rubbish-heap. Pack on the board whenever you can, but great care must be taken in unpacking from the board to the bases, and here you are especially liable to confuse the rotation of suits. The rubbish-heap may be turned once. Clearly success will see your bases headed from left to right, King of Hearts, of Clubs, of Diamonds and of Spades.

FOURS

TAKE a piquet pack, that is the Whist Pack without the four 2's, 3's, 4's, 5's and 6's, and so of thirty-two cards. Deal four

cards in a row, say, Ace of Diamonds, Queen of Spades, 7 of
Diamonds and 7 of Spades. Put 7 of Spades on 7 of Diamonds.
Deal four more cards on top of these three and the vacant
space: say, 9 of Spades, 10 of Clubs, Knave of Clubs, and 9 of
Hearts. Put 9 of Spades on 9 of Hearts. Deal again: say, King
of Spades, 9 of Clubs, Ace of Hearts, Ace of Spades. Place
Ace of Spades on Ace of Hearts; this exposes the 9 of Spades,
place the Club 9 on it. Deal 8 of Diamonds, 10 of Spades, 8 of
Hearts, 9 of Diamonds. You have now all four 9's together in
the fourth space: the object of the game is to get together
any four cards of the same value. When you get a 'four' packet,
put it away and go on dealing with the rest. You are allowed
as many deals as you like, but the order of the cards once
started must not be altered. To win you must get rid of all the
cards in packets of four.

At this point in our particular hand the 9's disappear and
the 8 of Hearts goes on the 8 of Diamonds.

Deal 8 of Spades, Queen of Diamonds, Queen of Clubs and
Queen of Hearts. Place the other two Queens on the Heart.

Deal King of Diamonds, Knave of Hearts, King of Clubs,
and King of Hearts. Place the Heart King on the Diamond
King. Deal Ace of Clubs, 8 of Clubs, 10 of Hearts and 7 of
Clubs. 'Nothing doing.' Finally deal 7 of Hearts, Knave of
Spades, Knave of Diamonds, and 10 of Diamonds. Knave
of Diamonds on the Spade Knave, 10 of Diamonds on 10 of
Hearts, 7 of Clubs on 7 of Hearts.

Now place packet two on one, on these packets packet
number three, on these packet four (from right to left). Don't
shuffle, but turn face-downwards and deal again from the top.

The first four cards will be Ace of Diamonds, King of
Spades, 8 of Diamonds, 8 of Hearts. Move 8 of Hearts on 8 of
Diamonds. Next four, 8 of Spades, Kings of Diamonds,
Clubs and Hearts. The two Kings go on the Diamond King,
and the 8 of Spades on the 8 of Hearts. (*Kings out.*)

Next, Ace of Clubs, 7 of Hearts, 7 of Clubs, Queen of
Spades. Seven of Clubs on 7 of Hearts. Next, 10 of Clubs,
10 of Spades, Knave of Hearts, 8 of Clubs. Ten of Spades on

Clubs. Next Knave of Spades, Knave of Diamonds, 7 of
Diamonds, 7 of Spades. Put Knave of Diamonds on the
Spade; the two 7's on the 7 of Clubs. (*Sevens out.*) Knave of
Hearts on Diamonds. Eight of Clubs on 8 of Spades. (*Eights
out.*)

Next, Knave of Clubs, Aces of Hearts and Spades and 10 of
Hearts. (*Knaves out.*) Two 10's on 10 of Hearts. (*Aces out.*)

Last, 10 of Diamonds, Queens of Hearts, Diamonds and
Clubs. The two Queens on the Queen of Hearts, 10 of Diamonds on 10 of Spades. (*Tens out, then Queens out.* QEF.)

The game does not always succeed as you will find out
when deal after deal the cards occur in similar order 'like a
recurring decimal', as Mr Bergholt says.

GOLF

DEAL five rows of seven cards face-upwards to form the
'links'; the remaining seventeen are the stock, and play is
begun by turning up the first of these. On it can be played the
lowest exposed card of any of the seven columns, regardless of
suit, provided it is next in order either upwards or downwards.
This goes on till no further exposed card is playable, when a
fresh card is taken from stock, and the process repeated. No
sequence can go further than a King, but on an 8 turned up
from stock (provided they were all exposed cards to begin
with, or subsequently became exposed, for, of course, each
card removed makes another 'exposed') you could have a
pick-up like this: 9, 10, Knave, another 10, 9, 8, 7. Often,
however, there will be no suitable card for the turn-up from
stock.

You should examine when you have a choice, whether it
will pay you best to start upwards or downwards, and a good
memory of cards already played will be useful.

When all the stock is played count the cards left on the links
and their number is your score for the 'hole'. Shuffle and redeal for a nine-hole course (Bogey 40!) nine times. If you
want a full round, repeat the dose eighteen times.

If you manage to clear the links, i.e. pick up all the thirty-five cards laid out, before you have used all your clubs (I mean, exhausted the seventeen cards of stock), the number of cards left in stock counts as a 'minus' score in your favour. If your last unbroken club (I mean, unused card from stock) just clears the links, your score for that hole is 'zero'.

Clearly a good game for two and a golfer can easily elaborate it for Medal Play, Flag-matches, etc., etc.

Bed-ridden during an earthquake the golf maniac would doubtless find it engrossing.

KING ALBERT

DISTINCTLY one of the less mechanical and more intelligent forms of Patience. (To the writer's mind quite the best single-pack game yet invented.) The lay-out is in nine rows, all cards face-upwards. In the top row are nine cards, in the second eight, in the third seven, and so to the ninth with one card only.

The whole lay-out of forty-five cards will form an inverted right-angled triangle, as it were. The seven remaining cards, laid out by themselves, also face-upwards, form 'The Belgian Reserve'. The lowest cards in each column and all the reserve are exposed. Exposed Aces are at once put out for foundations to be built on in ascending suit-sequence to their respective Kings. Packing among the exposed cards is in downward sequence of alternate colours. Only one card can be packed at a time, and no second deal is allowed. If an entire column is made vacant any exposed card can be moved there. This assists the movement of sequences from one part of the lay-out to another and prevents chockering. You may at any time 'worry-back' by returning cards one at a time from the foundations if they will pack on the board according to rule.

Remember that *one* vacant space enables the transfer of a sequence of *two* cards, *two* spaces of a sequence of *four*, *three* spaces of a sequence of *eight*, *four* spaces of a sequence of *sixteen*.

The odds against success are a little more than 2–1.
(*See* Appendix VI for two games worked out.)

LADIES' BATTLE

TAKE the Queens and Knaves from the pack, throw aside
three of the Knaves and place the fourth at the top of the
board, the four Queens being in a row below. Place three
cards from the pack on each side of the Knave in pyramid form.
See if any packing or building can be done with the cards
already on the board. The Knave is not covered, the cards on
the pyramid are packed downwards in alternate colours, the
Queens upwards in suit-sequence. The Queen whose sequence
is first finished claims the Knave and wins.

Whenever a vacancy occurs on the pyramid through packing
or building, fill from the pack. When no more manipulations
are possible, play out six more cards on the pyramid, laying
them on top of the others (the whole six must be placed before
playing again). If, when the pack is finished, no Queen has
won the Knave, pick up the pyramid packets, beginning from
the left, and, placing them on each other without shuffling,
lay out as before. This may be done twice. Towards the end of
the game one suit must not be abandoned for another: e.g. if
the Heart Queen has reached *seven* and the Clubs *nine* in their
respective heaps, whilst on the pyramid are 8, 9, 10 of Hearts
exposed. Even though by taking the 9 of Hearts you expose
the 10 of Clubs you must continue with the Hearts, and not
by stopping at the 9 and placing the 10 of Clubs on its pile,
give the Knave to the Clubs.

LADY BETTY

THE aim of this very old game is to build upwards in suit-
sequence from the Aces to the Kings. The pack is dealt into
six heaps which need not, however, all be formed at once, and
below these packets the Aces are placed as they come out.
Cards may not be transferred from one heap to another and

there is no second deal allowed. Care should therefore be taken not to pack a higher card over a lower one of the same suit, and one packet should certainly be reserved for Kings, another, if possible, for Queens and Knaves (or one for Kings and Queens, another for Knaves and 10's) till you are well on with the building.

The game much resembles Sir Tommy (which see), and is not easy to get out unless the run of the cards is favourable.

MARTHA

TAKE out the Aces and place them at the foot of the board to be built upwards in suit-sequences to the Kings. The rest of the cards are dealt out in twelve packets of four, the first and third card in each packet face-downwards, the second and fourth face-upwards. The free cards are available for building up the foundation-Aces and for packing on the lay-out itself in downward sequence and alternate colour. Concealed cards are turned face-upwards as soon as freed, and become available for building and packing. Sequences may be moved as a whole when opportunities occur, but if a space is made* only a single card may fill it. This restriction sometimes defeats the player, and building should not be too rapid.

THE MISSING LINK

SHUFFLE and cut the pack, then take a card from the middle which put aside face-downwards without looking at it; this is the 'Missing Link'. Lay out seven cards in a row face-upward; and, if an Ace occurs among them, take it out and place above the seven row, filling the vacancy from the pack. Treat the other Aces similarly when they turn up.

Deal out the rest of the pack on the seven foundations in any way you like, building, as opportunity occurs, on the Aces in ascending suit-sequence.

Naturally you will avoid, when possible, packing high

* By clearing the whole of a packet.

cards on low ones, though you will have to do so if all seven
foundations are low cards. Even then you have a chance, for
if you can work off the whole of a foundation row you may
place any exposed cards in the space, which will often get rid
of a high blocking card.

When all the pack is dealt turn up the 'Missing Link', and
if by its aid you can complete the Ace packets you have
succeeded. There is no second turn.

If you are lucky enough to have a King, Queen or Knave
in the first seven cards, keep one of your foundations for
Kings and Queens only, and, if doubly blest, another for
Knaves and 10's. (Cp. packing in 'Lady Betty' and others.)

MONTE CARLO

Also called 'Double and Quits' and 'Weddings'

LAY out four rows of five cards: if pairs are touching each
other up or down, side by side, or at their corners – within,
in fact, the King's move at Chess – throw them out.

Should three of the same value be touching you cannot
throw out all three, but can choose which pair to take.

Now close up the ranks, beginning from the left. Should,
for instance, the right-hand card of the second row have been
one of the successful pairs, the left-hand card of the third row
takes its place. Fill up from the pack, and repeat 'pairing'. If
successful you will get rid of all the cards when you have gone
through the pack; but the odds are against you, and it is, of
course, possible to be defeated at once if there are no pairs
adjacent in the first twenty cards, or to 'pair off' forty-eight
cards triumphantly only to find yourself in the end facing an
order of this kind, '7 of Hearts, 9 of Diamonds, 7 of Spades,
9 of Clubs!'

NINES

SUCCESS depends entirely on the fall of the cards; skill
simply doesn't come in. Deal three rows of three cards. If, *as*

the cards are dealt, a combination of two cards making 9 turns up, those two cards are covered at once by two more from the pack, *before completing the lay-out of three rows.*

If a 10, a Knave, a Queen, and a King are on the board together at the same time, all four are covered in the same way, so also each separate 9.

When neither the sequence mentioned nor a single 9 nor a combination of two cards (three cards as 2, 3, 4, or Ace, 3, 5, making 9 are not admitted) is present, you must shuffle and start again, success implying the covering of cards till the pack is exhausted.

After which the cards must be picked up in the combinations of nine or the sequence (King to 10) until the table is cleared.

If two cards of the same value are available for a new combination, choose the one with the smaller heap. Those underneath will not be blocked so much when you come to pick up.

NINETY-ONE

LAY out the pack in thirteen packets of four cards each, face-upwards. Reckon up the value of the top-cards according to pips, one (Ace) to 10 face-value, Knaves 11, Queens 12, Kings 13.

The aim is to get a total of exactly 91, and top-cards may be moved from packet to packet till you get it. A full sequence from Ace to King will do it, but so will many other combinations. A lay-out is given in Appendix VII with three different solutions.

Hardly a sedative for the tired housewife, who has been wrestling with the monthly bills!

NUMBER ELEVEN

DEAL twelve packets of four cards each in three rows with their top-cards alone face-upwards. Keep the last four as a reserve. Next take away any *two* cards that make 11. Court-cards cannot join in this combination, so are taken off if King, Queen and Knave are on the board at the same time. (Ace counts one.)

All 'eleven-ses' having been removed, turn up the new top-cards of the packets which have contributed, proceeding as before. When a packet is finished, fill with a card from the reserve.

Success implies getting rid of all the cards.

(Compare and contrast 'Block Eleven Patience'.)

ORACLE

IMAGINE that Venus (Goddess of Beauty) be represented by the card Queen of Hearts; Juno (Goddess of Wealth) by the Queen of Diamonds; Bellona (Goddess of War) by the Queen of Clubs; Minerva (Goddess of Wisdom) by the Queen of Spades. The following exercise, you must further suppose, will act as an Oracle to show which female will affect your existence most.

Place each Queen a little distance from the others with a card of her own suit, as dealt from the pack, one each side, one above and one below to form her court. The card above cannot be moved: the three others can both capture and be captured.

Clearly one court will be completed before another – it all depends how the suits turn up – and as soon as it is complete, *but not before,* that court is ready to attack the others. It cannot, however, commence hostilities till a sixth card of its own suit turns up. This card may capture any card of its own value from the other courts (*not* the one above the other Queens, which, as said above, cannot be moved). Captor and captives are laid above the Queen, whose three other courtiers can then also capture any others of their own value. These are placed beneath them.

Suppose the card turned up cannot find any courtiers to capture: it is placed on the top-card of the court, and another card turned from the pack. You go on, forming up temporarily

attenuated courts, and capturing whenever you can until the
pack is finished.

Then you count the cards and the 'Power' that scores the
most wins: Aces are worth 4, Kings 3, Knaves 2, common
cards 1 each.

'Quot homines . . . !'

PAIRS

ALMOST too simple to include, but it will fill in a vacant five
minutes if you are really so unfortunate as to have nothing
better to do.

Lay out nine cards in three rows: throw out pairs; fill vacant
spaces from the pack. If you get nine cards without a pair,
you may lay down one card more – which may set the game
going again. This privilege you can repeat whenever stopped
at the ninth card. But if this tenth doesn't give you a pair, you
have failed.

The pairs, of course, need not be adjacent.

POKER

DEAL the cards face-upwards, one by one. After the first card
each card must be laid down next to one already on the board,
either vertically, horizontally, or diagonally (the King's move
at Chess).

Eventually you must have an oblong lay-out of five rows
with five cards in each, and the cards are counted up either
across or downwards, scoring thus:

Straight Flush (sequence of five in the same suit) . .	30
Fours (four cards of the same denomination) . .	16
Straight (sequence of any five, different suits) . .	12
Full House (three of one denomination, two of another).	10
Threes (three cards of same denomination) . . .	6
Flush (five cards of same suit, not in sequence) . .	5
Two Pairs	3
One Pair	1

The maximum possible would be five Straight Flushes one way and four 4's the other=230, but anything approaching 100 in actual play is very good. The Ace can count for sequences as lower than two or higher than King.

Clearly the game can easily be adapted for any number of players, each with a separate pack, and be easily elaborated by using a Joker or playing with a Piquet pack.

PUSS IN THE CORNER

PLACE the four Aces together in two rows in the middle of the board. They are to be built upwards in colour, but not necessarily in suit, thus a 4 of Diamonds can go on a 3 either of Diamonds or Hearts, a Deuce of Spades on either black Ace. Deal from the rest of the pack, turned face-downwards, putting the card dealt on the Ace-sequence if suitable; if not, place it in one of the corners of the board apart from the centre formation of Aces. Proceed thus till the pack is finished. Then take up the packets in any order, but without shuffling, and deal once again. If the four Aces are not built up to their Kings this time, you have failed. You need not fill all four packets at once. When a 7 is turned up you have the privilege of moving any packet on to any other, and, having done so, may put either of the two remaining packets on the other.

Keep one packet for high cards (Kings, Queens, etc.) and avoid packing lower cards on higher ones, e.g. both black 5's under a black 6.

(A game is worked out in Appendix VIII.)

QUADRILLE

(Sometimes called 'La Française')

DEAL the cards on a rubbish-heap which may be turned twice, placing as they turn up Aces and Deuces on the board in the diagram below, to form the figure of a quadrille.

On these eight foundations build upwards in their suits but in *alternate numbers,* i.e. odds on the Aces (3, 5 ... J, K), evens on the Deuces (4, 6 ... 10, Q). Success will leave each King with his Queen on his right.

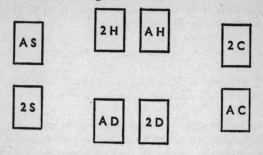

QUEEN AND HER LAD

PLACE the Queen of Hearts at the top, the Knave at the bottom of the pack; unless the two meet – a rare occurrence – the game has failed.

As you lay out the cards (beginning, of course, with the Queen) push out any card that comes between two others of the same suit or the same signification.

Push out any *two* cards of the same suit, or pairs which come between two others of the same suit or signification.

When readjusting the line you may find three or four pairs of cards adjacent of the same suit or signification, and then, if a suitable card comes along, the whole lot can be shoved, e.g. suppose after the Queen of Hearts comes the 7 of Diamonds followed by two Clubs, two Spades, two Knaves and then a Diamond. All the six between the two Diamonds go, but cards of the same suit must be adjacent to qualify.

REVERSE PUZZLE

PLACE twenty cards in a circle: turn one down, counting one, two, three, four; turn down the fourth. Go on turning first and fourth cards down, working always one way round the circle all until twenty are reversed.

Cards already reversed count in the fours, but you must neither begin nor end on one of them. If you do, you have failed, and must rearrange the circle and begin again.

(For solution *see* Appendix IX.)

ROSAMUND'S BOWER

TAKE from the pack the Queen of Hearts, the King of Clubs and the Knave of Spades. Place the Queen in the middle of the board with eight cards about her as the 'guards of her bower', two above, two below and two on each side. Above her to the right goes the King with a packet of seven cards face-downwards as extra guards; the Knave is below the Queen to her left.

Next form *three* rubbish-heaps, building whenever possible on the Knave in downward-sequence but regardless of suit, until he has attracted the whole of the pack. His aim is to capture the Queen, but he cannot do this while she has her guards and is protected by the King. Whilst you are building, if a card from the 'guards of the bower' becomes suitable, you *must* take it in preference to one from the rubbish-heaps, and fill the vacancy from one of the (King's) extra guards. When this extra guard is finished, Rosamund can have no others. Still she remains safe, though only the King is left her, as long as any cards remain in the rubbish-heaps. These heaps may be gathered up and distributed thrice; and what skill there is in the game consists in so arranging them that they all work off on the Knave's packet.

After which the King and Queen are also captured, and 'Paris triumphs'. You will find it useful to arrange your rubbish-heaps as far as possible in ascending values, keeping a wary eye on the way the knave packet is going.

SEVENTH WONDER

AFTER shuffling deal the cards out one by one in line, throwing out 7's as they occur. When you have a combination of cards on the table that by pips count seven, or a multiple of seven, remove them at once. (Knaves=11, Queens=12, Kings=13, Aces=1.)

Thus if the first two cards were a Queen and a 9, you have 21 (7×3), so remove. Commence again. Suppose the next four cards were 10 of Hearts, 3 of Diamonds, 5 of Clubs, 6 of Spades: total 24, and no multiple of 7!

But count back, and 6+5+3=14, or twice seven. So remove those three cards. Thus you can often remove three, four or even more cards.

You are successful if you remove all the cards. The game has been described as 'not an easy one to accomplish'. Assuming you have a knowledge of the multiplication table, and are not half asleep, you will possibly succeed nineteen times out of twenty! Selah!

SIR TOMMY

THIS may be called the original Patience, from which all others are ultimately derived. The object is to build up packets from the Aces to the Kings, but in this game you do not follow suits, only the ascending order.

You deal out the pack in four heaps and place the Aces as they turn up below these heaps, packing whenever you can. There is no rubbish-heap, no second chance, and no transference from one heap to another. So you must as far as possible keep one heap for high cards, and pray that the Kings will come out soon.

SPANISH

DEAL thirteen packets of four cards each, face-upwards. If there is an exposed Ace, take it out for the base of a sequence.

In this game the sequences are of number only, not of suit. Pack exposed cards in descending sequence, your great object being to free the Aces and the low cards.

When you come to an end of this, gather up the packets in any order, but do not shuffle, and lay out again in packets of

four. You may do this once again in order to complete the
Ace-packets for success.

SPRINT

LAY out face-upwards four rows of six cards each. The
twenty-fifth card and the other three of the same denomination
are the bases, to be built in upward sequence without regarding
suit or colour.

The right-hand and exposed cards of the lay-out can be
used for packing without regard to colour and suit, but in
downward sequence. Eleven cards are built on the bases, and
the thirteenth in sequence is the only card that can fill a space
made in the lay-out with or without a sequence attached, i.e.
if Queens were the base-cards, the Knaves could fill vacancies.
After the twenty-fifth card has been turned up the rest of the
pack is dealt on to a rubbish-heap in *threes,* the exposed one
being always available for packing or building, but only one
card may be taken at a time from the rubbish-heap; even
though, by its being taken, the card under it in the heap could
join on to the lay-out or base-heaps. Similarly for building
cards must be taken singly. The rubbish-heap may be dealt in
threes again without shuffling so long as a move can be made.
If a deal ends with one or two cards (i.e. there isn't a packet of
three left) the single card or both of the two are available.

STONE-WALL

LAY out six rows, each of six cards; the first, third and fifth
rows face-downwards, the others face-upwards. The remaining
sixteen cards of the pack are placed face-upward on one side
as a reserve, and may be used at pleasure. Aces exposed in the
lay-out or reserve are the bases, to be removed at once and
built up to their Kings in ascending suit-sequences; exposed
cards on the board to be packed in downward sequence and
alternate colours. Any concealed card becomes exposed and is
turned upwards as soon as the one below it is removed.

Sequences can be removed as a whole, or single cards taken from one column to another, provided an upper card in sequence is available. A vacancy in the top row can be filled by any exposed card or sequence.

But the eighteen concealed cards are not easy to get over, and you want a favourable run of cards to accomplish the game. Two 'tips' are useful:

(1) Go for getting spaces in the top row as hard as you can.

(2) Don't build too high, even if the cards offer the chance on both red or both black suits, while the opposite-coloured Ace-sequences are low. You'll want 9's and 7's, etc., for packing. (The game worked out in the Appendix was the first of its kind attempted by the writer, but was followed by many failures.)

TEN TO FIVE PUZZLE

LAY out the first ten cards (Ace to 10) of any suit in a row. The puzzle lies in placing them in such order that when you reduce them to doublets (packets of two) the top-cards shall show a sequence of one to five: whilst, to bring them to doublets, each card, by the conditions of the puzzle, must jump over two others when moved, either two single cards or one doublet. The cards can be moved in either direction.

(Two solutions are given in Appendix XI.)

TOWER OF HANOY

TAKE nine cards from the Deuce to the 10: shuffle and deal face-upwards into three rows, each of three cards. The idea is to move the cards till they are arranged in a single column with 10 at the top, 9 underneath and so on down to the Deuce. The cards may be moved only according to the following rules:

(1) One card only to be moved at a time; and this to be taken only from the foot of one column and placed at the foot of another, immediately under a card of (any) higher denomination.

(2) Whenever all the cards of a column have been moved, the bottom card of either of the other two columns can move into the vacant space in the top row.

(An example is worked out in Appendix XII.)

TRAVELLERS

A SIMPLE game: deal forty-eight cards in packets of four face-down (three rows of four packets are convenient); the last four form the reserve. Imagine the packets numbered one to twelve, number eleven for Knaves, twelve for Queens, thirteen for Aces.

Turn up the first of the reserves: if it is a 7, it goes beneath the packet number seven. This packet now has five cards and its top-card becomes a 'traveller'; that is, it is transferred to its proper packet (number 12 if it be a Queen).

If it's a King, it is thrown aside, for there is no thirteenth packet; and another card is taken from the reserve. Whenever you slip a card under a packet it is convenient to put it face-upwards: this helps you to see at a glance what cards have not yet travelled. Your aim is to divide all the cards (excluding the Kings) into twelve heaps, each made up of the four cards of the same denomination.

If the spare packet be exhausted before all the board packets are complete the game has failed. If a couple of Kings are in the reserve, or happen to be near the top of the packets, your chances of success – never very rosy – grow small indeed.

TRIPLE ALLIANCE OR TRIPLETS

LAY out sixteen packets of three cards, two of two cards. From the top (exposed) cards of the packets look for three of consecutive value regardless of suit, and place them either fan-wise or in packets apart from the original lay-out. More cards will then become exposed, and available for forming fans. The object of the game is to arrange the whole pack in fans, leaving one over (often a 7 or a 10). Kings count lower than Aces – King, Ace, 2 and Ace, King, Queen are both triplets. If successful, you will have seventeen sets of alliance, of which four (and *only* four) will be duplicate. Some discretion should be exercised in selecting the triplets, and the following hints will prove useful:

(1) When you have two cards of the same denomination, each available for a triplet, choose the one from the packet containing the more cards in order to have a larger number of 'exposed' cards.

In such cases you may, according to some authorities, look underneath and see which will leave exposed the more useful card.

(2) Avoid too many sequences of the like numbers.

(3) Arrange your triplets as far as possible to make a complete set, i.e. alliance from 3, 4, 5, etc., up to 1 from the Ace, one from the 2. This will help you to memorize cards out and to decide which sets you will have to duplicate.

VANBRUGH

PLACE the four Queens in a packet in the centre, the four Kings north, south, east and west of them, and the Knaves each to the right of his King. Deal the rest of the pack one by one, building on the Kings in upward suit-sequence, on the Knaves in downward alternate sequence, i.e. 9, 7, 5, 3. If the card turned up cannot be placed it goes on a waste-heap, the top-card on which may at any time be used for building.

Now suppose we've got one of the Knave-sequences down to 3 and its corresponding Ace up to the Deuce. The 3 is ready for transference, but can only be moved when the 4 of the suit is dealt. Then both 3 and 4 go on the King-heap, but the 5 must wait till the 6 appears, the 7 till the 8. But when the 10 appears, 9, 10 and Jack all go on at once and the packet is completed. The waste-heap may be turned and redealt twice; three rounds in all.

When any one Knave packet is finished by transference to its King's packet, the card dealt from stock fills the vacancy, if not available for building, and is *not* thrown on the waste-heap. In a successful result all the Knave packets work off on the Kings, and these are crowned by their respective Queens.

YORK AND LANCASTER

THIS, like Oracle Patience, demands a flight of fancy, since a red King for Lancaster and a black one for York are taken out of the pack and placed some distance from each other. The top-card of the pack is turned; and, if red, it is placed by the Lancastrian King; if black, by the Yorkist. And so with each succeeding card turned till each monarch has his 'camp' of his own colour, one card above, one below and three on each side. Suppose the red camp complete and more Lancastrians turning up before the black is finished – they go in a heap by the side, each party having a prisoner's camp. War starts as soon as both camps are completed. Then the first card turned up, if red, can take any black card of the same denomination, or of one point lower, both captor and prisoner(s) going to the Lancastrian prisoners' camp. A Spade or Club turned would behave in the same way to the Red Rose.

After which any card in the attacking camp can take prisoner any like card in the opposing camp – like or of one point lower – excepting the Kings in the centre, which, like kings at Chess, neither take nor are taken. When a King has only two guards left the attack ceases. Then an Armistice comes while the cards are turned from the pack, the camps filled up and, as before, any supernumeraries go to their own prisoners' camp till the other side is ready. When the pack is finished, count the cards (Kings 4, Queens 3, Knaves 2, rest 1 each).

The side with the higher score wins. (Cf. the Oracle.)

AGNES

Lay-out:

> 7 C, 8 and 4 H, 6 H, K S, 8 C, 9 D.
> J C, 8 S, 10 C, 3 D, 9 S, 6 D.
> 4 C, Q H, 5 S, K H, 8 D.
> K C, 5 D, J H, 10 D.
> 5 C, 9 H, Q D.
> K D, 10 H.
> 4 S.   *Turn-up* A C.

Place 9 D on 10 D. Q D in space seven. J H on Q D, 10 and 9 H on J H, 8 D on 9 D, 5 D on 6 D, 4 S on 5 S.

Deal seven more cards for foot of each column. Suppose cards dealt are in this order: 2 D, A D, 3 C, J D, A H, 5 H, 2 H; A and 2 H out, A and 2 D out. Q H on K D, J H to 9 H on Q H. J D on Q D, 10 D to 8 D on J D. Q to 9 of H on K H. Q to 8 D on K D. (Mark how the H and D are got into one uninterrupted sequence.) K to 9 H in space seven, 3 D out, 5 H on 6 H, 8 S on 9 S, 8 H on 9 H. *Vacant space.* We are not forced to fill space two before dealing again.

Deal seven more cards: 3 S, Q C, A S, 7 D, 2 C, Q S, 7 S. A S out, 2 and 3 C on A, 3 S on 4 S, 7 D on 8 D, 7 S on 8 S.

Deal again: 2 and J S, 10 S. 9 and 6 C, 7 H, and 4 D. 2 S out. (J S is on Q C.) 10 S on J S, 9 C on 10 S. 6 C on 7 S. 4 D out on 3, 7 H on 8 H. 3, 4, 5 S out. 9 C on 10 C. 5 and 6 H on 7 H. Q S on space four. 5 and 6 D out – rest of D from 7 out. 5 C on 6 C, 8 C on 9 C, K C in space six. 4, 5, 6 C out. 10 C, 9, 8 on J C. 7 to 9 S on 10 S. J to 7 S on Q, these on K of S. Q C on K C. J to 8 C on Q C. 4 H on 5 H, 7 C on 8 C. *Last two cards in pack* 6 S, out on 5; 3 H on 2. *All out.*

BISLEY

Lay-out:

Row I.   The four A's; 7, 8, 9 D; K, 2, 3 C; K H; 3 D, 6 C.

„ II   4, 6 H; 3, 7, 8 S; 2 H; K D; Q C; 6 S; 5 H; 4 S;
        3 H; 9 S.

„ III. 6 D; 10, 9, 8 H; 10 D; 2 S; 7 H; 10, 9, 8, 7 C;
        J C; 10 S.

„ IV.   J D, Q S, Q D; K S; 4 D, 4 C, J, Q H; 5 S; J S,
        2 D, 5 C, 5 D.

2 D on A; J H on Q; *K and Q S out for base below:* Q D on J;
10, 9, 8, 7 H on J; *K D out*; Q and J D on K; 4 C on 5; 2 S and H
on their A; 5 D on 6; 10 and 9 S on J; 4 D on 5; 10 D on J; 8 S
on 9; 9, 8, 7 D out; 8 to J S on 7, then out on Q S; 3 S on 2;
7 and 8 C on 6; 4 S on 3; *K H out*. 5 S on 4; 6 H on 5; 7 to Q on
6, all out to 5 on K. In Clubs 9 on 10, 8 to 6 on 9, 4 on 3, 5 on 6,
4 and 3 on 5. 6 S on 5; 2 to 10 C on A to J. Q K C, *all C out*. 3 H
and D on their Deuces; 4 to 6 D out. *All out.*

Lay-out:

4 Aces, 6 C, 9 D, K, J H, 5 S, 7 and 3 C, Q H, 2 C.
8 H, 10, 8, K, 4, 2 D, 6 S, 5 C, 6 and 5 D, 4 H, K C, 10 H.
3 D, Q and 3 C, K S, 7 D, 9 C, 3 and 10 S, 9, 5, 7, 3 H, 7 S.
J C; Q, 9 S, J D; 10 C, Q D; J S, 2 and 6 H; 2 S, 8 S, 4 C, 4 S.
Place 2 H and 2 S on their Aces.

J on Q D, *K S free* (place below), Q and J S on K.   10, 9, 8 S on
J, 3 and 4 S on A, 7 S on 8, *K D free.* J and Q C on 10; J D on 10;
Q, J, 10 on K D.   4 C on 5, 3 H upon 2. *K C free.* Q to 8 C on K.
2 D up.   9, 8, 7 D on 10.   3 and 4 D up on 2.   7 H on 8.   4 to 10 H
up.   2 to 6 C up.   5, 6 both of D and S up, 7 C either above or
below.   Rest out.

BRIGADE

Lay-out:

> 3, 9 H. 7 C. 2, K H. 10 C. 9 D.
> 3 C. K, 5, Q D. 8 H. 8 C. J S.
> 8 D. 2 C. K S. 6 C. 6 H. 7 D. 6 S.
> 5 C. 4 S. 6, J, 4 D. K C. 4 H.
> 5, Q H. 9 C. 10 D. 10 H. 2 S. 9 S.

Reserve S Q, 10, 8, 7, 5, 3. D: 3, 2. C: Q, J, 4. H: J, 7.

Play 2 S on A, Q H on K, J* C on Q, 10 H and 9 C on J. 3*, 4 S, 2 C out; 5 H on 6 D, 4 D on 5 H, 5 C on 6 H, 8 D on 9 C, 3 C out; 3 H on 4 D. (*Vacant space made.*) Put 10 D in vacant space. Q* S on K D. J D on Q, 10 D on J. (*Vacant space made.*) 9 S on 10 D. 7* S on 8 D. 6 and 5 C on 7 S. Q D in vacant space, 2 H out, also 3 and 4 H. 2*, 3*, 4 D out, 5 and 6 H out; 5* and 6 S out; 4*, 5, 6 C out; 7* and 8 H out. Q D on K H. J S on Q D, 6 D on 7 S, K S in vacant place. 5 D and 7 C out, 6 D and 7 S out. 8*, 9, 10*, J S out. *We have two vacant spaces,* put 10 D in one, J D on Q, Q and K S out, K D in vacant space; 10, 9, 8 D on J D. *Three vacant spaces.* 9 C on one space; 9 and 10 H out. J C in vacant space. J* H and Q out; K C in vacant space. *All out.*

COURT PUZZLE

Imagine the two diagonals of your quadrilateral. Put the Kings along one, the Aces along the other. Two opposite corners will hold Aces; the other two, Kings. Next to the Kings must be Queens, next to the Aces, Knaves.

* = Card taken from Reserve.

APPENDIX V

THE FLOWER GARDEN

Let the six flower-beds be:

```
2 S.  3 C.  7, 5 D.  A C.  J D.
A S.  6 D.  K C.  J S.  2 H.  9 C.
5 S.  4, 3, 10 D.  9 S.  K H.
3 H.  4 C.  Q H.  8 D.  5 C.  K D.
7 S.  9, 8, 6 H.  2 C.  6 S.
J H.  6 C.  4 S.  7, A, 5 H.
```

Bouquet:

Clubs: Q, J, 10, 8, 7. Hearts: 10, 4. Diamonds: A, Q, 9, 2.
Spades: K, Q, 10, 8, 3.

Place 5 H on 6 S, Q* S on K H, J D on Q S. (A H and A C free.) 10* C on J D, 9 C on 10 C, 2 H on A. A* and 2* D out. 8* S on 9 C. 7 H on 8 S. 4 S on 5 D. 6 C on 7 H. Q* C on K D, J H on Q C. *Vacant space.* 5 H on 6 C, 4 S on 5 H. Sequence K to 4 in vacant place. 10* S on J S, 9 S on 10 S, 10 D on J H, 3, 4, 5 D out. 8* C on 9 S, 7 D on 8 C, 6 S on 7 D, 5 S on 6, 3 C on 4 S, 2 S on 3 C, 2 C out. *Two vacant spaces.* 6 and 8 H on the vacant spaces, 9 H on 10 D, 8 H on 9, 7 S on 8, 6 H on 7 S. *Three vacant spaces.* Sequence to K D on one, sequence to J S on another. 5 C on 6 H. K C on vacant space. 6 D, A S, 2 S out, 3 C, 3* S out. 4, 5, 6 S out, 7, 8 D out, Q H on K C. J sequence on Q. 4 C 3 H out. Rest follows.

APPENDIX VI

KING ALBERT

Lay-out:

```
5 D, 9 C, 8 H, 4 C, K S, K H, 4 D, 7 S, Q H.
Q S, J, 8 D, 10 S, 5 H, 6 D, 5 and 2 S.
3, 4 S, A, 2, 3 C, 9 D, 9 H.
```

* Taken from Bouquet.

55

K D, 10 C, 7 D, Q C, 6 H, 8 C.
7, 5 C, 7 H, 6 S, 8 S.
6 C, Q D, A H, A D.
3 H, A S, J C.
2, 4 H.
J H.
Reserve: 2, 3, 10 D; 9, J S; 10 H; K C.

A D out, J C on Q H, A H out, 2* D on A D, 10* H and
9* S on J C, 8 C on 9 H, 7 H on 8 C, 6 S on 7 H, J H on Q C,
8 S on 9 D, 7 D on 8 S, 2, 3, 4 H out. A S and A C out, 6 C
on 7 D, 2 S out, 8 D on 9 S. 7 S on 8 D. *Vacant space.* 7 C on
8 H. Q C and J H to K D (via vacant space, thus: Place J on
space, Q on K, then J on Q, leaving space still vacant). 6 H
on 7 S. 2 and 3 C out, 10 S on J H. 4 C, 5 H, 3* D out. *Two
vacant spaces.* Sequence of 4 cards to 9 H on 10 S (via two
vacant spaces), 5 S on 6 H, 4 D out. *Three vacant spaces.* Q D
on K S. 5 and 6 C out. 10 C in vacant space. '*Worry back*' 5 H
on 6 S, 4 S on 5 H, J D on vacant space, 10 C on him. J* S
and 10* D on Q D, 9 C on 10 D, 5 S to 8 D (sequence) on 9 C,
9 to 7 D on 10 C, 8 H and 7 C on 9 S. *Four vacant spaces.* K D
to 4 S (sequence of 10 cards) out on the vacant spaces, 3 S out,
6 D on 7 C, Q S on K H. *Rest obvious.*

Or, *Lay-out:*
J, 9 H. A S. 8 and K D. 6 H. K S. 7 S. 2 H.
5 S. 2 C. 5, Q H. 8 S. 3 H. 5 C. 5 D.
A C. 10 H. 2 S. 6 C. Q C. 10 D. 4 S.
9 S. J C. 3, 4, J D. 10 S.
J S. Q, 6 D. 8, K H.
7, 9 C. 2 D. 3 S.
4 C. A D. A H.
4, 7 H.
6 S.
Reserve: K, 10, 8, 3 C; Q S; 9, 7 D.

A and 2 H out. *Vacant space.* Put K H there, Q* S on him,
J D on her, 10 S on that, 9* D on that, 8* C on that, 7 H and

* Cards from Reserve.

6 S on that. *A and 2 D out.* 5 D on 6 S, 4 S on 5 D, 9 C on 10 D,
3 S on 4 H, 7 S on 8 H. *Vacant space.* 6 D on 7 S, 5 C on 6 D,
3 S in vacant space. 4 H on 5 C. 3 S on 4 H. Q D on K S,
J C on Q D, 3 D on 4 S, 2 S on 3 D. 9 C in vacant space.
10 D then 9 C on J C. 3 H out. 5 H on vacant space. A S out.
2, 3 S out. 4, 5 H out. 6 H out. 3 D out. 4 S out. *Three
vacant spaces.* 8 H to 5 C on 9 C. 4 D out. 4 C on 5 D. 7 C,
J and 9 S in the three vacant places. A C out. 10 H on J S.
9 S on 10 H. 2 C and 5 S out. 3*, 4, 5 C out, 6, 7 also. 5, 6 D.
Rest clear.

APPENDIX VII

NINETY-ONE

Suppose a Lay-out:

> 4 C. 2 H. 5 D. K C. K D.
> Q H. 10 C. 8 S. 3 C.
> 3 S. A H. 7 S. K S.

This makes 94. You want to lose three. Move, say, the 10 C:
if it exposes a Deuce you have lost 8, but by putting the 10 C on
the 5 D you gain 5. Hence with 10 C on 5 D, any 3 as top-card
instead of 10 C you get exactly 91.

Or again: Suppose on moving the A H the 5 S is exposed –
you've gained 4. Put the A on the 8 S. That knocks off 7 –
net loss 3. Result 91.

Or again: Suppose on moving the Q H you find the 4 D –
you've lost 8; put the Q on the 7 S, you gain 5. Result 91.

* Cards from Reserve.

PUSS IN THE CORNER

Let A, B, C, D be the four side-packets: thus

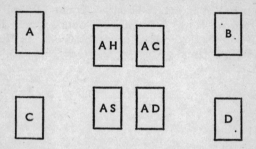

The cards are given as dealt: 4 H on B, 6 H on C, 4 D on B, 5 C on C, K H on A, 6 D on C, K S on A, 9 H on D, 7 S, *Privilege, place on D and transfer C block below 7 to D,* Q H on A, J S on C, 5 H on D, J D on C, 10 H on C, 9 D on C, *2 H on its A,* 8 D on C, *7 H on C (nothing gained by exercising privilege),* 3 C on B, 5 D on D, 8 H on A, 7 C *on C. Transfer B to D,* J H on B, 6 S on C, Q D on B, J C on B, 5 S on C, 4 S on C, 9 C on B, *2 C on its A,* 3 C goes out, 8 C on 9 C, 3 D on 2 H, *4 D out,* 4, 5, 6 S on 3 C, 7, 8, 9 C on them, 6 C on 7 H, *2 D out on A.* 3 H on 2 D, 4 H and 5 D on 3 H, 5 H, 6 D on 4 D, 4 C on D, 9 S on B, 8 S on B. 2 S on A. 7 D on 6 D. 8 H on 7 D. 10 S on 9 C. 10 D on A, Q S on A, 3 S out. 4, 5, 6 C on 3 S. 6, 7 H on 5 D; 8, 9 D on 7 H, 7 S on 6 C. 8, 9 S on 7. 9, 10 H on 8 H, J C and Q S on 10 S; 10, J, Q D on 9 D. J, Q H on 10. K S on Q S. K H on Q H. K and Q C on A, K D on Q D, 10 C on 9 S. Q and K C out. J S on 10 C.

APPENDIX IX

REVERSE PUZZLE SOLUTION

Let A to T stand for the cards (their denominations do not matter), and the figures one to twenty denote the order in which they are turned down. Start at C, C counting as one, two, three, four. F is turned. Skip two cards. Turn down I and L. Again skip two: O and R turn down. Now you must

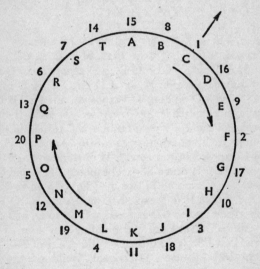

change the rotation. Start at S and turn down B. Skip two; start at E and turn down H. Skip two: start at K and turn down N. Skip two: start at Q and turn down T. Start at A and turn down D; at G and turn down J; at M and turn down P. 'Quod erat faciendum', as friend Euclid remarks.

APPENDIX X

STONE-WALL

Lay-out:

Row I.   (Q H, K D, A H, 2 C, 3 D, 9 C.)†
„   II.   10, J D, J, 4 H, Q D, 5 C.
„   III.   (K S, 6 H, A, 2 D, 7 H, 3 S.)
„   IV.   4, 5 S, 8 D, 9 H, 6 C, 10 H.
„   V.   (7, 4 D, 8 S, 9 D, 5 H, 10 C.)
„   VI.   J C, 6, 7, Q S, 8 H, K C.

Reserve:

5, 6 D. 7, 8 C.   9, A, 10, J S.
A C. 2, 3 H. 4 C.   Q C. K H. 2 S. 3 C.

A, 2 S, A C out. J C on Q D (7 D exposed), 10 D on J C
(Q H exposed: place on K C). J D on Q S (K D exposed;
place Q S and J D on him, 9 D exposed). K* H. Q* C from
reserve in vacant place on top row, place J H on. A H exposed.
Take out and build 2*, 3*, 4 on him. 2 C turned in top row
place on its A. You have now *2 spaces in top row.* 3*, 4*, 5, 6 C
out. 9 C exposed in top row, 7 H in third row. 7* C out.
10* S on J H, 9 H on 10 S. (2 D exposed.) K C and Q H to
top row. (10 C exposed.) Place on J D. 9 D on 10 C. 8* C
on 9 D, 7 S on 8 H (8 S exposed): place on 9 H. Q D, J C,
10 D in vacant space. 3 D exposed, 9 C on 10 D, 8 D on 9 C.
(A D exposed.) Take out and build 2, 3 on him. J* S on
Q H, 10 H on J S. (3 S exposed – build 3, 4, 5 of S – K S and
6 H exposed.) 6 S out, 4 D exposed. Build 4, 5*, 6*, 7 D.
7 S 8 H on vacant top space. 5 H (exposed) to 8 H built.
Rest come out.

† The cards between brackets in rows I, III and V were, of course,
dealt face-downwards, and had to be reconstructed when recording the
game.
   * Cards from Reserve.

APPENDIX XI

TEN TO FIVE PUZZLE

Arrange thus:

(1) 2 : 8 : 4 : 9 : A : 10 : 5 : 7 : 3 : 6.

Place 5 on 6; A on 8; 4 on 7; 3 on 10; 2 on 4; the last two moving over doublets already formed.

Or,

(2) 2 : 6 : 4 : 7 : A : 8 : 5 : 9 : 3 : 10.

Place 5 on 10; A on 6; 4 on 9; 3 on 8; 2 on 7: the last two moving over doublets.

APPENDIX XII

TOWER OF HANOY

Suppose this arrangement (calling for convenience the cols. A, B and C):

A	B	C
4	2	6
7	5	8
10	3	9

'Ten' gets into position in 5 moves thus: 3 to A, 5 to C, 3 to C, 2 to C, *10 to B*.

Next 9 and 8 – thus in nine moves: 2 to A, 3 to B, 2 to B, 5 to A, 2 to C, 3 to A, *9 to B, 8 to B*.

Next 7 – In eight more moves: 2 to C, 3 to B, 2 to B, 5 to C, 2 to A, 3 to C, 2 to C, *7 to B*.

Next 6 – seems to need thirteen moves: 4 to B, 2 to A, 3 to B, 2 to B, 5 to A, 2 to A, 3 to C, 2 to C, 4 to A, 2 to B, 3 to A, 2 to A, *6 to B*.

Next 5 – in eight: 2 to C, 3 to B, 2 to B, 4 to C, 2 to A, 3 to C, 2 to C, *5 to B*.

The rest thus: 2 to B, 3 to A, 2 to A, *4 to B*, 2 to C, *3 out, 2 out*.

Part Two

DOUBLE PACK PATIENCE

FOREWORD

THOSE who have confined themselves to Single-pack Patiences will probably find the games with two packs different, not merely in degree, but almost in kind; and the many card-players who feel (and sometimes express) a mild contempt for Patience, if they give even the first four games in this selection a fair trial, may, 'though they came to scoff, remain to' – play! For it is no exaggeration to say that certain games, such as 'The British Blockade', 'The Emperor', 'Grandfather's Clock', or 'The Spider', afford as much scope for foresight and ingenuity as any kind of card game.

With the single-pack varieties, if you exclude 'Bisley', 'King Albert' (above all), and a few others, there are hardly any forms where skill counts for more than the fall of the cards; but in more than half of the fifty double-pack games here selected intelligent play makes all the difference. Furthermore, even in the easier games, there are few or none which are merely 'mechanical' or 'silly'.

In the present series each game may claim to have justified its selection on one of the following grounds:

(1) Because skill has a chance against the run of the cards to a very considerable extent. To this class belong all games described by 'Cavendish' as 'Patiences presenting a definite problem', where, should the fall of the cards not absolutely preclude success, it is the player's own failure in analysis, and that alone, that is to blame if a solution is not attained. 'The Spider' is a striking example.

(2) Because of unusual and interesting sequences, e.g. 'Squaring the Circle' and 'Senior Wrangler'.

(3) Because of unusual or 'pretty' figures, e.g. 'Grand Round', 'Herring Bone', 'Double Pyramid', 'Right and Left'.

Varieties very like each other have been omitted. In most cases where solutions have been given the text has been so

65

arranged that a reader may try to solve a game 'on his own', before turning to the Appendix.

The compiler is indebted to many writers on Patience, but most of all to 'Cavendish's' sumptuous *Patience Games* (1889), and to some long-suffering friends who have worked through text and solutions to find out anything that might not be clear to the lonely reader and 'student'.

In explaining Patiences the 'live voice' is far more effective than the pen; but as yet our educational Bolsheviks have not founded a professorial chair for the teaching of Patience, though many things of much less value for the training of the young idea are taught with great energy and expenditure!

OXFORD, *December 1925.*

In preparing this new edition for the press a thorough revision of the text has been made, and particular attention paid to the appendices with their examples and solutions. The gentle reader will readily understand that on pages such as 91 or 95 the smallest error (e.g. 'J H' for 'J D') would stultify the whole demonstration.

Very few actual misprints were discovered, but many small alterations and additions have been effected that the procedure might be as clear as possible to the 'student'.

In conclusion the compiler has to offer his grateful thanks to the many readers who have written kindly letters with suggestions or commendations. Your true Patience player may be a 'solitary bird', but he (or she) is almost always genuinely courteous, and courteously genuine.

OXFORD, *January, 1932.*

ABOVE AND BELOW. *To form sequences following suit, four ascending and four descending.*

LAY-OUT. – The two packs are not to be shuffled together. (This is unlike the majority of Patiences, but compare 'Backbone', 'St Helena'.)

The first card turned up determines the eight bases, which are the numbers immediately above and below it. These are to be placed on the board as they turn up, and built on in suit, the higher ones *upwards,* the lower ones *downwards.* The first card turned up is placed by itself, the others of the same denomination being superimposed as they turn up.

PROCEDURE. – You are allowed four waste-heaps; and as you deal from the first pack, one by one, any card that will not build is placed on one of these. The top-card of each waste-heap and the top-card dealt are at any time available for building (of course, if in right sequence): thus you always have five available exposed cards for the eight foundation packets. The diagram shows the board after the first pack has been dealt through.

The cards have not gone well: on packet 2, for example, nothing has happened, nor on packet 8. Under the turn-up will be the other three 8's. On packet 1 will be seven cards from the 9 up; on packet 3 the 9, 10 and Knave of Diamonds; on packet 7 five cards from the 7 down to the 3 of Diamonds.

Now deal the second pack. All the 8's will still join the heap where lies the original turn-up, but the 10's and 7's will go like other cards on one of the waste-heaps or foundation-packets. Whenever in the course of building up or down one of the packets reaches an 8 it will take its own 8 from the turn-up heap and proceed.

Success will mean that this heap is absorbed, and each packet crowned with its appropriate 8 (or whatever the turn-up card may have been).

At the end of the first deal the four waste-heaps can be gathered up *without shuffling,* and played through again (once).

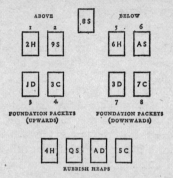

PRIVILEGES. – You may shift cards one by one from ascending to descending packets in the same suit if the cards are at the top of the packets and consecutive, e.g. in the diagram if packet 7 had worked down to a Queen of Diamonds, packet 3 could take the Queen and (under her) the King of Diamonds, and so get the Ace from the waste-heap, which Ace would probably be 'blocking' some desirable cards.

HINTS. – A difficult game to 'get out'. Without great care you will 'chocker'* the waste-heaps. But no care nor skill will avail if the cards are consistently unkind in 'turning up'. It is, for instance, obviously possible (though not very likely) for you to go through the whole of the first pack without building on a single foundation-packet. The longer the bases are in turning up, the more unmanageable become your waste-heaps, and the sheer luck of this prevents the game, interesting though it is, ranking among the best Patiences.

You will be guided immensely by the fall of the cards in arranging your waste-heaps; but, as far as you can, keep one

---

* Cards are said to be '*chockered*' when they are so blocked by other cards that by the laws of the particular game they are available neither for packing nor building.

heap for cards likely to be wanted soon, another for cards that after the game has advanced a little will clearly not be wanted till the end. (A game is worked out in full in Appendix I.)

BACKBONE. *To form eight ascending suit-sequences from Aces to Kings.*

LAY-OUT. – As in 'Above and Below' the two packs are not shuffled together. From the first pack deal twenty cards in a perpendicular column, arranged in pairs at an angle to each other, and (for economy of space) slightly overlapping: the twenty-first card is placed at the bottom of this 'Backbone', horizontally if you like. On each side of the Backbone place four cards horizontally to represent the 'Ribs'.

If any Ace occur among these first twenty-nine cards, it is not to be included in the Backbone or Ribs, but laid apart as one of the foundations.

Should a King chance to come as bottom of the Backbone (as twenty-first card) you may transfer him to the bottom of the pack and replace by the next card dealt.

PROCEDURE. – After the lay-out, 'pack': but *only* on the Ribs in downward, on the base-Aces (as they appear) in upward suit-sequence, and NOT on the Backbone. Only the lowest card on the various ribs and the from time to time bottom-card of the Backbone are available for building. (This explains the 'grace' or 'merci' of removing the King mentioned above.) ('GRACE' or 'MERCI': a special privilege waiving or contradicting for a unique occasion the usual laws of any particular game.)

Clearly as soon as the lowest card of all is removed from the Backbone you will have two lowest cards in it available, and it is important never to overlook a chance of getting rid of a Backbone-card; for unless the whole bone is cleared away you cannot succeed. Any vacant space in the Ribs is *at once* filled with another card from the pack, or with the top-card of the waste-heap when you have begun to form it. (This you do as soon as you have finished whatever packing is possible in the original lay-out.)

Cards taken from the Backbone are not replaced – which is a blessing – but they can only be moved, remember, to a Rib or an Ace-foundation. *They may* NOT *replenish the Ribs, i.e. start a fresh rib.*

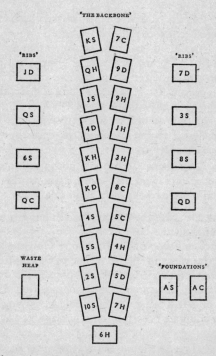

After exhausting the first pack, proceed with the second. This finished, the waste-heap may be turned over, and dealt once more. There is no other 'grace' or privilege.

HINTS. – The treatment of the Backbone is the key to this rather difficult but interesting game. Sometimes before you play a card you can tell from the Backbone that success is

impossible. If, for example, in the lay-out the high and low
cards of a suit are very much mixed and a King of that suit
turns up – you are done. Throughout the game you must be
on the watch to avoid 'chockering' and must frequently
refrain from packing available cards; for you are not bound to
make immediate use of consecutive cards.

The diagram shows the lay-out of a game which 'came out'
after turning the waste-heap.

Not a nice Backbone, for it is clear we cannot get at the
6 H (bottom-card Backbone) till the second pack,* but possible.

Cards arranged thus:

Rest of first pack: 10 C, 9 C, 2 C, J C, 4 C, 8 D, 6 D, 8 H,
3 D, 10 D, 2 H, A D, 6 and K C, A H, 10 H, 9 S, 7 S, 5 H,
3 C, 2 D.

In second pack: 9 D, 7 D, K D, A D, 4 H, 9 C, 6 C, 10 C,
10 H, 10 D, 2 C, J D, 9 H, 8 H, Q D, 6 H, 5 H, A H, 8 C, 7 C,
5 C, J S, A S, 4 C, 2 S, 5 D, 3 H, 2 H, Q H, 4 D, 3 C, 6 D,
3 D, J C, 10 S, A C, 2 D, 9 S, J H, K H, K and Q C, 6 S, 5 S,
3 S, 4 S, 7 H, K S, Q S, 8 S, 7 S, 8 D.

(This game is solved in Appendix II.)

BATTALION. *To form four ascending sequences from Ace to
King, four descending from King to Ace, following suit.*

LAY out twelve cards in a horizontal row to form twelve
depots. Should the row contain any Aces or Kings they are
to be taken and placed below as foundations: similarly any
other available cards such as 2's and 3's, Queens and Knaves;
their places being filled from stock until there are no available
cards in the first row. After this deal a second row, whence
only the first and last cards may be taken (their places being
filled as before from stock), but no *intermediate* cards here are
available. So proceed until both packets are exhausted, each

* Because both 3 H and 4 H are higher up in the right-hand side of the
'*Backbone*'.

subsequent row being treated like the second. The final row will probably not be complete.

From the bottom row – 'exposed' cards, as having none beneath them – any available card in suit-sequence to the established foundations may be taken; or fresh foundations started, should the row contain an Ace or King.

PROCEDURE. – The exposed cards may pack on each other in *Ascending* or *Descending* Sequence (Aces and Kings are mutually in sequence). If you make a space by getting rid of all the cards in a depot (or perpendicular column), any exposed Ace or King may be moved thither.

Two deals are allowed. When you can do no more packing or building after the first deal, take up first the left-hand column, then the second under it, and proceed towards the right-hand column, which will be placed at the bottom of this new-formed stock. This is dealt under the same rules as before *without shuffling* horizontally.

There are no peculiarities or 'graces'.

HINTS. – This is a really fine game, belonging to the class which Cavendish describes as 'Patiences presenting *definite* problems'. 'In them,' he writes, 'there is no middle course. Either it is right to take or move a certain card, or it is not; the proper play depends on analysis alone. If a player fails to solve the problem when a solution is possible, the failure is due merely to his want of analytical power.' Therefore look long at your lay-out, and make a definite plan before starting: 'respice finem', in fact.

Remember, too, how much you can benefit by the *varying sequence** in packing. When you have an ascending and a descending sequence going along simultaneously in the foundations, a depot packed like this – Jack, 10, 9, 10, Jack – is often most useful. Don't be carried away in building up one foundation to the neglect of others. Go for getting your foundations out, and remember how useful a space is. The

* Also called the '*Auxiliary*' sequence. Cp. '*Heads and Tails*', p. 101, and '*Russian*', p. 123.

example given below can be solved in one deal. (The Ace of
Diamonds in the left-hand corner of the second row could
not be taken for foundation purposes, as the other Ace of
Diamonds had already turned up.)

Lay-out:

```
7S   9D   3D   10D  7C   8H   9S   4C   KH  8D   4D   2C
AD   5H   10H  9C   10S  5S   QH   8C   6D  2D   4S   4H
9H   AS   6S   AH   JH   5D   3C   3C   KD  6C   6H   JH
2H   8S   JS   7D   2H   5C   3H   7H   QH  10C  3S   QS
5S   8S   4H   4D   8D   KC   QD   QC   7C  KS   6S   10H
6H   3D   7D   10D  AC   KC   6C   2S   3S  7S   9H   5H
3H   AC   QC   QD   10C  4C   AH   2S   4S  9S   8H   6D
5D   9D   JD   9C   8C   JS   10S  7H   2C  JC   JD   JC
5C
```

As foundations (turned up in dealing):
Ace and 2 of Diamonds, Ace of Spades.
King of Hearts, King of Diamonds, King and Queen of
Spades.
(Solution in Appendix III.)

BLOCKADE (THE BRITISH). *To form suit-sequences,
four ascending from Aces, four descending from Kings.*

LAY out ten cards in a row. In this row any Ace or King that
occurs (but only one Ace or one King of the same suit) may
be taken to form foundations, and placed apart from the main
lay-out, keeping for clearness the Ascending and Descending
Sequences separate. Any cards in correct sequence may also
be taken, and spaces thus made must be filled from stock,
proceeding from left to right. Continue thus till the top row
contains no card available for building. Then deal a second
row of ten below the first, taking as before any cards suitable
for the foundations, *but dealing the whole ten before taking any card.*

Any available card from either row may now be taken, and
the vacancies filled from the top of stock. You have the choice
of taking more than one available card before filling, or filling
after each card taken; but when once you start filling, you
must fill all vacancies before taking another card.

Naturally, cards taken from the second or succeeding rows will often make earlier cards now available for building. If vacancies occur both in first and second rows, the first row must be filled from left to right before the second; and even if an Ace turns up or a card available for an existing foundation, it *must first* be placed in its proper vacancy, and all the other vacancies filled before it is built on its foundation. Next deal a third row as before; but now the second or middle row is '*blockaded*', and a card in it can only be got at when a card has been taken from the space immediately above it in the first row, or immediately below it in the third.

The same applies when you go on to a fourth and further rows: in short, the top and bottom cards of any depot or column are at any time available for building, and their vacancies are filled as explained above.

PROCEED thus till stock is exhausted, each subsequent row blockading the rows between it and the top-row.

PRIVILEGES. – Though there is neither moving to a space nor from one depot (or column) to another, cards may be moved from the foundation sequences if the top-card of an ascending formation is in sequence with the top-card of a descending one in the same suit, or vice versa. Also if after the stock is exhausted, the Patience is blocked, you have the 'grace' or 'merci'* of taking any one blockaded card which releases the cards immediately above and below it, e.g. with six rows dealt a 'merci' card taken from the blockaded fourth row will release a card in the third and a card in the fifth. Some players allow a second 'merci' – there is only *one* deal.

In the strictest form of the game no 'merci' is allowed, and as soon as the second row is laid out, the top is not available until the last row has been dealt. But this is very rarely successful, and places the player too much at the mercy of the fall of the cards.

* See p. 69, line 25.

HINTS. – Because vacancies have to be filled at once, after
dealing the first row look at the top-card of stock before
taking an available card for building. If this stock-card is
likely to be soon wanted, take your building-card and fill the
vacancy; but don't take more than one till you have seen the
next card. If the stock-card, however, is not likely to be
wanted soon, deal the second row to gain the advantage of
seeing ten more cards. Use the privilege of looking at the
top-card of stock throughout, though some players do not
allow it – which, as Cavendish remarks, makes the game to a
great extent one of chance.

The play principally consists in manoeuvring top-cards of
stock so as to get the ones wanted in the first row for choice,
or in the last if you cannot manage a vacancy in the first. There
is room for skill in moving about the foundation sequences,
and when the whole stock is laid out, or a 'merci' card taken,
you have, of course, a Patience 'presenting a definite problem',
and requiring deep analysis.

It is a fine game, and though you play with care and look
at the top-card of the stock, is still not easy. Cavendish estimates
it as with one 'merci' slightly against the player, with two
'mercis' as in his favour.

The example shows the Patience in a game actually played
at a point when the whole stock was exhausted. You may
exercise your ingenuity by solving from this point. It comes
out with *one* 'merci'.

Columns:

8 D	4 C	10 D	J D	9 D	A C	5 C	7 D	2 D	4 D
10 H	8 H	A S	10 S	A D	3 C	J C	Q H	6 D	7 S
6 S	A H	10 H	Q D	Q S	5 S	7 H	J S	J H	5 H
K H	7 C	2 H	K C	8 D	4 H	3 S	4 S	2 S	3 H
Q C	K D	5 D	9 S	6 H	3 D	6 C	K S	9 H	2 C

Ascending Foundations (from Aces): 9 H, 10 C, 7 D, 8 S.
Descending Foundations (from Kings): J H, 8 C, 9 D, 8 S.

(This game is worked out from the beginning in Appendix
IV.)

COCK O' THE NORTH. *To form sixteen ascending suit-sequences, eight from Aces to Kings, eight from Deuces to Queens; from the Aces on the uneven, from the Deuces on the even cards.*

LAY out eight packets of four cards each, four packets face-downwards, four face-upwards in the form shown in the subjoined example.

Make a ninth packet of eight cards, and place face-upwards in the centre (as the packet headed 7 C in the diagram).

This Star is only a kind of feeder; for the real foundations

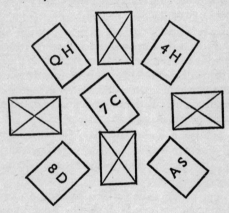

are the Aces and Deuces as they turn up, which are placed apart as shown below:

$$
\left\{
\begin{array}{llll}
\text{A H} & \text{A S} & \text{A D} & \text{A C} \\
\text{2 H} & \text{2 S} & \text{2 D} & \text{2 C} \\
\text{A H} & \text{A S} & \text{A D} & \text{A C} \\
\text{2 H} & \text{2 S} & \text{2 D} & \text{2 C}
\end{array}
\right.
$$

If an Ace or Deuce happens to be the top-card of one of the four upturned packets in the Star, remove it to serve as a foundation.

The Ace packets are built up in ODD numbers to the Kings, the Deuces in EVEN numbers to the Queens.

PROCEDURE. – Deal the cards one by one from stock, immediately placing any Ace or Deuce as a foundation, and building on these whenever a top-card in one of the upturned packets in the Star or the card dealt from stock is available.

Other cards from stock go on a rubbish-heap, of which the top-card can at any time be taken if in available sequence to any foundation. Should the top-card from the rubbish-heap be the same as one of the exposed cards on the Star (e.g. both Knaves of Hearts) the card from the Star has preference.

At the end of the deal take the eight cards from the centre packet of the Star (or those that remain), spread them out; and, if any are available, place them at once on their proper foundations. Next turn the top-card of the unexposed packets, and build, if available, proceeding thus till no more cards can be used. Then take up these packets, shuffle them with the rubbish-heap and deal as before. Two deals are allowed. Very clearly there is no skill in the game, and success depends very largely on the quickness with which the foundation cards appear.

THE CORONA OR ROUND DOZEN. *To build four ascending suit-sequences from Aces to Kings, four descending suit-sequences from Kings to Aces.*

LAY out twelve cards in a circle, then a second and a third outer circle of twelve, so that you have a CORONA of twelve rays, each containing three cards. Remove four Aces and four Kings (one of each suit) that are, or become, exposed to serve as foundations.

PROCEDURE. – Exposed cards are those which lie on the outer points of the Rays, and these only can be moved for building on the foundations. Any exposed card can be moved to another exposed card of the same suit in sequence either upward or downward. The vacancy thus made can be filled by moving any other exposed card, but only one at a time. Sequences, that is, cannot be moved *en bloc,* but only one card

at a time (thus reversing the sequence) if there is a suitable
exposed card or a vacancy to start on.

From the Rays to the foundations sequences may be lifted
bodily. When nothing more can be done with the Corona as

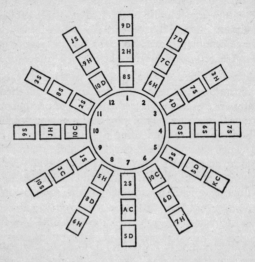

originally dealt, proceed from stock, filling up vacancies or
forming a waste-heap as you think preferable.

There is no second deal.

HINTS. – Though much depends on the fall of the cards, the
game is not really difficult and gives scope for some skill.

Get out foundations as soon as you can; plan to free buried
cards; and make the best use of vacancies, *which need not be
filled up at once.*

Keep a wary eye on the way your foundations are going;
and, while you may, arrange your sequences in the proper way.
It is annoying to find yourself towards the end of a game with
a long sequence unavailable because it is not in the right order.

Also don't 'get the wind up', even if you have a dozen or
more cards in the waste-heap. It is surprising how you can get

rid of them on Rays or foundations when a few vacancies
come along. The game of which the example below is the
lay-out came out very sweetly with the cards in the packs in
this order:

(After lay-out, thirty-six cards.)

2 C (top-card), Q D, 4 H, A H, 9 S, K C, A H, 7 H, 2 C,
3 H, 7 C, 4 C, K D, 2 D, 6 S, A D, 8 C, 5 and K S, J D, J C,
A S, 5 C, 6 C, 8 H, 5 S, J C, 4 D, K H, 8 C, 5 H, 6 and 9 D,
Q and A D, Q C, Q H, 10 and 8 H, 2 and J H, 6 C, 7 D, 10 D,
4 C, 9 C, 8 D, J D, 9 H, A C, 3 D, 3 D, 10 S, K H, 2 D, 4 and
Q S, Q C, 4 H, 5 C, Q H, 3 C, K S, 4 S, 9 C, A S, K D, 10 H.

(Solution in Appendix V.)

(The pack played face-upwards enables you to see the next
card to be dealt and to plan ahead.)

DIAMOND. *To form eight ascending suit-sequences from the
Aces.*

LAY out nine rows in the shape of a diamond, a single card,
three cards for the second row, five in the third, seven in the
fourth, nine in the fifth (the middle and longest row): after
which the rows decrease by twos, seven in the sixth row
corresponding to the fourth, five in the seventh, three in the
eighth, and again a single card.

PROCEDURE. – 'Outside' cards are 'exposed cards': i.e. to
begin with, the top and bottom single cards and the first and
last of each row. Any Aces in these positions in the original
'Diamond' are removed at once for the foundations; then any
cards in sequence that are, or become, exposed. There is no
freeing of the cards in an upward or downward direction.
The remaining cards are dealt out one by one from stock on to
three waste-heaps, if not Aces nor available for foundations
already established; but *you have no choice as to which heap* on which
to place any particular card. The cards must be placed on the
heaps in rotation from left to right.

A top-card of a waste-heap is always available for building.

You may take which you like, when you have a choice between a card on the waste-heaps or in the 'Diamond'.

Cards are taken from the latter only for building and their places in the original lay-out not filled till the end of the first deal (when, by the way, the player may consider himself fortunate if he has all the Aces out for building, and some of the sequences started). He now must take the left-hand waste-heap, turn it over, and fill the spaces in the 'Diamond' until it resumes its original shape. He may exercise his choice as to the order in which he fills the spaces and thereby perhaps gain some advantage; but note that *building on the foundations ceases* as soon as the first deal is over and only begins with the second deal on to the heaps when the 'Diamond' has been replenished.

After the 'Diamond' is filled up, the three heaps are well shuffled together and play begins again as in the first deal.

Should the game be unusually advanced you may have to take some cards from the second waste-heap: if, on the other hand, you are unlucky enough to have made no vacancies in the 'Diamond' you do not shuffle the heaps till the third deal.

After the third deal – played as the two previous ones – collect *all* the cards left, *including those on the 'Diamond'*, shuffle and lay out a small 'Diamond' like the first, but with seven lines only with seven cards in its middle row. This should bring the game out, but not necessarily.

There is no chance – or next to none – for skill in this game; but it is leisurely, and far from uninteresting.

DISPLAY. *From a single card to form a descending sequence of thirteen regardless of suit and arranged in a horizontal line; and under each card of this sequence to form an ascending sequence of eight, regardless of suit and arranged in a vertical column.*

LAY-OUT. – Start with a single card in the top left-hand corner of the board.

PROCEDURE. – Deal from stock one by one on to one of three waste-heaps. Assume your first card is a 7: a 6 of any

suit may be placed to its right; a 5 must wait till the 6 is in
position; an 8 can be placed below the 7, and so on: that is,
though the top row cards must wait their proper turn, those
already in position there may pack downwards freely.

Each column will have eight cards, each row thirteen.
(Take care not to build downwards more than *eight* cards.)
Again, assuming the first card is a 7, success will show in the
end the whole two packs laid out – a top row in descending
sequence from 7 to 8, the second row in descending sequence
from 8 to 9 and so on, the bottom row reading from an Ace
to a Deuce; while the downward columns will read 7 to Ace,
6 to King and so on to the last, an 8 to a 2.

When stock is finished gather up the waste-heaps and deal
again, but *only on one heap.*

PECULIARITIES AND HINTS. – Unique, as far as I know,
among Patience games in starting from a single card and
ending in all the 104 laid out. It requires more watchfulness
than skill; but there is room for intelligence in the handling of
the waste-heaps, where care must be taken to avoid 'chockering'.

These tips may be useful:

(1) Don't put many cards of the same denomination on the
same waste-heap.

(2) Get out the top row as quickly as you can.

(3) Develop the columns equally as far as you can.

An interesting and popular game.

THE DOUBLE FAN. *To form four ascending sequences from
Ace to King, four descending sequences from King to Ace, following
suit.*

LAY out the pack in depots of three face-upwards, thirty-four
'fans' in all with two cards over, each of which forms a separate
depot. These will be conveniently arranged in contracting
rows of eight, seven, six, five, four, three fans and a bottom

row containing the two single cards and one fan of three. Aces and Kings (one each of the four suits) on the top – that is the right-hand of the fans – may be taken for foundations.

PROCEDURE. – Top-cards of fans in sequence with the foundations may be taken for building, and a top-card of any fan may be moved on the top-card of another fan if in sequence (either above or below). Any number of cards may be moved to one depot. It is no advantage to clear all three cards of any particular fan, as the vacancy cannot be used.

Only one deal is allowed.

HINTS. – With so many exposed cards (thirty-six) the Patience is much in favour of the player, and does not require so much analysis as most of the 'Definite'* Patiences; but still you must plan ahead to get out foundation cards as soon as may be, and be very careful when running off one sequence in a suit that you are not leaving the cards you will need for the other sequence in the same suit (ascending or descending as the case may be) 'chockered'.†

Thus if a 'fan' contains from left to right the 9, 10, 8 of Spades and you build the ascending sequence in Spades with the other 8 up to the 9, forgetful of the awkward arrangement of this particular fan, you have blocked your descending sequence; for you can get at the 10 neither from above nor below. Similar situations are likely to occur in every game of Double Fan, but can always be got over if you are not in too great a hurry to get on with one sequence to the neglect of its opposite. It makes a very pretty game, not too exacting.

VARIATION of the game is to form Eight *Ascending* Sequences from the Aces, when, of course, Kings are not taken for foundations, and packing from fan to fan is only in descending suit-sequence. The other rules are unaltered.

The game given below comes out quite easily, but you have to be careful with the Spades.

* See p. 72, *ad imum*.

† See p. 68, footnote.

(7 C, 4 and Q D); (8 C, 7 S, 5 C); (6 C, 10 H, 4 D); (6, 5 and Q D); (K S, 10 C, 2 H); (6 D, 9 D, 5 H); (4 H, 3 H, 9 C); (J H, 8 D, 9 H).

(9 S, 10 and 3 C); (2 D, A and 8 C); (7 and 5 D, 4 H); (10 D, J S, 8 D); (7 D, 3 S, 7 C); (6 H, Q C, J D); (8 S, K H, A C).

(10 S, 9 D, 6 S); (9 H, J S, 7 H); (8 and 5 H, 6 S); (7 and 8 S, 5 C); (4 and 2 S, 3 D); (A H, K C, 6 C).

(7 H, 4 C, 5 S); (6 and 3 H, 2 D); (A S, K and Q H); (3 S, 2 C, A S); (K and Q C, 10 S).

(Q H, K and A D); (2 H, K D, 4 C); (Q S, J C, 9 S); (5 S, K S, 4 S).

(A H, 9 and J C); (10 and J H, 2 S); (A, J, 10 D).

3 C; (2 C, 3 D, 8 H); Q S.

(For solution see Appendix VI.)

THE DOUBLE PYRAMID. *To build eight ascending sequences without regard to suit.*

LAY-OUT. — The first card turned up from the shuffled pack is the apex of the outer pyramid. Put a line of ten cards on each side of it in a downward-slanting row. (You may economize space by overlapping these.) The twenty-second card determines the bases of the inner pyramid, built up inside the first without regard to suit. (See diagram.)

PROCEDURE. — Four waste-heaps are allowed for cards from stock not immediately eligible for building, in which great care must be taken against blocking cards, as there is only one turn. Any card from the sides of the first pyramid is at any time available for building, as also the temporary top-cards of the four waste-heaps.

HINTS. — (1) Lose no chance of taking cards from the first pyramid; but when you have a choice between cards in it and the waste-heaps, take the latter.

(2) Keep one of the waste-heaps for the last and penultimate cards of the foundations: e.g. if a 9 is the twenty-second card, keep a waste-packet for 8's and 7's. Naturally, when you can

account for all these except two, or even three, you can put a few lower cards in the heap.

The game is interesting and deserves inclusion in this selection because good play with the waste-heaps will go far to overcome a bad run of cards.

(This game is worked out in Appendix VII.)

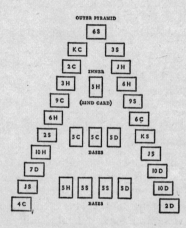

OUTER PYRAMID

6S

KC   3S

2C   INNER   JH

3H   5H   6H

9C   (22ND CARD)   9S

6H   6C

2S   5C   5C   5D   KS

10H   BASES   JS

7D   10D

JS   5H   5S   5S   5D   10D

4C   BASES   2D

THE EMPEROR. *To form eight ascending suit-sequences from Aces to their Kings.*

LAY out face-downwards ten packets each of three cards – which are called *'sealed'* packets; underneath them deal a row of ten single cards face-upward. Take out any Ace that appears in this row for a foundation.

PROCEDURE. – Examine the row to see if any packing can be done downwards and in alternate colours (e.g. a red 7 on a black 8). If now or later a vacancy is made in the row, turn up the top-card of the packet immediately above, thus 'breaking the seal'. Then deal the cards from stock one by one, building or packing if you deem it advisable, leaving on a rubbish-heap if otherwise. When you get rid of the whole of a sealed packet any exposed card can be placed in the vacancy and become the haed of a column. Continue to the end of stock, building up

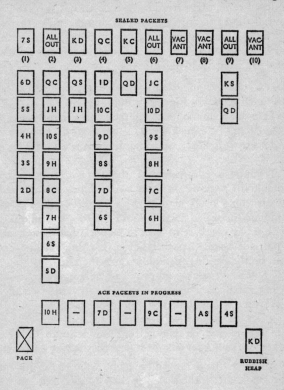

SEALED PACKETS

7 S	ALL OUT	K D	Q C	K C	ALL OUT	VAC ANT	VAC ANT	ALL OUT	VAC ANT
(1)	(2)	(3)	(4)	(5)	(6)	(7)	(8)	(9)	(10)

ACE PACKETS IN PROGRESS

on Aces and forming columns whenever you can. If you succeed, each Ace-foundation will end in its proper King.

PRIVILEGES AND PECULIARITIES. – You may at any time move an exposed card from one packet to another, if in due sequence. You also have the privilege of 'worrying back', i.e. putting back cards already on the Ace-foundations to the columns, if by this device you can get at obstinate cards and make better combinations.

After finishing stock you can take up the rubbish-heap and lay down three cards from it. If you can find a place for any or all of these, do so; and fill their number up to three from the rubbish-heap again. This can continue till none of the three can be placed, in spite of any 'worrying back', etc., when you have finally failed.

HINTS. – A very fine game – one of the very best Patiences – with much scope for ingenuity and forethought.

(1) Do not be in too great a hurry to pack, hardly ever doing so on a King or Queen, *except at the head of a column when the sealed packet is finished* – when naturally you want Kings at the top.

(2) Suppose two cards of the same denomination are available for packing on – say two red 10's are exposed and you turn up a black 9 from stock – exercise your power of looking at the sealed packets above the 10's, to find out which it would pay you best to free: in fact you had better examine its particular sealed packet before packing on any card to avoid bottling up Aces and low cards therein.

(3) Make all the use you can of interchanging columns and gaining vacancies which are invaluable towards the end.

(4) Don't be frightened of a big rubbish-heap.

(5) Get out the sealed packets as soon as you can: this is more important even than getting foundations. (In the game worked out two Aces did not appear till the very end of stock.)

Assume you have carried the game as far as the diagram on p. 85: there are in the sealed packets row (1) two cards, row (4) two cards, row (5) one card concealed: the rest are all out: in the rubbish-heap from top-card down are K D, 10 H, 10 D, 9 S, 3 H, K H, Q S, 2 C, 8 D, 2 H, K S (eleven cards).

You can account for eighty-one cards: there are therefore left in stock twenty-three (which are in this order – 4 D (top card), J C, 9 C, 5 C, 5 H, 8 D, J S, A D, 3 D, Q H, 5 S, 10 C, 6 C, 8 S, 9 D, Q H, 3 C, 7 S, 2 S, A H, K C, A C, 4 C).

The cards in the sealed packets are J D, K H (row 1); 10 and J S (row 4); 4 S (row 5).

(The game of which this is a later stage is worked out fully in Appendix VIII.)

FOUR CORNER. *To build four ascending sequences from Aces, four descending from Kings, following suit.*

LAY-OUT. – Lay out twelve cards as in the diagram, starting in the top left-hand corner with a card at an angle of 45° to a column of four; then another card in the bottom left-hand

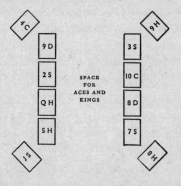

corner at an angle; leave space for two columns of four to be filled by an Ace and King of each suit, as they appear; then a card at the top right-hand corner, another column of four and a twelfth card in the bottom right-hand corner.

PROCEDURE. – Deal on these cards in the same order until stock is finished, taking the Aces and Kings as they appear and building thereon *with this restriction*: Corner cards are always available (if in sequence), but cards in the vertical lines only if in the same row as the packets on which they are placed. This restriction ceases when stock is exhausted. Then you can take for building any top-card of the depots, and can also pack on these in ascending or descending suit-sequence.

On coming to a stop, take up the twelve outer packets in the same order as originally dealt, and again deal round *without shuffling*. This can be done twice, but the game does not easily come out. (Three deals in all.)

The only useful HINT – for the game, though interesting, calls for no skill and depends almost entirely on the fall of the cards – is to make the most you can of the 'reversing' sequences.

THE FOUR MARRIAGES. *To form eight ascending sequences, following suit; four from an Ace of each suit, rising by twos (Ace, 3, 5, 7 . . . 2, 4, 6 . . . Queen), four from a Deuce of each suit, rising by twos (2, 4, 6, 8 . . . Ace, 3, 5 . . . to Knave, King).*

LAY out cards face-upwards, rejecting any card of the same value as one already dealt until you have thirteen cards of different value (not regarding suit). Place these in a packet face-upwards on the table in whatever order they happen to lie.

Begin then to deal a waste-heap, and as Aces and Deuces appear place them (one of each suit) around the thirteen packet, the Ace and Deuce of each suit next to each other, so that you have in the end eight foundation cards.

PROCEDURE. – Build on these in the sequences described above, having at any moment the choice of three cards, the card dealt from stock, the top-card of the waste-heap, and the top-card of the central packet.

The waste-heap may be turned twice.

Success will show each King next to his Queen at the top of a packet of thirteen cards, the central packet being absorbed.

Clearly the game is entirely one of luck and depends immensely on the quickness with which bases turn up.

GEMINI. *To form eight ascending sequences, irrespective of suit.*

LAY out four cards of different value, allowing space between them for each to have a 'twin' of its own denomination next to it, when turned up.

PROCEDURE. – Form four waste-heaps. When a card turns
up one degree higher than any of the first four, place it above
the original card and build on it, *but not until the original card
has its twin beside it.*

Success sees the 'twins' each with a packet above it, finishing
in the card next below them in value.

You may collect the waste-heaps after the stock is finished,
and have another shot, but this time only *two* waste-heaps are
allowed. Thus if your first four cards are 3 H, 6 S, 9 C, K D,
your result should show:

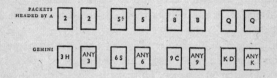

THE GENERAL'S. *To form eight ascending sequences, following suit.*

LAY out a row of thirteen cards; then turn up the next three
cards, selecting one of these for the base, and placing the two
rejected in a line below with seven others.

PROCEDURE. – The other seven bases will be placed in a row
with the first chosen as they turn up: upon the nine cards in
the lower row pack in alternate colours downwards. The cards
from the top row (the first thirteen dealt) can only be taken to
be placed on their proper base-packet, and that only in the
order they are arranged from right to left. Thus in the diagram:

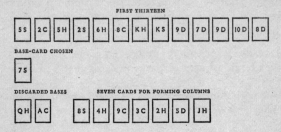

the 10 of Diamonds can only be taken on its foundation when the 8 has been taken, the 6 of Hearts when all on its right up to the 8 of Clubs have been placed.

In choosing the base-card you will have to look very carefully at the top line to make sure certain cards are not blocking each other. Thus in the diagram, 7 being chosen as base, you can get to the 10 of Diamonds, but not to the 9 of Diamonds beyond it, for behind that lies the second 7. You have, however, the privilege before beginning the game of transposing any two cards in this top row, and here you can save the situation by changing the 9 and 10, or the 7 and 10.

If more than one suit is blocked like this – deal a fresh thirteen.

This danger of blocking persists throughout the game, both as you build and pack; and you must in either process keep constant watch on the row. Thus again – in the diagram game – in your first Heart sequence should a 6 turn up from the pack, you *must* not take it for building; for this would block the 5 of Hearts (third card dealt), which lies to the left of the other 6. In such an event you must wait till you can get at the 6 in the first row.

Deal the cards one by one from stock, placing such as will neither pack nor build on a waste-heap. A vacancy made in the lower row may be filled by any exposed card either from the packets or the waste-heap. Clearly one or two vacancies will be useful in moving sequences from one column to another. The top-card of the waste-heap is available for building or packing at any time.

After exhausting stock take up the waste-heap and turn up the first card: if you can place it, play the next, and so on.

When you can find no place, the game has failed.

HINTS. – A very good but difficult game.

Don't be in a hurry to pack on cards that will be wanted soon.

Work with your vacancies to transfer sequences as much as possible.

Try to get the cards that will crown the foundations at the top of sequences in vacancies.

The example given came out on the turning of the waste-heap, the cards being arranged as follows:

9 II, A H, 3 C, 2 D, 8 C, A C, 2 S, Q S, J C, Q D, A D, 7 H, 5 C, 6 S, 5 S, Q C, 5 C, 4 D, J S, 2 D, 7 C, 3 H, K C, 4 C, 10 C, K H, 10 S, 5 H, 7 C, K D, 5 D, K S, K D, 6 C, 2 H, A H, K C, 7 H, 7 D, J D, 6 D, J S, 6 H, A S, 10 H, 9 S, 8 H, Q H, 9 H, 3 S, 2 C, J C, 10 H, 9 C, 4 H, 6 D, A D, 6 S, 10 S, J D, A S, 3 D, 3 S, 8 H, Q C, 4 S, Q D, 7 S, 3 D, 8 D, 6 C, 10 C, 4 S, J H, 9 S, 8 S, 10 D, 3 H, Q S, 4 D, 4 C.

(See Appendix IX.)

GRANDFATHER'S. *To form four ascending sequences from Aces to Kings, and four descending from Kings to Aces, following suit.*

LAY out two parallel lines, each of ten cards, putting out an Ace and King of each suit, below and above the two lines respectively as they turn up. The duplicate Aces and Kings take their places like other cards.

PROCEDURE. – If any vacancy occurs in the lines, fill up immediately from stock: then form a waste-heap, which may be turned once; but you have the privilege of placing one card on any or all of the twenty in the two rows. Here you must avoid the superimposed cards 'chockering'* the lower.

HINTS, ETC. – The game is only included as a companion to 'Grandmamma's Patience'. It becomes a little more sporting if you either try to do without the waste-heap altogether or limit it – say, to half a dozen cards. There is no room for skill.

GRANDMAMMA'S. *To form four ascending, four descending sequences, following suit.*

LAY out two rows each of eleven cards; the twenty-third card

* See p. 68, footnote.

determines the upper foundations and is placed above the two rows with three cards of the same denomination, one from each of the other suits. These are taken as they turn up and built upwards.

The four lower foundations are similarly formed by the cards one pip higher than the upper ones, and built upwards.

PROCEDURE. – Thus if a 6 be the twenty-third card, the upward sequences will be built on four 7's. If any cards in the two rows of eleven are suitable for building, take them and fill vacancies from stock at once. You may place one card upon each of the twenty-two, still working off on foundations whenever possible, and filling vacancies. You may also take four 'grace' cards and place them on one side. If, after you have covered all the twenty-two and put out the 'grace' cards, you can go no further, you have failed.

HINTS. – The game is easy enough, though a better one than 'Grandfather's'; if you take elementary care, in the choice of which cards you cover with which, to avoid blocking. Be especially careful of penultimate and ultimate cards in your sequences and when ascending and descending sequences approach each other.

Failures are estimated as 1–10; and then they are generally right at the end, and the result of improvident covering of the first cards.

GRANDFATHER'S CLOCK. *To form twelve ascending sequences, following suit, the top-cards to correspond with the hours on a clock face.*

LAY-OUT. – Take from the pack a sequence of twelve cards from the 2 to the King, three of each suit, choosing the cards in a regular rotation of suits, i.e. if you have 2 H, 3 C, 4 D, 5 S, go on 6 H, 7 C, 8 D, 9 S, 10 H, etc. The cards of each suit must, that is, be equidistant (2, 6, 10: 3, 7, Jack); but it is of no importance what suit you start with, as long as you keep to the same rotation.

Arrange these twelve in a circle with a 6 to correspond to one o'clock, a 7 for two o'clock, . . . a Jack for six o'clock, a Deuce for ten o'clock, a 5 for midday (or midnight!). These are the twelve foundation cards. Next deal twelve packets of three cards each, one behind each hour, starting at one o'clock (which is represented by a 6 of some suit), and following as a clock's finger goes.

PROCEDURE. – The top-card (i.e. the last dealt) of each packet, if in ascending sequence and in suit with any foundation card, may be taken for building, *provided it does not carry the sequence beyond the corresponding hour of the clock.* Thus suppose you have placed the 6 of Hearts as a foundation card at one o'clock, there you will build Hearts up to the Ace *and no further*; the Deuce of Hearts to the 5 will be wanted on the 10 of Hearts, which you will have placed for five o'clock. (For this part of the game Aces are in ascending sequence with Kings.)

Any top-card of the outer packets in descending sequence and in suit with any other top depot card may be moved from one depot to another. (Here Kings are in descending sequence from Aces.)

After taking and moving as many cards as you think best, you must *at once* fill up the packets till there are three in each. (They may have *more,* but must not be allowed to have *less,* than three.)

When all packets have been made up to three, *but not before,* the top-card of stock may be dealt (if in ascending suit-sequence) to any of the foundation cards, or (if in descending suit-sequence) to any top-card of the packets, or to the waste-heap (called in this particular Patience 'The Clockmaker').

The top-card at the 'Clockmaker's' can only be moved on to foundations, can neither fill up packets nor be packed on them; and, so long as there is any card in stock, all packets must be filled up before a card can be taken from the Clockmaker.

Only one deal is allowed. In the finish all cards will be absorbed in the clock-face with a Knave for eleven, a Queen for twelve o'clock.

Hints. – (1) Since you have to fill up the packets (or depots) at once, it is advisable to play this Patience with stock held face-upwards. As Cavendish remarks, if you are not allowed to look at the top-card of stock, the 'Clock' (like the British Blockade, *q.v.*) becomes a game of mere chance.

(2) If this top-card of stock is likely to be soon wanted, only take or move one card, and then fill the depot. If the top-card is unlikely to be wanted soon, or is one of which the duplicate card can be easily got at from another depot, take or move two cards from a depot whose bottom-card is not immediately required and then fill.

(3) As cards sent to the Clockmaker are so hard to get back, avoid sending any as far as possible. You have twelve foundations and twelve depots to play on.

But there are occasions when a card must go to the Clockmaker: suppose your Heart sequence at five o'clock has been built up from 10 to Ace, and the other Heart Ace appears in stock.

Once only can this second Ace reach its foundation, i.e. when the one o'clock Heart sequence has been built up to the King. Consequently, if the vacant place in the outer packets where the second Ace would have to go would leave it over any Heart between 9 and King, you are ruining your chance of success, and go to the Clockmaker's it must.

Hearts between 2 and 9 in such a position will be wanted for the nine o'clock foundation, and could with safety (if with inconvenience) be placed under the second Ace in packets, though you would have to wait till the whole of the one o'clock packet was finished before using them.

(4) Keep in reserve some positions which allow you to move one or two cards at pleasure from a packet, according to the nature of the top-card in stock.

(5) It is not wise – except very occasionally – to empty a packet while more than two cards remain in stock, as filling any space may block the Patience.

Played thus, the game – perhaps the finest of all Patiences, certainly a first-class game – is in favour of the player, but it wants real foresight and ingenuity.

In the event of success there will be eight suit-sequences of nine cards, and four of eight.

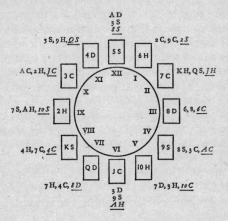

The diagram gives the game solved in Appendix X; the underlined cards are the top-cards of their respective packets.

The rest of the pack was arranged as follows:

5 D (top-card), 5 C, 6 H, 3 D, 8 H, 8 H, A S, 10 S, A S, Q H, 2 S, 6 S, 4 S, 7 H, 2 D, 9 D, 9 C, K H, 3 S, 2 D, 10 D, 3 H, J S, 8 C, 9 H, Q C, K D, 10 H, 7 S, 5 H, 2 C, 6 D, Q C, 9 D, K C, 4 H, J D, J S, Q H, K D, 10 C, 6 S, 5 H, 7 D, K C, 5 D, J H, 10 D, J D, Q D, K S, 6 D, 5 C, A D, 4 S, 4 D (last card).

GRAND ROUND. *To make a circle, its circumference formed of packets of four cards, each packet consisting of three cards together counting eighteen and crowned by a court card.*

LAY out the eight Aces in the form of a cross: they take no part in the game, but look pretty and help to prevent your circle being lop-sided. Deal out two rows of six cards each. If any three of them count eighteen and there is a King, Queen or Knave to crown them, pack together and start the circumference of the 'Grand Round'.

PROCEDURE. – If not, cover the two rows with another dozen cards, and, *using only the exposed cards*, try again for the combination eighteen and a court card. Fill any vacancy in the rows at once from the pack (a superimposed card when removed makes the one under it exposed): otherwise deal twelve at a time. If you have a choice of more than one card of the same value, you may look underneath to see which it will pay you most to take. This is the only point where the game gives any scope for ingenuity.

You may only make up the eighteen with *three* cards; any two cards, such as a 10 and an 8, or any four cards, such as 2, 3, 6 and 7, are not allowed; and you must have a court card to top off with.

If you succeed, the Aces will be surrounded by twenty-four packets of four cards each; and, if you like, you can make the effect more gorgeous by arranging the court cards alternately red and black.

HADEN. *To work off the cards dealt in packets by couples counting eleven 'pips', or sequences of King, Queen, Knave.*

LAY out the two packs in twelve packets, each of eight cards, face-down with the exception of the top-card of each packet. The remaining eight cards are placed face-upwards and singly in a row to form the 'dummy hand'.

PROCEDURE. – Examine the exposed cards for any two that make eleven (e.g. 5 and 6, Ace and 10) and remove: remove also a sequence of Knave, Queen, King if the three are at any time exposed together. If there is only one picture-card on the board and the two others are in dummy, you may take those two; but if there are two on the board also, only one can be taken from dummy. You only have recourse to dummy when, without it, you cannot find two cards to make eleven; and the longer dummy is untouched, the better the chance of success. When more than one available card is of the same signification, you may look at the cards underneath to see which it would be better to take. When no more combinations can be found, turn up the (new) top-cards of the packets from which cards have been taken, and look for fresh combinations.

HINTS. – You may compare the single-pack Patience called 'Number Eleven'.*

THE HARP. *To form eight ascending sequences from the Aces, following suit.*

LAY out face-downwards a row of eight cards with a ninth card face-upwards; under it a second row of seven cards downwards with an eighth card face-upwards; a third row of six with a seventh face-upwards, and so to a row of two, the right-hand one upwards, and finally a single card upwards.

PROCEDURE. – If any card among the exposed nine is an Ace, take it for a foundation, and turn over the card immediately above it, which thus becomes available for packing or building. Exposed cards in the lay-out may be packed in descending sequence and alternate colour, each card moved exposing the one above it, and Aces going out for foundations.

This finished, deal from the remaining cards one by one on to a waste-heap, looking for chances of packing or building. A vacancy made in the top line can only be filled by a King or King-sequence – no other sequence may be moved. If neither King nor King-sequence is available when a vacancy is made, the first card of stock, whatever it be, or the top-card of the waste-heap must fill the vacancy *at once*. The waste-heap may be turned twice and its top-card is always available for packing or building.

HINTS. – A stiff game and difficult to get out – your 'rights' are so very limited, and you are so much at the mercy of the distribution of the lay-out. But these 'tips' may be useful.

* See my *Games of Patience – Single Pack*, pp. 36 and 14.

(1) Play with the stock held face-upwards (as recommended for 'Grandfather's Clock' and 'The Blockade').

(2) This will often help you to hold up making a vacancy until a King or suitable card comes along.

(3) Do not pack too eagerly on the first deal *unless on a King,* which you have a chance of getting into a vacancy, or with low cards that ought to work off on foundations. Otherwise you will never uncover the cards in the lay-out.

(4) Often it will pay you to pack with a card available for building, if you can thus get a longer sequence on the board and expose more cards.

With the lay-out and arrangement of stock as given below the game comes out after turning the waste-heap (which contains twenty-three cards at the end of the first deal) once. Cards between brackets are face-down.

Lay-out:

[J D, K C, 6 S, 2 S, K S, 10 H, 7 C, 2 H], 2 S.
[Q C, Q D, 5 S, A D, Q C, 4 D, 3 C], 9 S.
[10 C, 3 S, 6 H, 9 H, 10 S, 2 D], K H.
[6 C, 7 D, 3 D, 8 D, 10 D], 5 D.
[8 S, K S, 10 H, 5 C], A S.
[5 H, A C, J H], Q H.
[J C, 4 C], 9 D.
[Q S], 8 C.
3 H.

Stock in this order:

J D, A D, K D, J 5, 3 H, 8 H, A H, 9 C, 7 C, 2 C, K C, 3 C,
6 D, 7 H, 8 D, 7 S, 2 D, 7 H, 4 S, J S, 3 D, 7 D, 10 S, 4 C,
5 S, J C, 4 D, 9 S, 6 D, 6 S, J S, 10 D, 6 C, Q D, A S, K H,
5 D, 8 C, 10 C, A H, Q S, 4 H, 3 S, Q H, 8 S, 9 C, 7 S, A C,
9 D, 9 H, 2 H, 4 S, K D, 4 H, 5 C, 2 C, 6 H, 8 H.

(The game is solved in Appendix XI.)

THE HAT. *To form four ascending, four descending sequences, following suit.*

LAY out eight cards into two perpendicular rows of four cards

each, beginning with any selected Ace or King. These are to
form the sides of the hat; and room is left between them for
four Aces and four Kings, one of each suit, taken as they
turn up for foundations to be built upon in the usual manner.
Deal six depots of four cards together from left to right, two
at the bottom of the side of each column, two below them to
form the brim. Thus the original lay-out will look like an
old-fashioned curly-brimmed 'topper'. The side-cards and the
top-cards of the brim-depots – that is, the last card dealt, or
put on them – can be taken, if available, for the foundations.
A diagram should make the lay-out clear.

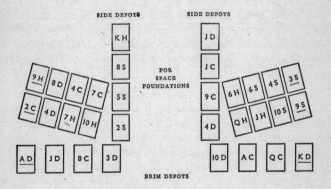

(The cards underlined in the brim-depots are exposed.)

PROCEDURE. – No side-depot may contain more than one
card, but any top brim-depot card can be moved to a space
in the side-depots. If a space is left by taking or moving all
the cards from a brim-depot, that depot must be filled by
dealing to it four cards together from the top of stock. When
you have finished moving or taking such cards as you think
wise, deal four cards together to each of the brim-depots *in
order* from left to right without moving or taking any card till
the whole six lots of four have been placed.

Repeat procedure till stock is exhausted.

Cards on the ascending and descending foundations may be moved from one to another when in sequence.

Three deals are allowed, and after each deal the brim-depot cards are to be taken up, shuffled and redealt by fours on the brim-depots, but the side-depots are not touched.

PRIVILEGES AND VARIATIONS. – If blocked after the third deal some players allow a 'grace' of taking any one brim-depot card other than a top-card, which makes the game with good play decidedly in favour of the player; without this 'merci', though very uncertain, 'it is believed', says Cavendish, 'to be on the whole somewhat in his favour'.

Some players deal to the brim by three cards at a time – this makes the game easier, but then the right of moving cards from one foundation to another is not granted. Some players do not shuffle the cards taken up after the deal, which makes it possible (with a good memory) to know the position of every card in stock.

HINTS. – (1) The way you manage the side-depot spaces is all-important. Always try to keep at least one vacancy until the very end of the third deal, or unless you see that filling it implies getting out a card from a brim-depot that will release other side-cards and make another vacancy at once.

(2) When the ascending and descending sequences are approaching the point where they meet and a card turns up that will soon be able to go on either sequence, hold it in a side space till you have seen several more cards.

(3) When drawing near the end of the second or third deal with less than twenty-four cards in stock, remember that the remainder of the deal will not cover the right-hand depots.

The game worked out in the Appendix was only successful on the third deal, the first shuffle of the brim-depots being very malignant. The lay-out was that given in the diagram, and stock was in this order:

9 C, J S, 4 S, *A S*; K S, 2 and 10 C, *Q D*; 7, J and 6 C, *2 D*; 7 D, 10 H, 10 D, *A H*; 5 H, 5 H, 7 and *9 S*; 7, 5, 2 S, *Q D*; A H, K D, K C, *9 D*; 8 H, K H, 3 C, *8 C*; 9 D, J S, A C, *5 C*;

2 H, Q H, 3 C, *6 D*; 5 D, 7 H, 4 C, *K S*; 3 H, 4 H, 7 D, *8 H*; Q S, 2 H, 5 D, *10 S*; A, 6, 8, *3 S*; K C, 2 D, 3 D, *Q S*; Q, 10, 5, *6 C*; A D, 4 H, 6 D, *J H*; 8 D, 6, 3 and *9 H*.

(Cards in italics were exposed cards of brim-depots.)

HEADS AND TAILS. *To form four ascending sequences from the Ace, four descending from the King, following suit.*

LAY out a single row of eight cards, then below this a row of eight packets, each of eleven cards, below this again the remaining eight cards in a single row. (The first row as the 'heads', the third the 'tails'.)

An important *variation* – which makes the game easier – is to make the middle packets of ten each only, and to have a reserve of eight cards to be employed at pleasure.

PROCEDURE. – One Ace of each suit and one King, as they occur, either now or later, are to be placed below and above the three rows, and built upon as usual.

Cards for the foundation-sequences can only be taken from the 'heads' or 'tails' – *not* from the middle packets. These are only to be got at when a vacancy occurs in the top or bottom row, when a card from the packet immediately above or below the vacancy is taken. Thus, if you succeed, all the middle packets are absorbed. Should the whole of any middle packet be absorbed and a vacancy occur above or below its place, that vacancy is filled by the top-card of the packet immediately to the left, or if it be the extreme left-hand packet that is finished, then from the extreme right-hand packet. (But another *variation* allows you your choice among the top-cards of the packets, which gives scope for some discretion.)

Cards in 'Heads and Tails' can be packed on each other if in sequence and following suit in *either* direction. This so-called *'auxiliary'** sequence is most useful. You can pack an 8 on a 7, then another 7 on that 8, and so forth.

HINTS. – It is in the handling of this packing (with due regard

* Cp. *'Battalion'*, p. 71, and *'Russian'*, p. 123.

to the cards in the middle which are to come and the way in which the foundation-sequences are going) that the skill of the game comes in. You have also the privilege when foundation-packets are within one of each other (in the same suit) of moving cards from one to another. This will often enable cards in the 'head' and 'tail' rows, which seemed hopeless, to be moved, and so fresh ones set free from the middle.

HEAP. *Upon a sequence of thirteen cards from a 7 to a 6 in alternate colours to form twelve sequences of eight cards following colour, and one sequence in alternate colours.*

LAY out a sequence of thirteen cards in alternate colour from a 7 to a 6 (suit does not matter). Then lay out twenty-two packets of four cards and one of three. There is no packing in the game.

PROCEDURE. – Now build from the 'exposed' cards of the twenty-three packets – that is, the right-hand cards of each packet – in numerical sequence and the same colour upward on the first twelve bases; on the thirteenth base build in alternate colours. Success will show a sequence from Ace to King in alternate colours save for the last two (headed by Queen and King), which will be of the same colour.

When every available card has been built, gather up the remainder, shuffle and redeal in packets of four – any cards over (one, two or three) have a packet to themselves. A packet if exhausted may not be filled by cards from other heaps.

There are only two deals.

HINTS. – An excellent game which with the exercise of sufficient foresight is in favour of the player.

(1) Try to keep the sequences roughly level.

(2) Turn down the eighth card of each sequence to prevent careless overbuilding.

(3) Pay particular attention to the troublesome 'alternate colour' sequence (the thirteenth).

(4) Calculate as you go on how many of each 'pip' you have used, and how many you still want.

(5) As far as possible work the packets to get out buried cards. You gain nothing by clearing the whole of a packet, so if two cards of the same denomination are available at the same time choose the one from the packet with the more cards in it.

(6) Keep a watchful eye, especially towards the end, to prevent the last few cards blocking each other.

VARIATION. – Some players make twenty-nine packets of three cards each, and two of two instead of twenty-two packets of four cards. This, of course, as giving more exposed cards, makes the game easier.

(Cp. and contrast 'Display' and 'S' Patiences.)

With *Bases*; 7 D, 8 S, 9 H, 10 S, J D, Q S, K H, A C, 2 D, 3 C, 4 H, 5 S, 6 H, and *Packets*; A D, Q H, J C, *9 D*; 6 and 7 D, 2 and *8 H*; 3 and Q H, 3 D, *7 C*; 2 and 3 C, 7 H, *8 C*; 7, 6 and Q C, *8 D*; 5 and 6 H, J D, *A S*; 9 S, 4, 5 and *2 D*; Q and 10 D, 10 S, *K D*; 10 H, 9 S, Q and *10 D*; 8 D, 6 and 5 S, *8 C*; K and 9 D, J and *2 S*; 2 and K S, 10 C, *3 D*; 4 and 3 S, 9 C, *5 D*; A H, 5 C, 9 and *J H*; 8 H, 7 and Q S, *A D*; A and 4 S, A H, *4 D*; Q C, 5 H, 5 C, *4 C*; A C, 6 and 7 S, *9 C*; J H, K S, K C, *3 S*; K H, 6 D, 10 and *2 H*; 10 C, 3 H, 4 C, *7 H*; 6 C, 4 H, 2 and *K C*; J C, 8 S, *J S*. The game comes out without a second deal. (*See* solution.)

Cards in italics are exposed.

HERRING BONE. *To form four ascending and four descending sequences, following suit.*

LAY out twenty-four cards by fours, arranged under each other as follows: three cards in a fan shape and one below them; three fan again and one below. Thus you will have a column (the Herring Bone) of six sets of four. Next place a card sideways to right and left of the herring bone both at the top and the bottom, four cards in all, which are called '*ends*'. Then two more perpendicularly, called the '*sides*', on each side of the bone. The next card – the thirty-third – determines the bases. It and its fellow 7 (as they turn up from stock, or are got at in the herring bone) are placed, four to the right, four to the left of the lay-out, to be built in suit-sequence, four upwards, four downwards.

PROCEDURE. – Deal the rest of the cards one by one on a waste-heap, which may be turned once, packing and building when you can. 'Packing' is on the four *sides* in either direction, and cards for this come either from the waste-heap or the exposed cards of the herring bone starting at the base. In the diagram the taking of the 2 of Clubs exposes both the 3

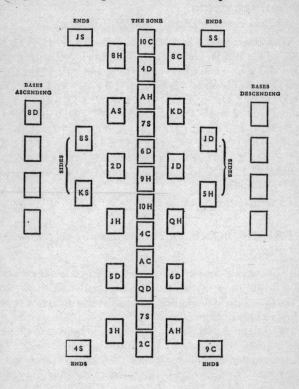

and Ace of Hearts; the taking of the 3 of Hearts exposes the
5 of Diamonds, but both 3 and Ace of Hearts go before the
7 of Spades is exposed. The *ends* can be taken only for building,
may not be packed upon, nor moved except to a base-packet.
When this happens, the vacant space is filled from the herring
bone. If a *side* is emptied by building, it may be left vacant or
filled from the waste-heap.

After laying out, study the 'bone' well. If there are several
base-cards in it – especially if near the top – or several duplicates, the chances of success are small. In any case the game
is not easy to get out.

INTRIGUE OR PICTURE GALLERY. *To form eight ascending sequences from the 6's to the Knaves, eight descending sequences from 5's to Kings, irrespective of suit.*

LAY out any Queen, and deal upon her cards from stock till
either a 5, a 6, or another Queen occurs. If a 5, place under the
Queen; if a 6, place over; if another Queen, place in a row with
the first Queen, and a bottom one of 5's and their sequences.

Proceed thus from Queen to Queen, placing the 5's and 6's
in a row with each other as they are turned up, and building
till all the Queens are out, the stock exhausted, and you have
three rows: a top one of 6's, with or without sequences; a
middle one of variously sized packets covering the Queens;
and a bottom one of 5's and their sequences.

PROCEDURE. – Lose no chance of building from exposed
cards on the Queen-packets or the pack, and, whenever
possible, exhaust a middle-row packet, as exposed Queens
'come in very handy' later on. When stock is exhausted it is
just possible that you have three rows, one of Knaves, one of
Queens, one of Kings; but most likely some (or most) of the
Queens will still be covered.

You may then take the top-card from any packet in the
middle row, and put it on an exposed Queen. You may put as
many top-cards on as many exposed Queens as there are, but
you may not transfer to a Queen more than once; and if these

transferences do not start the game again, you are done.

Generally, if you go for diminishing the fuller packs, you will succeed.

KING'S PATIENCE. *To form eight sequences from the Kings, four ascending and four descending, following suit.*

LAY-OUT. – Take out the Kings from two packs and arrange in two rows of four. Deal out the rest of the stock, face-upwards, in thirteen packets, counting as you deal 'Ace, 2, 3, etc.', to Kings. If any card turns up when you are calling it (e.g. as you say 'seven', and turn a card, 7 it is) place it beside the Kings, face-*downward,* to form a reserve.

PROCEDURE. – After exhausting stock you may spread out the thirteenth (or 'King' packet) – on which, of course, no Kings *can* have fallen – and use any card from it; but prefer to take cards of similar denominations, if available, from other packets. Begin now to build in suit on the Kings, on one of each suit in descending order, on the other of the suit in ascending, using the top-cards of the packets and those that become top (or exposed) as you go on.

When all suitable cards are exhausted, take the top-card of the reserve. If suitable, use it and take the next. If not in proper sequence, place it beneath the unspread packet that corresponds to its number (e.g. under the fifth if a 5, under the eleventh if a Knave). Then take the top-card of the packet thus used and slip that under its proper packet till you uncover a card which can be used for building, or come across one which is already in its proper packet.

This cannot be moved, and you must take again from the reserve.

When this is exhausted, take up the thirteen packets from the table in regular order, and, without any shuffling, deal afresh as before.

You are allowed *four* deals, but the chances are said to be about two to one against you. (The writer has not found this so, having only failed once in over twenty games.)

KC. *To form eight ascending sequences from the Aces, following suit.*

LAY out face-upwards twelve packets, each of four cards, in two rows. If there are any Aces and cards in sequence to them among the top-cards, remove them for foundations.

PROCEDURE. – The top-cards may also pack among themselves in a downward direction; but this must be done sparingly for fear of 'chockering'.* Next form the waste-heap, building or packing at every opportunity. Should at any time a card on one of the packets be of the same significance as the top-card of the waste-heap, the latter *must* be taken, and thus quite possibly a good run is stopped: e.g. you have packed Spades from the 8 down to the Deuce. Waste-heap has for top-card a 5 of Spades, then the Ace. You can build from the packet to the foundation as far as the 4, but then *must* take the 5 from the waste-heap, and thus are cut off from the packed 6, 7 and 8.

A vacancy in the two rows is filled (1) according to some players by any top-card – when you will certainly choose the highest available, a King for preference, (2) but others say you *must* take the top-card of the waste-heap.

Prefer the former, and also follow those players who allow a second turn at the waste-heap, for the Patience even with these indulgences does not easily come out.

PRIVILEGES AND HINTS. – (1) The top-card of one packet may be moved to another, if it is thought advisable and the cards are in due sequence.

(2) Suppose you have two sequences in the packets in the same suit – say one sequence of Hearts from King to 9, another from Knave to 2. Your Ace duly turns up, and you start building from the Knave sequence up to the 8. You can now choose which 9 you like, and so switch off to the other sequence, and your decision will be influenced by examining the packets behind the sequences. If the Knave at the head of one sequence covers a lower Heart it must be taken; if the King, he must.

Of course, you can often see success is out of the question,

* See footnote, p. 68.

e.g. if both 10's of a suit cover up a lower card in that suit, you are done.

Players who adopt the second turn at the waste-heap and the free choice of any top-card to fill a vacant space can make quite a good game of this, though it can never rank with the very best.

Since you will naturally look at the packets to see if you are hopelessly blocked from the lay-out, it logically follows that these might as well be dealt upwards. Playing thus, reserving a vacancy, i.e. not necessarily filling it up at once, and holding stock upwards you give some chance to foresight and ingenuity. Consider the game worked out in full in the Appendix, where at one time you have thirty cards in the waste-heap and under 'strict' rules could never have succeeded.

KING'S WAY. *To remove forty cards from the lay-out in descending sequences of alternate colour on to cards dealt from the stock to a waste-heap.*

LAY-OUT. – Take out the eight Kings from the packs and place them in a row. Deal four rows of eight cards face-downwards under the Kings, with a fifth row of eight face-upwards.

PROCEDURE. – Deal from stock one by one to a waste-heap. As soon as a card turns up on which any of the exposed bottom row in the lay-out can go *in ascending or descending sequence, but alternate colour,* remove that card from the lay-out; the faced-down card above it being now turned upwards, becoming exposed; and, if available, joining the first two in the waste-heap.

Aces have especial treatment:

(1) If turned up from stock they can take with them to the waste-heap an exposed Deuce of alternate colour from the lay-out, if one such be available, and subsequent sequence cards. If there is no available Deuce they go to a separate packet till stock is exhausted; when, if any cards (*except the Kings*)

are left on the board, their number is the number of cards that may be taken from the waste-heap for a second attempt to clear the King's Way.

(2) If an Ace is, or becomes, exposed in the lay-out it can only go to the waste-heap if a Deuce of alternate colour turns up from stock.

Success will see no cards of the lay-out left but the top row of Kings, whose 'royal road' is now cleared.

PECULIARITIES. – The game is unlike any Patience with which the writer is acquainted, and for that reason is included in this selection. There is no 'packing', of course, on the lay-out, and the game has no place for skill.

But it is short, amusing and unusual, and you are by no means sure of success.

LIMITED. *To form eight ascending sequences from the Aces, following suit.*

LAY out three rows, each of twelve cards face-upwards, taking out any Aces that occur in the *lowest* row and placing above for foundations.

PROCEDURE. – Packing on the board is '*limited*', i.e. any exposed (bottom row) card may have *one* of lower consecutive value in the same suit placed upon it, taken either from other exposed cards on the board or from the waste-heap, but *only* one; and the couple thus made may not be moved till taking their place on their proper Ace-packet. Single available cards as turned up from stock can build on their foundation Ace-packets at once.

When stock is finished you are allowed a '*limited*' second turn, being granted four 'grace' cards. These are set out in a line, and if you can place any of them in a column, or a vacancy, or on an Ace-packet, you do so; once more fill up the 'grace' row to four and so proceed till none of the 'graces' will fit.

As a final respite, you may look at the fifth card; but if that

fails you all is over. A vacancy made in the top row can be
filled by any single exposed card, but need not be filled at once.

HINTS. – (1) Be chary of packing: one of your great objects
will be to free low cards in the first two rows blocked by
higher cards of the same suit in the third. Hence the great
value of vacancies, which also come in most usefully in the
second turn.

(2) Do not hurry to fill vacancies.

(3) Do not be alarmed at a large waste-heap – in the game
given there are at one period over forty cards in the heap.

The *lay-out* was:

10H	10D	JS	7S	3S	4D	9C	9S	8D	7S	6D	QH
JC	QD	3D	4C	3H	4D	5C	4H	3C	10C	9D	KD
4C	2H	2D	AD	2S	6S	8C	7D	7C	6D	QC	JII

And the pack was in this order:

K D, 7 H, 2 H, Q H, 3 S, 8 C, 2 D, K H, 4 S, Q D, K H,
J D, 10 S, 2 S, 10 C, 7 H, 6 H, Q S, 8 S, 9 H, 6 C, 7 D, 8 D,
3 D, 7 C, J D, 6 H, 5 S, 4 H, A S, A H, 4 S, K S, K C, 5 D,
A C, 5 H, A C, 9 C, J S, K S, A S, 8 S, 9 D, 3 C, 3 H, 2 C,
Q C, J H, A H, 8 H, 9 S, 2 C, 10 H, K C, J C, 5 D, A D, Q S,
6 S, 6 C, 5 H, 5 S, 5 C, 10 D, 9 H, 10 S, 8 H (last card).

MILTON. *To form four double sequences (twenty-five cards),
     following suit.*

LAY out any eight cards in a row – this is called the index row.

If it contains any two consecutive cards of the same suit,
place the higher below the lower to be packed in upward
suit-sequence.

Any vacancy in the row must be filled at once either from
the pack or the top-card of the waste-heap.

PROCEDURE. – Deal this waste-heap, a single card at a time,
from stock, as soon as the index row is arranged, keeping
watch for higher cards to put on the various 'index cards'.
As soon as you place a card in a sequence which is just below
the value of some index card (of the same suit), take that

index card down to put on the packet together with any cards that have already been built on it. But this index card must *not* be the one immediately above the packet to which you are transferring it, or, of course, you could never get the second half of your sequence. The first Ace of each suit that occurs will be placed like other cards, but the second can only go into a vacancy in a top row; for otherwise you could not succeed in the final result, which will show an Ace of each suit by itself with a packet of twenty-five cards of the same suit underneath it, headed by the Kings; thus:

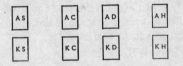

Similarly avoid putting the second Deuces of any suit in the index row. It is possible to succeed if you do so, but only right at the end when there are vacancies handy, and you *may* have the luck to be able to work a second Deuce off on its own second Ace in another part of the index row.

You may turn the waste-heap twice – three deals in all; but you want the cards to be kind if you are to succeed, in addition to great watchfulness on your part; for, although there is very little power of choice in the game, and, therefore, little room for skill, one card wrongly played wrecks the whole game.

The end game worked out below will, it is hoped, make all clear. Packet I contains 4, 5, 6 to Ace of Spades, 2, 3, 4 (again) to 9. Packet II, Diamonds 3 up to Ace, 2, 3 (again), 4, 5 Diamonds. Packet III, 2, 3, 4 Clubs. Packet IV, only two cards.

To prevent building too far, it is convenient to mark the first Aces in some such way as shown.

This is taken at the end of the first deal. In the waste-heap are twenty-two cards: 6 H (top-card), 2 H, Q D, 10 D, J S, 10 S, 3 H, 4 H, K D, 7 D, 2 S, 9 D, 7 H, 8 D, A H, 5 H, 6 D, K H, A S, 6 C, J D, 5 C.

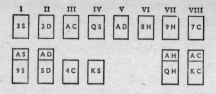

Deal *6 H* and *2 H* on WH, *Q* and *10 D* on WH, *J S* on WH,
10 S on col. (1), take J S and col. (4) to 10 D to col. (4) from
WH. Deal to WH till *6* D on col. (2), *KH* on col. (7), A S on
WH, *6 C* on WH, *J D* on col. (4) on 10 D, *5 C* on col. (3),
6 C from WH. All col. (8) on this and *Clubs out.* Col. (2) on to
col. (5), A S out to vacant space, 9 H col. on to 8 H. 5 H and
A H from WH to vacant spaces.

Board now like this:

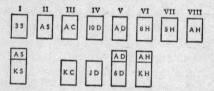

Turn. 6 H on 5, 2 H on A, Q D on J, 3 H on 2, 4 H on 3,
col. (7) on col. (8). K D on Q, 7 D on 6, 2 S on A, col. (1) on
col. (2). Spades out. 9 D in vacant space. 7 H on 6. Hearts out.
Col. (6) on col. (8). 8 D on 7, 9 on 8. Diamonds out.

MISS MILLIGAN. *To form eight ascending sequences from the
Aces, following suit.*

LAY out eight cards in a row, removing any Aces for foundations, and packing, where possible, in downward sequence
of alternate colour. This done:

PROCEDURE. – Deal eight more cards in order from left to
right, filling such vacant spaces as there may be, and placing
the new cards below the old where these have not been

moved, or have been covered by others in downward sequence. *No packing may be done till the whole eight have been dealt.* Continue thus till stock is exhausted, taking out Aces whenever they appear, *but not till the eight-lot in which they come is all laid out;* building on these foundations, and packing downward whenever possible.

A vacancy made in the top-row may be filled only by a King or King-sequence, but you have two important privileges.

PRIVILEGES, HINTS, ETC. – (1) In packing on the columns a sequence may be moved as a *whole* if it fits. Thus, if col. (2) ends in a black 10, and the bottom of col. (3) consists of a red 9, a black 8 and a red 7, the 9 down to the 7 can be placed on the 10 *en bloc*.

(2) If, when stock is exhausted, you find an exposed card blocking a packing, or series of packings, but when these are finished you can see how to place the blocking card in proper sequence, you may lift this card and hold it till you have finished the movements of the others and have found it a proper resting-place.

This is called '*waiving*', and the process may be repeated, of course, only waiving one card at a time. By this privilege many desperate positions can be remedied.

This is a popular and ingenious game which is by no means easy to get out. Much may be done by adroit shifting from column to column, and naturally your great idea will be to get Kings on the top of these.

The game of 'GIANT' is practically the same as 'Miss Milligan'; the two points of difference being that –

(1) Any exposed card or sequence may be moved to a vacancy and you are not restricted to Kings and King-sequences.

(2) The privilege of 'waiving' is not allowed, but you may 'worry back', i.e. return the top-card of a foundation-packet to the foot of any column, if it will fit there by the rules of packing.

(A game is fully worked out in Appendix XVI.)

NUMBER FOURTEEN. *To discard the stock by twos, each combination counting fourteen.*

LAY out twenty-five cards in five rows, face-upwards.

PROCEDURE. – Search the lay-out for couples of cards together either in the same row or the same column making fourteen (reckoning Kings as 13, Queens as 12, Knaves as 11). Any two that do so, you lay aside. After removing all you can, fill the vacancies from stock. If you come to a stand you may alter the position of two cards. This you will naturally do in such a way as to obtain two 'fourteens', and so gain four vacancies. If the pack is finished and cards still remain on the table, take up the lowest row, and fill the vacancies beginning at the top left-hand corner.

Go on till all the cards pair out.

A good game for children. Your combinations are, of course, fixed, fifty-two in all, eight each of Aces and Kings, Deuces and Queens, 3's and Knaves, 4's and 10's, 5's and 9's, 6's and 8's, and four combinations of 7's.

OCTAVE. *To form eight ascending sequences from Ace to King, following suit.*

LAY out face-downwards a row of eight cards with a second row of eight below it also face-downwards, and a third row face-upwards. (Some players, making success more difficult, lay out *three* concealed rows and a fourth exposed.) From the bottom row take any Aces and place above for foundations.

PROCEDURE. – Pack on exposed cards in downward sequence and alternate colour. Any card taken from the third row exposes the card in the second row immediately above it, and that, being in its turn taken, exposes the card above it in the first row. Deal the rest of the cards one by one from stock, packing and building as occasion offers. If the stock is exhausted and the foundations not completed, you may take the top eight cards of the waste-heap and lay them out in what is called a

'*grace*' *row*. These eight you may use for building or packing,
filling the vacancies in the 'grace' row till it at last consists of
eight cards for none of which can a place be found. Lastly, you
still may turn a ninth card from the waste-heap which, if available, will start you off again. Otherwise – failure! You may move
cards, if suitable, from one column to another; and when you
make a vacancy in the top row, may fill it with any exposed
card. But if you are wise—

HINTS. – (1) You will not be in too great a hurry to fill
vacancies, and when you do you will fill them with high cards,
such as Kings and Queens, or cards you know are blocking
a run suitable for the foundations.

(2) Similarly, until the concealed cards are exposed, you
will be chary of packing on high cards, because in the ordinary
course of events it will be long before these are worked off.
Low cards do not matter so much. But, of course, you are in
for a stormy passage if most of the Deuces and 3's are concealed.
In a word, use restraint in a game which is interesting, but
calls for little skill (cp. and contrast 'The Emperor', where,
unlike this game, the privilege of 'worrying back' is allowed;
and for the use of 'grace' cards cp. 'Limited').

(3) It will sometimes pay you *not* to build, when by packing
the available card you can get a longer sequence, or procure a
vacancy. Two vacancies – still more three – are most useful
for getting sequences from one column to another, or a King
(on which you have been obliged to pack) into a vacancy, and
so at the head of a column.

The Ace-foundation packets are only built up to the 10's,
leaving three rows of Knaves, Queens and Kings of alternate
colour beneath them.

ODDS AND EVENS. *To form eight ascending sequences,
following suit, but in alternate cards, from one Ace of each suit
proceeding by odd numbers to the Queen, from a Deuce of each suit
by even numbers to the King.*

LAY out on each side of a middle space reserved for the foundation Aces and Deuces sixteen cards in four rows of four cards each. An Ace of each suit and a Deuce to be placed in the middle in two columns as they turn up now or later from the stock. This is dealt, one card at a time, on a waste-heap.

PROCEDURE. – Decide which lot of sixteen cards, the one on the left or the one on the right, is to be the '*Active*', which the '*Passive*' side. From the Active side any available card can be taken; from the Passive, only 'uncovered' cards (i.e. those with none below them).

Your choice will depend on which side has the most low cards; but should the whole of either bottom row be made up of cards which cannot be wanted for some time, you will make that the Active side. Vacancies on the Active side are filled up from stock or the waste-heap. You build up on the Aces by alternate cards 3, 5, 7, etc., to King, whence 2, 4, 6 to Queen; on the Deuces 4, 6, 8, 10, Queen, whence Ace, 3, 5 to King. Thus success sees eight sequences of thirteen cards, the Ace packets ending in Queens, the Deuces in Kings.

If the same card is available for building in each lot of sixteen, the one from the *Passive* side *must* be taken.

HINTS. – There is no skill in the game; for you never have the power of choice, and those players who only allow one turn at the waste-heap must often be disappointed of success.

You get a better chance if you allow six '*grace*' *cards* on the principle of 'Limited' and 'Octave' after stock is exhausted.

PERSIAN – SOMETIMES CALLED BEZIQUE. *To form eight ascending sequences, following suit.*

LAY-OUT. – From two Piquet packs – i.e. Whist packs without the 6's, 5's, 4's, 3's and 2's, and so of thirty-two cards each – deal eight depots, each of eight cards, as shown in the diagram.

PROCEDURE. – Any Ace in the last row of these depots is to

be taken as a foundation and built on in suit and ascending sequence, 7 coming next to Ace. The exposed cards in the

I	II	III	IV	V	VI	VII	VIII
KD	10 C	7 C	8 H	8 H	8 C	10 C	10 S
7 D	8 D	8 S	10 D	7 H	9 H	J D	Q S
A D	J D	10 H	A S	J H	9 S	7 S	7 S
9 H	Q H	J C	10 S	K C	Q D	10 D	K D
J H	A C	A H	J S	J S	7 D	8 C	K S
K H	K H	9 D	8 D	9 C	A D	J C	K C
Q D	9 C	Q C	Q H	Q S	Q C	10 H	9 S
8 S	9 D	K S	A C	7 C	A H	7 H	A S

DEPOTS

FOUNDATION ACES

depots may also be moved from one depot to another in descending sequence and alternate colour. If a space is made by taking all the cards from a depot, any exposed card may be moved there and packed on. You can have three deals: if no card can be taken after the first deal, it does not count as one of the allowed three.

The untaken cards are shuffled after each deal and dealt as before; and, as some (if not all) of the depots will now have less than eight cards, it is as well to deal in horizontal lines towards the end to avoid mistakes.

HINTS. – (1) Aces should be taken whenever available.

(2) Always play to obtain a vacant space.

The Patience is a fine example of 'games presenting a definite problem', and requires deep analysis before beginning. It is in favour of a skilful player.

With this arrangement (adapted from Cavendish's sumptuous

book on Patience, 1890, now out of print) the game can be solved in one deal.

(See Appendix XVII.)

RIGHT AND LEFT. *To form eight ascending sequences from the Aces, following suit.*

LAY out two squares of sixteen cards each. The left-hand square must be finished first and dealt thus: if the first card turned is a 6 or under, the row must be dealt from left to right; if the fifth card is above 6, the second row must run from right to left. This rotation applies also to the other two rows, whose direction of dealing depends on their first card. In forming the second square reverse this order: thus a row commencing with a low card (6 or under) goes from right to left, and vice versa.

The aim of all this – which takes longer to write than to understand – is to get low cards on the outside of the squares, for these outside cards are the 'exposed' ones, and only exposed cards are available for building on the foundation Aces.

These are taken when they are, or become, exposed cards – (an outside card taken, the next in the run naturally becomes 'exposed') – or when they turn up in the process of dealing from the packs on to the waste-heap.

PROCEDURE. – Examine the lay-out for possible packing on the outermost cards – this in a downward direction, but regardless of suit. Cards may be moved from one square to another, but sequences cannot be taken as a whole, only one card at a time.

Whenever a space is made by removing all four cards of a row, a King may be put there: therefore don't pack on Kings as a rule, but keep them free on the chance of a space being 'to let'.

HINTS. – 'It's the packing that does it'; and you must take

care about blocking inner cards, for there is only one turn at the waste-heap, and no 'graces', privileges and the like.

So in the diagram you won't pack on the Queen of Diamonds, which blocks the Ace behind her.

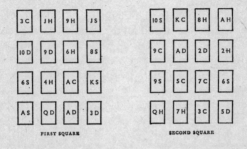

FIRST SQUARE   SECOND SQUARE

Packs in this order: K H, 10 H, J S, J C, 8 S, 8 C, 2 C, 4 C, J D, 7 D, 8 H, 5 S, K D, 10 H, A S, 9 C, 10 C, 3 H, Q H, 7 H, 6 D, 5 H, A H, 7 S, 5 H, 2 S, 4 D, 6 C, 4 S, 8 D, J D, 8 D, K S, 2 D, Q D, 3 D, 3 S, 5 D, A C, 2 C, J H, 4 D, 2 S, 5 S, K D, 7 C, 3 H, 2 H, 10 S, 4 S, 7 S, 8 C, Q S, 9 S, Q C, 10 D, 3 S, 10 C, K H, 9 H, J C, 4 C, 6 D, 7 D, 6 C, 6 H, K C, 4 H, 9 D, Q S, 5 C, Q C (last card).

(The game is worked out in Appendix XVIII.)

ROVERS. *To form sequences, following suit, four ascending from Aces to Kings, four descending from Kings to Aces.*

LAY out two cards at the top of the board to be called 'Rovers'—then four down one side in column: then two more 'Rovers' at the bottom and a column of four up the other side. Leave room between for an Ace and a King of each suit to be taken as foundations as they turn up.

PROCEDURE. – Continue dealing thus, taking cards for building as they turn up, *if dealt on the Rovers:* if dealt on the sides cards cannot be moved till stock is finished. Then packing on exposed cards begins either in upward or downward sequence. Kings and Aces may now be taken from side rows as well as from the Rovers.

When you come to a stand, gather up the cards (*not*, naturally, the foundation packets) and lay out again as before. Some allow a third deal.

If a card available for building is dealt in a Rover's place the first round – use it, and fill the vacancy. In the second and

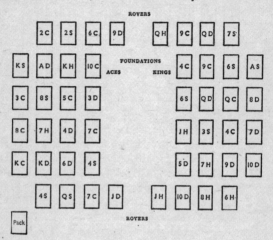

subsequent rounds you may take such a card, but the deal is continued without filling the vacancy.

If you get rid of a whole row, you can put an Ace or a King in the vacancy. If at the end you seem done, there is a 'grace' of drawing *one* card from any part of the board, but it is a forlorn hope.

HINTS. – The whole game lies in the packing. You *must* free cards wanted for building on the foundations.

Don't hurry about packing, therefore, if there is any fear of 'chockering'. Obviously the sooner you get out your foundations the better. Not at all a bad game.

The diagram shows the Patience commenced – no foundation has as yet turned up in either Rover row.

ROYAL PARADE – ALSO CALLED ROYAL PROCESSION AND THREE UP. *To build ascending sequences, following suit, eight on the Deuces, eight on the 3's and eight on the 4's, by intervals of three cards.*

LAY out three rows, each of eight cards, face-upwards. Take away any that happen to be Aces, filling any vacant space thus made in the first row by a 2, in the second row by a 3, in the third row by a 4. These 2's, 3's and 4's along with any that can be got into their proper rows are to serve as foundations as described above: thus in the first row 2, 5, 8, Knave; in the second 3, 6, 9, Queen; in the third 4, 7, 10, King. Aces are thrown out as they turn up throughout the game.

PROCEDURE

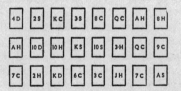

Thus, if the original lay-out were as above, after removing the Aces you will have a vacancy in each row: take the 2 of Hearts to the top row (in the seventh place where the Ace of Hearts was), the 3 of Clubs to the place of the departed Ace in the second row, the 4 of Diamonds to the vacant RH corner in the third. The 6 of Clubs then is built on its 3, the 9 on the 6. This gives you another space in the second row, on which you at once put the 3 of Spades. One of the Queens of Clubs will go on the 9 and complete that packet. Take the one in the middle row, because it is never wise to leave a crowning card in the row to which it belongs. A Knave in the first, a King in the third row, in the same way, are occupying a place which, if you are to succeed, must eventually be taken by a 2 or a 4 with their sequences.

After making all possible arrangements with your first lay-out deal a fourth row of eight, a little below the others. Suppose this fourth row to our three above were:

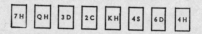

Put the 2, 3 and 4 of Spades in their proper rows; the 6 of Diamonds will go on the 3 of Diamonds, 7 of Hearts on 4 of Hearts, 10 of Hearts (from middle row) on 7 of Hearts. This packet now only wants the King for completion, and though you have one in the new row, there is no need to take it instanter. It will go to its own place in the end; and when you deal the second King of Hearts, you may be very glad of a spare place.

Now deal another row of eight over the fourth row, but not completely covering it, so that the sight of the cards beneath may influence your play with a view to freeing them.

The game becomes more complicated with every deal, as you keep on burying cards which will need both ingenuity and good luck to get out again to their proper sequence.

Right at the end when you are dealing the last round on the fourth row, but *have not yet put down the last card,* if you discover some necessary card is blocked, you have the *privilege* of taking up what cards of the last round you have already put down, and dealing them from *right to left,* the reverse to the usual way.

This may save the game, but the privilege lapses as soon as the last card has been dealt. Success shows a row of Knaves in the first row, Queens in the second and Kings in the third.

HINTS. – Always go for vacancies in the first three rows. They are the only chances you get of planting fresh foundation cards.

Also positions not infrequently arise when you must refrain

from building for a time, e.g. one Spade sequence from the 4
has started and is covered with a 7; the other 4 of Spades is
waiting for a place in the third row, but has been covered in
subsequent rounds of dealing by the 10 of Spades: if the other
10 of Spades turns up and you carelessly take it to build, you
have irretrievably blocked the second 4.

RUSSIAN. *To form sequences, following suit, four ascending from
   Aces, four descending from Kings.*

LAY out twelve cards in a row, taking out and placing below
any Kings or Aces that occur – (one of each suit, no duplicates).
Any card in sequence to these foundations (as Queens or
Deuces) in the first row can also be taken, their places being
filled from stock. But in the succeeding rows – for the whole
of the two packs are laid out – this privilege stops.

PROCEDURE. – Aces and Kings for foundation, only the
first and last of each row are available for building. When these
are taken the card above them becomes 'exposed', and, if
available, may be taken and its place filled from stock. When,
however, all the cards have been dealt this restriction ceases.
You will then have eight rows of twelve cards each, minus the
few (generally very few!) you have been lucky enough to
build.

Now you may start packing in suits to any extent upwards
or downwards on exposed cards, building the whole on
foundations.

When you are held up, unable either to pack or build,
gather up the cards in columns from *right* to *left,* and place
one on another *without shuffling.* Lay out again and proceed
as before. A third deal is allowed. Into a vacancy made in the
top row any exposed card may be moved.

HINTS. – At the third and last try be very careful in packing
to avoid blocking upper cards. Some players do not allow the
foundation Aces and Kings to be taken unless they come in the
top row, which makes a game, where the chances of success

are in any case sufficiently remote, hardly worth the bother
of trying.

It is, however, a fine exercise in manipulating the mobile
sequence.* The game in the diagram can be got out without
a redeal.

(*See* solution in Appendix XIX.)

2H	JC	6S	9S	3C	5D	3D	10D	4D	QC	2C	7S
6S	QD	2D	4C	KS	QH	8S	8S	5C	10C	QD	7C
6D	7S	9S	5S	4C	10D	JD	9C	9D	QC	8C	5S
6H	4D	9D	6C	2S	QS	8H	KD	4S	JH	3H	5C
5H	AH	3S	2H	4S	AD	10H	JC	4H	3S	10C	6D
3D	8H	AS	3C	7H	JS	8C	5H	2D	AC	JH	9C
8D	6H	KH	2S	5D	7C	10S	KC	JS	6C	8D	9H
7D	3H	7H	10S	9H	4H	10H	QS	7D	JD	QH	——

Foundations: A H, A D, A and 2 C, A S,
K H, K D, K C, K S

'S'. *To form thirteen ascending sequences, each of eight cards, regardless
of suit, upon thirteen bases, themselves a complete sequence.*

LAY out a full sequence without regard to suit in the shape of
the letter S, beginning with the 7 at the bottom tip and ending
with a 6. (*See* diagram.)

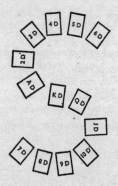

PROCEDURE. – Build on these in ascending sequence, not regarding suit, so that if you succeed you will have thirteen packets of eight cards each, crowned by an Ace, a Deuce, a 3 and so on to a King.

Deal the cards from stock, putting those that will not fit on two waste-heaps. There must be no shifting from one packet to another, and care must be taken not to overbuild, i.e. put more than eight cards on one packet. There is no second deal, so you must not block cards likely to be wanted soon in the two waste-heaps.

HINTS. – This game is not nearly so easy as it seems at first, and can be made very tantalizing if you build in suits according to rotation – say, Diamonds, Spades, Hearts and Clubs. In this form lay out the 'S' in Diamonds, the next layer in Spades, the third in Hearts, the fourth in Clubs, then Diamonds again. You are in this variety allowed *four* waste-heaps, which can be taken up twice and shuffled. The final layer should show a sequence of Clubs. But success is rare through the danger of 'chockering', and the difficulty of remembering, as you place each card, the suit-rotation. (Cp. 'Heap' Patience, p. 102.)

ST HELENA. *To form four ascending sequences from the Aces, four descending from the Kings, following suit.*

LAY-OUT. – From one of the two packs – which are not shuffled together, compare 'Backbone' and 'Above and Below' Patiences – take the Aces and Kings, arranging them in two rows, the Aces underneath.

Deal out the rest of the cards in twelve packets round and round these eight foundations in the order shown by the diagram on p. 126.

Cards are built on their foundations with this restriction: from packets 1–4 on the Kings only, from 7–10 on the Aces only, from the side-packets (5 and 6, 11 and 12) on either.

PROCEDURE. – Before dealing a second round look for any Deuces, Queens and cards in sequence, and after building any

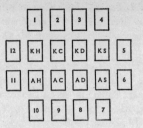

that may have occurred, fill the vacancies by fresh cards from stock. These may in their turn give opportunities for further play. If not, deal a second round on the outer packets, noting *card by card* any chance of building. This '*card by card*' point is important, for in later rounds it may often make a difference to your building; when, if you had to complete the round before building, you might cover suitable cards. When stock is exhausted – (that is, of course, both packs. You do not stop on finishing the first pack, but go straight on to the second, in which Kings and Aces are dealt with other like cards) – the restriction as to building is relaxed, and cards may be taken from any one of the outside packets – if in due sequence – to any one of the foundations. Furthermore, you may now pack between the top-cards of packets 1–12, in either ascending or descending sequence, following suit.

Thus if among your top-cards were an Ace, King and Deuce of the same suit, you could pack the Ace on the Deuce, the King on the Ace; or, if you had a 9, a 10 and (the other) 9 of one suit, you could put the 10 on one 9 and the second 9 on the 10.

Here clearly is some chance for memory and ingenuity.

When no more building or packing can be done, pick up the twelve outer packets in reverse order to their dealing, i.e. from No. 12 to No. 1, *without shuffling*. Turn over and deal again, starting at place 1 as before. Again the restriction as to building comes into force, to relax once more when stock is finished.

A third deal is permitted under identical conditions. Although too mechanical to gain a place in the best class of Patiences, the game is strangely interesting.

SENIOR WRANGLER – SOMETIMES CALLED MATHEMATICS. *To form eight ascending sequences, at intervals of 2, 3, 4 to 9 respectively, not regarding suit.*

LAY out eight cards of any suit from 2 to 9 inclusive face-upwards in a row. Then count out eight packets of twelve cards each, placing a packet under each card of the first row. These are the board-packets and their top-cards are face-upwards, 'exposed', and ready for play.

PROCEDURE. – Next try to find foundation cards, each to be twice the value of the card above its own packet: 4, 6, 8, 10, Queen are clear enough for the first five, and an Ace for the sixth. Now bring in the 'Imaginary Thirteen' rule, so that for the seventh foundation twice $8=16$, subtract 13, and a 3 is your card, with a 5 for the last packet (twice $9=18-13=5$). These foundation cards are not likely all to come at once. Meanwhile, build upon whatever foundations are out according to the following rules:

The card above each board-packet shows the constant difference by which the correspondence sequence is to be built up. (Non-mathematical readers are urged to keep calm: it's really quite simple!) Thus the first sequence proceeds from the 4 by *twos*, 6, 8, 10, Queen, Ace, 3, 5, 7, 9, Knave, King; the next goes up from the 6 by *threes*, 9, Queen, 2, 5, . . . 4, 7, 10, and so on. A complete scheme is shown in the diagram.

Build till no more available cards are exposed, then take up the first board-packet, and deal it round on the others, beginning at the space from which you have taken the packet. Look first at the bottom-card of the packet you are about to deal out: it will decide whether it will be better to deal with the packet face up or down. If a King is at the bottom you may thus make certain of its not falling into a space where it will block the game. More frequently, you will find, it is a King at the top that has already blocked the game, when you will hold the packet upwards and deal the King, as top-card, into the vacated space. This is an important 'grace', as a packet once dealt may not be touched again (save, of course, to take cards from it in due order for building). On a second stoppage proceed to deal out the second packet, and so on till you reach the last.

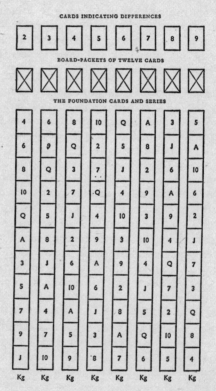

CARDS INDICATING DIFFERENCES

2	3	4	5	6	7	8	9

BOARD-PACKETS OF TWELVE CARDS

THE FOUNDATION CARDS AND SERIES

4	6	8	10	Q	A	3	5
6	9	Q	2	5	8	J	A
8	Q	3	7	J	2	6	10
10	2	7	Q	4	9	A	6
Q	5	J	4	10	3	9	2
A	8	2	9	3	10	4	J
3	J	6	A	9	4	Q	7
5	A	10	6	2	J	7	3
7	4	A	J	8	5	2	Q
9	7	5	3	A	Q	10	8
J	10	9	8	7	6	5	4
Kg	Kg	Kg	Kg	Kg	Kg	Kg	Kg

By now, if you are to succeed, the foundation pockets ought to be nearly full.

Hints. – Don't be in too great a hurry to close your sequences by their ultimate Kings, or even the penultimates of each series (though, of course, there are occasions when this has to be done when a King or penultimate card is blocking some necessary lower one). For once placed on their sequences Kings cannot be moved. Before this happens cards may be moved from one sequence to another, one at a time, if in due sequence; and thus quite frequently a place is found for cards on the board.

If a game goes well you will have all, or most, of the foundation sequences mounting together more or less evenly, while the board-packets are worked off to a few cards each *with Kings at the bottom*. In the end the central row will be blank, the bottom will be a row of Kings, and the original eight cards will remain on the top.

THE SNAKE. *To form eight ascending sequences from the Aces, following suit.*

Lay out eight columns, each of eight cards, taking any Ace that occurs in the lowest row for a foundation. The other Aces are taken as they become 'exposed' in the lay-out, or are turned up from stock.

Procedure. – Pack on the lay-out in downward sequence, but regardless of suit. When you have done all you can, begin to form the 'Snake'; i.e. continue the left-hand column with cards from stock which gradually pile on it till it *may* coil round the other columns. The longer the Snake, the less your chances of success.

Privileges. – You may pack from the Snake to the columns, or vice versa, provided it is in downward sequence, moving sequences *en bloc*. You may 'worry back' from the Ace packets, a device that frequently puts the game on its legs again. A vacancy in the top row may be filled by any exposed card or sequence, and start on its own; but despite all these 'graces' and the undoubted scope the game offers for ingenuity, you are very much up against the fall of the cards, and straightening out the Snake is not easy. The example shows a game in progress where the Serpent is becoming ominously elongated, but:

Foundations: A D, A H, A C, 6 D (i.e. a packet from A to 6), 5 H (A to 5), 7 S (A to 7).

Twenty-three cards in stock in this order:

7 H, 6 C, 3 C, 9 C, 7 D, 4 C, 9 C, 7 S, 5 C, K D, A S, K C, Q C, Q S, J D, 10 S, J D, 8 S, 4 D, 8 H, J S, 9 S, K S.

The game easily comes out. (*See* solution.)

Q C	10 C	K H	9 S	5 D	10 H	8 D	K S
7 D	4 H	10 H	K D	K H	8 D	Q D	9 H
9 D	2 C	10 C	Q H	Q S	4 C	5 H	3 C
8 C	J C	5 S	J C	7 H	8 H	K C	Q D
3 S	Q H	6 H	6 S	4 S	6 D	8 S	5 C
2 H	6 C	10 D	J H		A C	9 H	3 D
7 C	9 D		2 D		J H	10 D	8 C
6 H			10 S		10 D		2 S
7 C							
2 C							
J S							
3 H							

THE SPIDER. *To form four ascending and four descending sequences, following suit.*

LAY out the Aces and Kings from one pack and place them in columns for foundations. Shuffle the remainder of the packs together and deal twelve cards, one to each depot, so as to surround the foundation cards. You must deal in a fixed order – the particular order you select does not matter, but once chosen you must adhere to the same in subsequent deals. (In the specimen game [and solution] given below the very usual order of left to right is adopted, starting over the top left-hand corner, then down the left-hand side, along the bottom, then up the right-hand side, the twelfth card being placed on the top of the right-hand corner.)

PROCEDURE. – You may take any card for building which is in proper sequence with the foundations, descending from the

Kings, ascending from the Aces, from the two top and the two bottom depots. Cards in the side depots can only be taken if dealt in the same line as the card on which they are to build.

The available cards, if any, being taken, deal twelve more in *the same order*. (You don't fill vacancies, so the depots will end in different lengths.) Build again, *but the whole batch of twelve* must be dealt before any card is taken. (Contrast in this respect 'St Helena'.)

Continue thus till stock is exhausted, when the restriction about side depots is removed, and any top-depot card, if in due sequence, may be taken for building. Now also top-cards, if in suit, and in either *ascending* or *descending sequence,* may be moved from one depot to another. (Aces are in sequence with Kings and Deuces.)

If, after stock is finished, the whole of a depot can be moved, any top Ace or King can be moved into the vacated space. Two deals are allowed, the rules for the second remaining unaltered. After the first deal take up the depot cards *in the order of the original dealing.* The stock thus formed is dealt to depots as before *without shuffling.*

HINTS. – Some players only take foundation cards as they appear, which makes a difficult game harder than necessary. It is slightly in favour of a player who plays well.

You will be well-advised, before taking up the depot cards after the first deal, to move sequence cards to the depot which will be at the bottom, or near the bottom, of the new stock, in order that on the redeal they may come out as top-cards or near the top.

The Patience frequently calls for very deep analysis and deservedly ranks among the very best.

The diagram shows a game at the point where stock is exhausted. The foundation packets have all been built on except the King of Hearts; on the ascending Heart packet, for example, are the Ace, 2, 3, 4, 5 and 6; on the descending Clubs the King, Queen, Jack.

(For solution see Appendix XXI.)

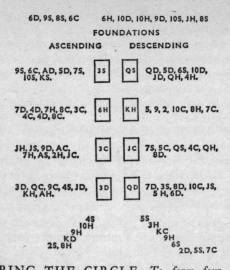

6D, 9S, 8S, 6C   6H, 10D, 10H, 9D, 10S, JH, 8S

FOUNDATIONS

ASCENDING   DESCENDING

9S, 6C, AD, 5D, 7S, 10S, KS.   [3S]   [QS]   QD, 5D, 6S, 10D, JD, QH, 4H.

7D, 4D, 7H, 8C, 3C, 4C, 4D, 8C.   [6H]   [KH]   5, 9, 2, 10C, 8H, 7C.

JH, JS, 9D, AC, 7H, AS, 2H, JC.   [3C]   [JC]   7S, 5C, QS, 4C, QH, 8D.

3D, QC, 9C, 4S, JD, KH, AH.   [3D]   [QD]   7D, 3S, 8D, 10C, JS, 5 H, 6D.

4S
10H   5S
9H   3H
KD   KC
2S, 8H   9H
          6S
        2D, 5S, 7C

SQUARING THE CIRCLE. *To form four contracting sequences, following suit.*

LAY out the Aces from one pack and place together in a 'square'; shuffle the rest of the two packs together, and deal twelve cards in a circle round the Aces. If a King occurs in these twelve, place it on its proper Ace and fill the vacancy.

PROCEDURE. – Form now from stock four waste-heaps, or reserve packets, taking every chance of building on the central Aces in suit, but in the following sequence: on the Aces their Kings; then 2, Queen; 3, Knave; 4, 10; 5, 9; 6, 8; 7 and 7. Now the order changes and becomes 8, 6; 9, 5; 10, 4; Knave, 3; Queen, 2; King, Ace.

Any vacancy made in the circle is filled from one of the waste-heaps, so that you have at all times seventeen cards to choose from for building (twelve in the circle, four top-cards of the waste-heaps and the top-card from stock). You need not deal on the waste-heaps in any fixed order.

HINTS. – Success indeed depends largely on how you manage the waste-heaps. Keep one, if you can, for Kings, Aces and

Queens, one for cards likely to be wanted soon, the other two for medium cards.

You may shuffle the heaps once; but the real difficulty of the game lies in keeping in mind the sequence.

THE SULTAN. *To form eight ascending sequences (one from Ace to Queen, the others from King to Queen), following suit.*

LAY out all the Kings of the two packs and one Ace of Hearts, as shown in the diagram. These are to be the foundations with the exception of the central King of Hearts, who remains

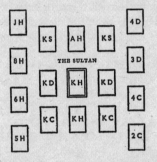

undisturbed throughout the game to blossom at the end into the 'Sultan'. Then place four cards on each side at right angles to the central arrangement. (If an Ace be one of these, place it on its King, but an Ace of Hearts will go, of course, on the lower of the two Heart Kings.)

PROCEDURE. – Deal the stock to a waste-heap, building in ascending suit-sequence on the foundations, whenever possible: the cards on the top of stock and the waste-heap are always available, like the eight side-cards for building.

When a side-card is taken, its place may be filled *either* with the top-card of stock *or* the top-card of the waste-heap, but need not be filled immediately.

Three deals are allowed and cards in the waste-heap are shuffled at the end of each deal.

HINTS. – The chief point of play lies in the management of the side spaces, what cards you select for vacancies and when you leave a vacancy unoccupied. Choose as far as you can cards likely to be wanted soon, cards that fill gaps in sequences (e.g. if a 7 and 9 of a suit are there already, choose an 8).

Don't take cards which cannot be wanted during the immediate deal (e.g. if one foundation is built up to an 8, but both 9's of the suit are already deeply buried in the waste-heap, higher cards [10 upwards] of the suit are wasted in side spaces). Frequently, therefore, examine the waste-heap and deal with the stock face-upwards. Then the Patience is in the player's favour, if he allows himself three, or even two, deals.

With the side-cards as in the diagram, the Patience can be solved in one deal in several ways, stock lying in this order:

9 H (top-card), Q C, A C, 2 D, A D, 10 S, A H, 3 C, J D, 9 H, J S, 8 H, 2 D, 7 H, Q D, 8 C, 9 C, Q C, 2 H, 7 S, 2 C, 4 H, 8 S, 7 D, 5 C, 3 H, 8 S, 9 D, 3 C, Q S, 5 D, A S, 9 D, 6 D, A S, Q H, 7 C, 5 D, 6 S, 2 S, 3 S, J C, 4 S, 10 H, 6 C, 10 C, J S, 2 S, Q D, 5 S, A D, 7 C, 3 S, 8 C, 7 S, 3 H, 5 H, 2 H, 5 S, 6 D, 7 H, 9 C, A C, 6 C, 10 S, 8 D, 3 D, Q S, 10 D, Q H, 9 S, 4 S, 6 S, J D, 4 H, 4 D, 7 D, 6 H, J H, 10 C, 8 D, 10 H, 5 C, 10 D, 4 C, 9 S, J C (bottom-card).

WHEAT-EAR. *To form eight ascending sequences, not regarding suit.*

LAY out face-upwards twenty cards, overlapping if space be a consideration, with four reserve cards on each side. (*See* diagram.) The next card (the twenty-ninth) with the seven others of similar value – to be taken as they come to hand – serve as the foundations to be built up in ascending sequence, not regarding suit.

PROCEDURE. – Use cards from the Wheat-ear when a card in suitable sequence becomes exposed, or, failing that, from the eight reserve cards. These can be replenished from stock, or the top-card of the waste-heap, on which you place all unavailable cards while dealing from stock.

RESERVES

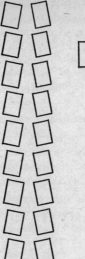

RESERVES

etc.

FOUNDATIONS

THE WHEAT-EAR

You may turn the waste-heap once without shuffling.

HINTS. – Spaces in the reserve need not be filled immediately, and the play comes in here. As the game proceeds you must keep an eye on what cards of each denomination are out and act accordingly.

WHEEL OF FORTUNE. *To form four ascending sequences from Aces, four descending from Kings, following suit.*

LAY-OUT. – The two packs are not shuffled together (cp. 'Above and Below', 'Backbone', 'St Helena'). From the first lay out sixteen cards in a circle. If there are any Aces and Kings among them, place them in two perpendicular lines within the circle to serve as foundations.

Every vacancy in the circumference is at once filled from the pack before another card is dealt.

PROCEDURE. – After building up, if and where possible, deal another circle upon the first (superimposed), and look again for chances of building. You *must* deal all round the circle before commencing to build, and always fill a vacancy immediately.

When stock is exhausted you have two privileges:

(1) Cards can be transferred from an ascending to a descending sequence, or vice versa on the foundation packets, if within one of each other. Manoeuvring this way often makes a card on the 'wheel' available for building.

(2) If a vacancy can now be made in the wheel, a top-card of any of the wheel packets may fill it. Make therefore as many vacancies as possible at this stage of the game.

THE WINDMILL. *To form, without regarding suit, four ascending sequences and a pile of four descending sequences.*

LAY out eight cards as depots as in the diagram; a King among these *may* be placed as a centre foundation, an Ace *must* be placed as a foundation. If no King be dealt, take any King out of the packs and place it in the centre to form the sail-axle of the windmill.

PROCEDURE. – Deal from stock to a waste-heap, the first four Aces that appear becoming foundations and being built on in ascending sequence, regardless of suit. On the central King build in descending sequence, again irrespective of suit.

Cards may be taken from the depots, if in sequence, on any of the five foundations, but other cards may not be moved or dealt on depot cards, whose places, when taken for foundations, are filled (*not necessarily at once*) either by the top-card of stock or the top-card of the waste-heap.

On the central King no less than four descending sequences are to be piled: it is a good idea to mark the limit of each of these by placing the following sequence at right angles to the former, forming a figure like this:

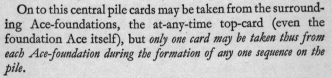

On to this central pile cards may be taken from the surrounding Ace-foundations, the at-any-time top-card (even the foundation Ace itself), but *only one card may be taken thus from each Ace-foundation during the formation of any one sequence on the pile.*

The waste-heap may be turned once, and if the top-card can be taken, or moved, the Patience proceeds, but there is no second deal.

HINTS. – (1) Complete two, and most of the third, central pile as quickly as possible; and therefore, when not inconvenient, leave cards on the tops of Ace-foundations uncovered, if they happen to be in sequence among themselves.

(2) Do not be in too great a hurry to fill vacancies, especially with cards unlikely to be wanted very soon. If, however, you

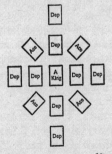

have more than one space at your disposal and duplicates turn up, save one of them.

The Patience is interesting and not really difficult.

APPENDICES

APPENDIX I: ABOVE AND BELOW

Example :

(Figures in brackets refer to the waste-heaps, counting from left to right.)

PACK ONE in this order: Turn up 2 C.

10 H, 9 C, 6 H, 10 D, J C, J D, Q H, 8 C, 10 S, 3 D, 7 C, Q S, 8 H, 6 C, 8 D, A H, Q D, 9 D, 8 S, 2 D, 10 C, 9 H, 5 C, 7 S, 7 D, 6 D, K C, A D, 3 C, 3 H, 2 H, 4 D, A C, J S, 4 S, 6 S, 4 H, J H, 5 S, K S, 5 H, A S, 2 S, K D, 3 S, 5 D, K H, Q C, 4 C, 7 H, 9 S.

Put 10 H on (1), 9 C on (2), 6 H on (3), 10 D on (3), J C on (3). J D on (3), Q H on (3), 8 C on (4), 10 S on (4). *3 D out for ascending foundation.* 7 C on (1), Q S on (3), 8 H on (4), 6 C on (1), 8 D on (4). *A H out for descending foundation.* Q D on (2), 9 D on (1), 8 S on (4), *2 D on turn-up packet.* 10 C on (4), 9 H on (1), 5 C on (4), 7 S on (3), 7 D and 6 D on (3), K C on (1). *A D out. 3 C out. 3 H out. 2 H on turn-up. 4 D out. A C out.* K C from (1) out on A. J S on (1), 4 S on (4), 6 S on (3), 4 H out. J H on (2), 5 S on (1), K S on (2), 5 H out. *A S out,* 2 S on turn-up. K D out on A. *3 S out,* 5 D out, K S and 4, 5, 6 S out. 6 and 7 D out, 7 S out, Q and J S out. K H dealt and out, Q and J H out from heaps, Q C (dealt) and out. Q and J D out. J C out, 4 C (dealt) and out, 5 C out, 10 C out, 8 S out, 10 D, 6 H, 8 D (from heap 4) out, 7 H (dealt) out on 6 H, 8 H out. 9 S (last of pack) dealt and out. 10 S out. 9 H out on 8 (ascending), 9 D on 8 (ascending), 6–9 C out (ascending). 10 H out (ascending). Transfer J S and 10 C from descending to ascending packet.

At end of first pack:

PACK TWO in this order: A H, 7 S, 6 S, 10 H, 7 H, 8 C, 7 C, K D, 6 C, A D, 5, 4 and 3 H, K C, 2 S, A C, 2 H, 5 C, 6 D, 4 D, 6 H, 5 D, 9 D, J S, 8 H, Q S, 5 S, 9 H, K S, J H, A S, Q H, 8 S, 9 S, J D, 8 D, 7 D, 2 C, 4 C, K H, 3 C, Q C, 3 D, 2 D, 10 D, J C, 10 C, 4 S, 3 S, 10 S, 9 C, Q D (last card).

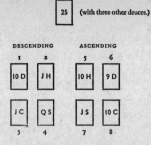

PLAY A H on (1), 7 S on (2), 6 S on (3), 10 H out, 7 H on (2),
8 C on (1), 7 C on (4). *Take 10 and 9 C from foundation packet*
(8) to foundation packet (3), then 8 C and 7 C out from waste-heaps.
K D on (1). 6 C out. A D on (4), 5 H, 4 H, 3 H on (2), K C on
(4), 2 S on turn-up, A C on (3), 2 H on turn-up, 5 C out. 6 D
on (3), 4 D on (2), 6 H and 5 D on (1), 9 D out, J S on (4),
8 H on (1). Q S out on foundation packet 7, take J S from
waste-heap on foundation packet 4, 5 S (dealt) on (2), 9 H out
(descending); *take out 8 H*; K S out, J H out, A S out, Q H out.
8 S and 9 S on (4), J D on (1), 8 D out (descending foundation
packet 1), 7 D out, *take 6 D from waste-heap.* 2 C on turn-up,
4 C out. K H out, 3 C out. Q C on (4), 3 D on (3), 2 D on
turn-up. 10 D out. *Take out J D and 5 D.* J C on (4), 10 C on
(4), 4 S on (1), 3 S on (1), 10 S and 9 C out. *Take out 10, J,*
Q C (ascending); 9 S, 8 S (ascending). K C out, Q D dealt and out.
End of pack.

Take up waste-heaps from left to right without shuffling
and deal:

A D, 6 S, A C, 3 D. A C out. Take 2 C from turn-up.
7 S out, take out 6 S, also from table. 7 H out, 5 H on (2),
4 H on 3 D, 3 H on A D, *4 D out, 5 S out,* A H out, take 2 H
from turn-up. K D out, *6 H out.* Take from waste-heaps 5 H,
4 H, 3 H with 2 H from turn-up. Also A D out. Take 2 D
from turn-up. 3 D out. Take 2 D from turn-up. *4 S, 3 S and*
2 S out. All out.

APPENDIX II: BACKBONE – *Solution*

TAKE same figure: cards in italics dealt.

J D on Q D, *10 C* to vacant rib, *9 C* on 10, *2 C* on A, *J C* on Q, *4 C*, *8 D* on WH. *6 D* on 7 D (rib), *8 H* on WH. *3 D* on WH, *10 D* on J (rib), *2 H* on WH. *A D* out for foundation, *6* and *K C* on WH. *A H* out for foundation. *10 H* and *9 S* on WH. *7 S* on 8 (rib), 6 S (rib) on 7 S, *5 H* to vacant rib, *3 C* out on foundation, 2 D out on A. *End of first pack*.

PACK TWO. *9 D* on 10 D, 7 D on WH, *K D* on WH, *A D* out. *4 H* on 5 H (rib), *9 C* on WH. *6 C* on WH. *10 C* on J (rib), *10 H*, *10 D*, *2 C*, *J D*, *9 H*, *8 H*, *Q D*, *6 H*, *5 H* all on WH. *A H* out. *8* and *7 C* on 9 C (rib), *5 C* on WH. *J S* on Q S (rib), *A S* out. *4 C* out on 3 (foundation), 5 C out from WH. *2 S* out. 3 S from rib, *5 D* on 6 D (rib), 5 H from WH to vacant rib, *3 H* on 4 H, 2 H out on foundation, 3 to 5 H out from rib, 6 and 7 H from backbone, 10 S on J (backbone to rib), 2 S (backbone) to A, 6 H from WH to rib, *Q H* on WH, *4 D* on 5 D (rib), *3 C* and *6 D* on WH. *3 D* out on 2 D, 4 D from rib, 5 D from backbone out. 5 S (from backbone) on 6 S (rib), 4 S (backbone) to 6 S out, 6 D from WH on 5 in foundation. 5 H (rib) on 6 H (rib), 4 H from backbone on 5 H, *3 C* from WH to vacant rib. 7 S and 8 S from rib to foundation. *J C* on vacant rib, *10 S* on WH. *A C* out. 2 D on A. *9 S* on 10 S (rib). *Spades out to Q*. *J H* in vacant rib, *K H* on WH. K and *Q C*, *6* and *5 S* on WH. *3 S* out on 2 S, *4 S* on 3, 5 and 6 S from WH on foundation. *7 H* on WH. K S on Q (foundation), *Q S* on WH, *8 S* on WH. 7 S and 8 S (WH) out on 6 S, *8 D* on 9 D (rib). *End of pack*.

REVERSE WASTE-HEAP. *4 C*, *8 D*, *8 H* on WH. *3 D*, *2 H*, *6 C* all out. *K C* on WH. *10 H* on J H in ribs, *9 S* on WH. 7 D out, 8 D to Q D (from rib) out, K D from backbone out, *K D* on vacant rib. *9 C* on 10 C (rib), *6 C* on 7 C (rib), 5 C from backbone on 6, 8 C from backbone on 9 C, 3 H from backbone, 4, 5, 6 H from ribs out on 2 H (foundation). 9 S from WH on rib, *10 H* on WH. *10 D* on WH. *2 C* on A, 3 C from rib out on 2 C (foundation). *J D* on vacant rib, 10 D from WH on

140

J D (rib), *9 H* on 10 H (rib), *8 H* on 7 H (foundation), 9 H and
10 H from rib, J H from backbone out on foundation, 10 H
from W H to J H in rib, 9 H from backbone on 10 H in rib.
Q D on K D (rib). *Q H* out on foundation, K H from backbone
out, 4 D from backbone out on foundation; 9 S from rib,
10 S (dealt), J S from backbone on 8 S (foundation), 9 D from
backbone on 10 D (rib). 7 C on 6 C (backbone to foundation).
8 C to Q C out from rib, K C from W H on 7 C. 8 H from W H
on 9 H, 8 D (now top-card of W H) on 9 D, 4 C on 3 C (foundation). All Diamonds (5 to K) out from three ribs to foundation.
All Clubs out to Knave.

Deal: K H, K C, Q C, 7 H, Q S on vacant ribs. *All out.*

APPENDIX III: BATTALION – *Solution*

T A K E J and 10 S, *A H* out, 8 C on 9 C, 10 C on J C (in twelfth
column). *A and 2 C out.* 6 C on 5 C, Q D on K D (out). J D
(row 11) on Q D, J C (over 9 S) on 10 C, 9 S out on 10, 8 D on
9 D, 2 and 3 H out. 3 and 4 C out, Q and J H out, K C (lower
one) to foundation, 10 S on 9 S, 7 C on 8 C. *Second K C in
vacant space.* 5, 6, 7, 8, 9 of Clubs out. Q D on J D, 10 D on J
(foundation), 4 D on 5 D, 8 D and 9 D on 7 D (col. 4), A C on
K C, 3 D out, lower 8 S out, 4 and 5 D out, 7 H on 8 H (col. 11),
lower 2 S out, 4 S on 5 S; 3, 4, 5 S out. 7, 8, 9 H on 8 H (col. 6);
6, 7, 8 S out (ascending), K S on A S (col. 2), J C on 10 C (col.
10), 10 C and J C out (ascending), 6 D out, 3 S on 2 S, 5 H on
6 H, 10 H on 9 H, Q S on K S, J H on 10 H (col. 6). 4, 5, 6 H
out. 3 and 2 S on 4 S (col. 11). Q, J, 10 C out (descending).
7 C on 6 C. Q H on J H. K D on Q D. 9 D, 8, 7, 6 out (descending). Q H, J, 10, 9, 8 on K H. 7 H (from col. 8) out on 6 H.
*Hearts out up to K, leaving 9th column vacant. A C into it, followed
by K C. K, Q, J of D into vacant 5th column.* Q and K C out.
7 D on 6 D (ascending). 3 C on 2 C, 8 C on 7 C, 4 C on 3, 5 C
on 4 (all in col. 12). 5 D on 6 D (descending), 4 H on 3 H
(col. 1). J, 10, 9 S on Q S. *Spades out to the K. A H in one of
the vacant spaces, say col. 7. All descending Clubs out from 9 to A.
A S up to vacant space.* 2, 3, 4 S on A, 4 D out on 5 D, 4 and

3 H on 5 H, 6 H on 7 H, 5 S on 4 S, 6 S on 5 S, 2 H on A H,
3 to 10 H on 2 H. *All Hearts out down to A.* 3, 2, A D out.
8, 9, 10 – K D out. 7 to A S out.

APPENDIX IV: THE BRITISH BLOCKADE –
Solution

ARRANGE pack thus:

A C (top-card), 4 and 5 C, K D, A S, A C, 5 C, Q D, 6 S, K C,
J and Q C, 6 and 5 H, 4 D, 7 and 2 H, 5 D, 8 H, 6 D, 8 C, 10 S,
3 and J C, Q H, 8 S, A H, 7 S, J D, 6 S, 3 H, 10 C, 4 S, 7 C,
5 S, 9 D, J S, J H, 5 H, K S, A H, 6 C, 5 S, 7 C, 2 H, 4 H, J S,
8 H, 3 D, 9 H, 3 S, 3 H, J D, K H, 7 D, 10 D, 4 H, 9 C, 9 D,
4 D, 4 C, K and 7 D, 10 C, J H, 7 S, 2 S, 2 D, A D, 9 S, 10 S,
9 C, 7 H, 8 C, 3 and 4 S, Q S, 8 S, 3 and 2 C, Q H, 8 D, 10 D,
2 D, 10 H, A S, A D, 6 D, 10 H, Q D, Q S, K H, K C, 8 D,
2 S, Q C, 5 D, 9 S, 6 H, 3 D, 6 C, K S, 9 H, 2 C (end card).

Deal 1st row from left to right:

A, 4, 5 C, K D, A S, A C, 5 C, Q D, 6 S, K C.

Take A C, deal J C. Take K D, deal Q C. Take A S, deal
6 H. Take Q D, deal 5 H. Take K C, deal 4 D. Take Q C,
deal 7 H. Take J C, deal 2 H.

Deal 2nd row:

5 D, 8 H, 6 D, 8 C, 10 S, 3 C, J C, Q H, 8 S, A H.
Take A H, deal 7 S. Take 2 H, deal J D.

Deal 3rd row:

6 S, 3 H, 10 C, 4 S, 7 C, 5 S, 9 D, J S, J H, 5 H.
Take 3 H, deal and take K S. Deal A H. Take J D, deal 6 C.

Deal 4th row:

5 S, 7 C, 2 and 4 H, J S, 8 H, 3 D, 9 H, 3 S, 3 H.
Take Hearts 4, 5 (top row), 6, 7, 8, 9. Fill up in due order
with J D, K H, 7 D, 10 D, 4 H, 9 C. Take K H, play 9 D.
Take 10 D, deal 4 D.

Deal 5th row:

4 C, K and 7 D, 10 C, J H, 7 and 2 S, 2 and A D, 9 S.

Take A and 2 D, 2 and 3 S, 3 D, 10 and 9 C (descending),
9 D (in 3rd row – descending), 4 D (in row 4), 4 S and 8 C.

Fill up vacancies in due order: 10 S (in 2nd row next to 10 S),
9 C, 7 H (3rd row), 8 C, 3 S, 4 S, Q S in 4th row; 8 S, 3 C,
2 C, Q H in bottom row.

Take Q and J H, Q and J S, 2, 3 and 4 C from bottom row.
5 S, 6 S (from top row), 7, 8, 9 S. 5 C (the one nearer left-
hand), 6 C, 7 C. 5, 6, 7 (below) of Diamonds, 10 S (under 9 D –
descending). *Transfer 9 S from ascending sequence and take 8 S.*
Take 8, 9, 10 C ascending.

Fill vacancies: 8, 10, 2 D in top row. 10 H, A S, A D, 6 D
in 2nd row. 10 H, Q D, Q S in 3rd row. K H, K C, 8 D, 2 S
in 4th row. Q C, 5 D, 9 S, 6 H, 3 D, 6 C, K S, 9 H, 2 C in 5th
row.* Take 8 D, ascending. 10 H, 9 H, descending. *Transfer
9 to Q D to ascending sequence.* Take K D from bottom row.
Take 7, 6, 5, 4 C, descending. J, Q C, ascending. 9 S, ascending, 8 H, 7 H, descending. K C, ascending. Q, J, 10, 9 D,
descending. 6 H, descending. 8 D, 7 D.

Take as 'merci' card 6 D: then 6, 5, 4, 3, 2 D possible, 7 S and
6 S out, 5 H to A H, 10 H to K H, 10 S to K S, 5 S to A S;
3, 2, A C, A D. *All out.*

APPENDIX V: THE CORONA – *Solution*

(Cards in italics dealt.)
TAKE K C. 7 H on 6 H, 5 D (ray 7) on 6. Take A C. 3 S on 2,
7 S on 8, 6 S on 7 (ray 11), J, 10, 9 S on Q. Deal *2 C*, place on
A and take 3. Deal *Q D* on W H, *4 H* on 3, *A H* out, 9 S on
W H, *K C* on W H, *A H, 7 H, 2 C, 3 H, 7 C* all on W H, *4 C* on 3
(foundation), *K D* out, *2 D* and *6 S* on W H, *A D* out, *8 C* on
W H, *5 S* on 6, *K S* out, *J D* on W H, *J C* on W H, *A S* out,
5 C on 4 (foundation), *6 C* out, *8 H* on 7. *Take 8, 7, 6 H on 9 H*
(*ray 12*), 8 D on 9 D (ray 1), 5 H on 6 H, *leaving vacancy,* 4 H on 5,
8 D on 7, 9 D on 8, *leaving 2 H exposed in ray 1. Now Hearts out*

---

* At this point your board should correspond with the diagram given
in the text.

up to 9. 8 S on 7 S (ray 3), 9 to Q S on 8. *Now Spades out down-wards to 7 S and a third space left.* 5 D (from ray 6) on 4 D, 9 D to 4 D on 10 D. *Now are vacant rays 1, 3, 4, 8.* Take J C from W H to ray (1), 10 C from ray (6) on him, J D from W H on ray (3), 7 C from ray (2), 8 C from W H on foundation, 6 S (W H) on 7 S (descending), 2 D (W H) on A, 7 C (W H) on ray (4), 3 H (W H) on ray (6), 5 S (dealt) out on 6 (descending foundation), *J C* on W H, *4 D* on 5 D (ray 5), *K H* out, *8 C* on 7, *5 H* on 6, *6 D* and *9 D* on W H, *Q D* on K D. J D follows. *Vacant ray. A D* in vacant ray (3). *Q C* out on K. *Q H* on K, J H on Q, *10 H* on 9 (ascending), *8 H* on W H, *2 H* on 3, *J H* on 10 (ascending), *6 C* on W H, *7 D* on vacant ray (8), *10 D* on J, *4 C* on W H, *9 C* on 8 C (ray 4), 10 and J C on this. *J C to 7 C out on Q.* 4 C (W H) to vacant ray. 6 C (W H) out on 7, *8 D* on 7 (ray 8), *J D, 9 H, A C* all on W H. *3 D* on 2, *4 to 10 D out from ray 12.* 3 D in vacant ray, 4 and 5 D on it. *10 S* on J. *K H* in vacant ray, *2 D* on W H, *4 S* on 5, 3 and 2 S (ray 7) on 4. *Spades out from 2 to 8.* 3 S on 2. 2 D (W H) on A D. A C (W H) on vacant ray (5). 9 H (W H) on vacant ray. J D (W H) out on 10 (foundation ascending). 8 H (W H) on 9. 9 D (W H) on 10 D. 6 D (W H) on 5. *All descending Diamonds out.* J C (W H) on ray (3), 10 C on him, 2 C (W H) on A, 7 H (W H) on vacant ray, 8 H and 9 H on him. A H (W H) on vacant ray, 2 H, 3 H on him. K C (W H) on vacant ray, 9 S (W H) out on 8 foundation, 10 and J S out, Q D (last card in W H) on J D. *Q S* (dealt) on J, *Q C* on K, *4 H* on 3. *Take 5 and 6 from ray (2)* on 4 H, *5 C* out on 6, 4 C on 5, *Q H* on J, *3 C* on 4. *Clubs out;* K H on Q, *K S* on Q, *4 S* on 5; 3 and 2 S out. *9 C* on 8. *Ascending Clubs out. A S* out on 2, *K D* on Q, *10 H* (last card in stock) on J. *Descending Hearts out.*

APPENDIX VI: DOUBLE FAN – *Solution*

PUT 4 C on 3 C (singleton). Take A D and K D (over 2 H) for foundations. Take Q D out (descending); put the other Q D on K D (over Q H). Put 10 D (over J D) on J D (over Q C). Take out J D (over A D) and 10 D (descending).

Take out 2, 3, 4 D (over 10 H) ascending. Put 5 C (over 8 S) on 4 C, 6 C on 5 C. Take for foundation K C and A H; A S and 2 S (over J H); A and 2 C. Put 4 S on 5 S (over 4 C). Take out K and Q S; 2 H (over 10 C), 3, 4, 5, 6 H. Take out K H, Q H (over other K H) descending, J and 10 H. Put 9 H on 10 H (over 6 C), 8 H on 9, 7 H on 8. Take out J S, 9 H (descending), 10 S, Q and J C; 9, 8, 7 S and 6 S (over 9 D) – all descending. Put 3 S on 2 (over 4 S), *not* on foundation; put 4 S on 3. Take out 5 S (over 4 C), 4, 3, 2 S (descending). Take out 3, 4, 5 C (ascending), 5 D (over 7 D). Put 5 D (over 6 D) on 4 D (over 7 C). Take out (descending) 9 D (the one over 10 S), 8 D (over J S), 7, 6, 5, 4, 3 D. Put J D on Q D, Q and J C on K C, 10 C (over 9 S) on J C, 9 C (over 3 H) on 10, 8 C on 9, 7 C (over 3 S) on 8 C. *Take out 3 to Q S ascending.* Put 10, 9, 8, 7, 6 D on J D – *then all ascending Diamonds out*. Put 3 H on 2, 4 H on 3, 5 H on 4, 6, 7, 8 H all on 2 – *then descending Hearts out to 2, likewise ascending Hearts all out.* 7 C (left alone) on 6, 8 on 7, 9 and 10 C on 8. 6 C on 7 C – *then all Clubs ascending and descending out.* K S out, 2 and A D, A H, A S. *All out.*

APPENDIX VII: DOUBLE PYRAMID – *Solution*

TAKE figure in diagram. Cards in italics are as dealt from stock.

Put 6 S on 5 H. Deal *9 H* on W H (1), *7 S* on 6 S, *5 C* in position in inner pyramid, take 6 C, *8 H* on *7 S*, 9 H from W H, 10 H and J H from pyramid out on foundation. *4 S* on W H (1), also *8 C*. Take 7 D from pyramid, 8 C from W H, 9 S, 10 D, J S from pyramid out on 6 C. *6 C* on W H (2), *5 C* in position, take 6 C from W H, *2 S* on W H (2), *4 C* on W H (1), *A S* on W H (3). *3 C* on W H (1), *8 H* on W H (4), *K D* and *6 D* on W H (2). *A C* on W H (3). *5 D in position*. Take 6 D from W H. *4 H* on W H (1), *J D* on W H (2). *5 H* in position, take 6 H from pyramid. *A H* on W H (3). *2 D* on W H (2), *Q S* out on J S, K S out from pyramid, A H out from W H, 2 D from W H, 3 S from pyramid, 4 H from W H. *10 C* on W H (2), *Q H* out on J H. K C from pyramid, A C from W H, 2 S from pyramid,

3 and 4 C from WH. *3 S* on WH (1), *5 S* in position. 6 H from
pyramid. *Q D* on WH (3), *A C* on WH (1), *9 D* on WH (2),
2 H on WH (4), *A D* on WH (4), *10 S* on WH (4), *Q C* on WH
(3), *K H* on WH (1), *7 H* out on 6 H, *6 D* on WH (4), *8 D* out
on 7 H; 9 D, 10 C, J D, Q C, K H, A C from WH, 2 C from
pyramid, 3 and 4 S from WH. *10 C* on WH (2) under K D;
5 S in position, 6 D from WH, *7 S* on 6 H, *4 D* on WH (1),
K and Q H on WH (4), *7 D* on 6 D, *Q D* on WH (3), *4 D* on
WH (1), *7 C* on 6 C, *3 D* on WH (1), *A D* on WH (3), *4 H* on
WH (1), *J D* on WH (3), *K D* on WH (1), *J C* on WH (4),
J H on WH (1), *K C* on WH (3), *Q S* on WH (2), *8 S* out on
7 S, 9 C and 10 D out from pyramid, J H from WH (1), Q S
from WH (2), K C from WH (3), *4 S* on WH (1), *5 D* in
position, *3 D* on WH (1), *J C* on WH (1). *Q C* on WH (3),
9 D on WH (1), *7 H* out on 6 D, *10 H* on WH (4), *A S* on K C,
8 S out on 7 D; 9 D, 10 H, J C (from WH (4)), Q H, K H out
from WH. *10 S* on WH (4), *9 H* on WH (4), *K S* on WH (1),
8 C out on 7 C, 9 H and 10 S from WH, J S from pyramid,
Q C and K S from WH, *8 D* out on 7 H, *9 C* dealt and out on
8 D, 10 S, J D from WH. A D from WH on K H, second A D
from WH on K S, 2 H on A D, *6 S* on 5 D, *3 H* on 2 H, *2 H* on
A D, *7 C* on 6 S, 8 H (from WH) on 7 C, *3 C* on 2 H, *A H* on
WH (4), *2 C* on WH (4), *9 S* out on 8 H. 10 and J C, Q and K D,
2nd Q D (out on J D). A S, 2 C, 3 D, 4 S out. K D, A H, 2 S
out. *All out.*

APPENDIX VIII: THE EMPEROR – *Solution*

Sealed packets from left to right:

(1) K H, J D, 7 S (top card); (2) 8 H, 5 S, 6 H; (3) K D, 7 H,
10 D; (4) J S, 10 S, Q C; (5) 4 S, K C, Q D; (6) 2 H, 5 D, 7 D;
(7) 6 H, 7 C, 9 D; (8) Q S, 4 D, 6 S; (9) A, 8, 3 S; (10) 10 H,
6 D, J H.

Top line. A D, 4 H, 7 and 9 C, 10 S, Q C, 8 C, 5 and 7 H, 5 C.

Take A D – exposes 7 S. 4 H on 5 C – exposes 6 H. 6 H on
7 S – exposes 5 S. 5 S on 6 H – exposes 8 H. 8 H on 9 C.

Vacancy. Put Q C in, exposing 7 D. 7 C on 8 H – exposes 10 D. 7 D on 8 C – exposes 5 D.

Deal from stock (cards dealt in italics): *K S* on W H, *6 S* on 7 D, 5 D on 6 S, exposing 2 H. *6 C* on 7 H, 5 H on 6 C – exposes 6 S. *J H* on Q C, 10 S on J H (exposes Q D). *2 H* on W H. *4 H* on *5 S*, *3 H* on W H.

2 C on W H. *5 D* on 6 S. *A S* to foundation, *9 H* on 10 S, *J C* on Q D, 10 D on J C (exposes 7 H), *8 C* on 9 H, 7 H on 8 C (exposes K D), *2 S* out on A, *2 D* out. *A H* out, 2 H out. Put 2 C from W H in this vacant space. 3 H out from W H, 4 H (over 5 C) out, *3 S* out, *8 D* on W H, *K S* on W H, *6 D* on 7 C, 5 C on 6 D (exposes J H), *4 C* on 5 D (row 7), *A C* out. 2 C out, 5 D in vacant space, 6 S on 7 H (col. 2), 5 D on 6 S, 4 D exposed in row 8, place on 5 C, exposing Q S. Place this on K D, J H on Q S, exposing 6 D. 5 H out on 4. (*Two vacant rows 6 and 8.*) Put 4 H in one, 5 S in the other. 6 H out on foundation, 6 D from col. 10 on 7 S, exposing 10 H. 5 S and 4 H back to col. 1. 10 D to col. 8. J C to col. 6. 10 D on J C. K S from W H to col. 8, Q D on him, exposing K C. *2 C* (dealt) on W H. *3 C* out on foundation, 4 C out. *Q S* on W H, *3 D* out, 4 and 5 D out (5 from col. 7), 5 and 6 C out on foundation, 7 H out, exposing in 9th column 3 S, which goes on 4 H, exposing 8 S. *K H* on W H. *9 S* on 10 D, 6 D out, *3 H* on W H, *8 H* on 9 S. 7 C (col. 4) on 8 H (col. 6), 8 H out (from col. 4), 9 C on 10 H, exposing Q C. *9 S* on W H. *Q D* on K C, *10 D* on W H. *7 D* on 8 S, 6 S (col. 7) on 7 D. Other 7 D and 7 C out. 8 C out (9 D exposed), 9 C out. *J D* on Q C, *2 D* on 3 S. *9 H* out, 10 H out. *Vacant space.* (Second) *10 H* on W H. *4 S* out. *K D* on W H. 10 C on J D. *9 D* on 10 C (exposing 7 C, which place on 8 H, exposing 6 H, which place on 7 C). *Two vacant spaces.* 6 S on col. 7, 7 D on col. 10, 8 S on 9 D, 7 D on 8 S, 6 S on 7 D. *A S exposed place on foundation.**

Transpose K C and Q D to col. 10 – exposes 4 S, place on 5 D. *You have now three vacant spaces (call them cols. 5, 7, 9). Transfer the sequence J C to 6 H to Q D col. 10. Transfer K D to J H to col. 9 and by help of the four vacancies (cols. 3, 5, 6, 7) transfer sequence*

* At this point consult diagram in text.

J D to 6 S to col. 9 after putting J H on 10 foundation. Put K D
from W H to col. 7, Q C on him, exposing 10 S. *'Worry back'
J H on Q C, take 10 S, exposing J S.* Put 10 H from W H on J S,
10 D from W H in vacant space, say row (6), 9 S from W H
on 10 H, 3 H on 4 S, K H (from W H) in vacant space, row (5),
Q S on him, 2 C on 3 H. 8 D on 9 S. 8 D out on foundation.
4 D on W H. J C on Q D. 10 D on J C. *'Worry back' from
foundation 9 C and 8 D on 10 D (col. 8).* Get from 5 S to 2 D on
6 H (row 10). You have two vacancies to work on. 7 S and 6 D
on 8 D (col. 8), exposing J D. Put this on Q S, exposing K H.
*Shove up rows to the right, leaving K H alone in row 3, rows 2 and 1
vacant.* Get from 5 D to 2 C on 6 S in col. 9, from 9 H to 6 S
on 10 S in col. 6, from Q C to 10 S on K H, leaving rows 3, 2, 1
vacant. (*You have now not only three vacancies, but all the sealed
packets out, and only three cards in the W H. Success should be
assured.*)

Deal *9 C* out on 8 C. *5 C* on 6 D (row 8), take 4 D from W H.
5 H on 6 S. *8 D* out on foundation. *J S* on W H. *A D* out.
3 D, take out 2, 3, 4 D. *Q H* in vacant space, row (3). Transfer
to her J S to 9 S, and replace in row (5). *5 S* out on foundation,
10 C out, *6 C* on W H. *8 S* on W H. *9 D* on 10 S. Take 8 S
from W H. *Q H* on W H. Transfer 10 S–8 S to J D and take
J H and Q H (from W H) on foundation. *3 C* on W H. *7 S* on
W H. *2 S* out. *A H* out, *K C* on row 2. Put Q H to 9 S on him,
and the whole back in row (5), *A C* out. Put 7 S from W H in
vacancy. Take out 2, 3 C. Deal *4 C* out on foundation. 5 and
6 C out (the last from W H). J S from W H on vacancy, 2 H
from W H on A, leaving K S alone in W H. *All out.*

APPENDIX IX: THE GENERAL'S – *Solution*

IN diagram transpose 9 D and 10 D. Put 8 S on foundation.
Pack 3 C, 2 H, A C on 4 H. *Deal* (cards dealt are in italics) *9 H*
on space (2), *A H* and *3 C* on W H, *2 D* on W H, *8 C* on 9 H.
Put 2 and 3 from W H in vacant space (3). *A C* on them. *2 S* in
row (6), A H from W H on 2 S. *Q S* on row (7), J H on her
from row (9), *J C, Q D, A D* on W H. *7 H* out for foundation,

5 C on WH. *6 S* on row (9), with *5* D on it, transfer to row (8). *5 S*, *Q C*, *5 C*, *4* D on WH. *J S* on Q H, *2* D on WH. *7 C* out for foundation, 8 C and 9 C out. *3 H* over *2 S* (by vacancies). *K C* on A H. *4 C* on *5* D. *10 C* on J H. 9 H on 10 C. Sequence 3 H to K C on 4 C in row (9), Q H and J S on K C. *2* D from WH into vacancy. 4 D from WH over 3 C, 5 C over 4 D from WH. *K H* on A C (row 3). Q C from WH. 5 S from WH in vacant row, transfer 4 H to Q C beneath him via vacancies. Close up rows. *10 S* in vacancy. *5 H* on WH. *7 C* out for foundation. *K D* on A C. *5 D*, *K S*, *K D* on WH. *6 C* in vacant space. *2 H* and *A H* on WH. *K C* on WH. *7 H* out, *7* D out, *8, 9, 10 and 7* D out from top line. *J D* out. *6 D, J S, 6 H, A S* on WH, *10 H* on J S, *9 S* and 10 S out. A S from WH on 2 D. 6 H from WH in vacancy. J S from WH on 10 S. *8 H* out, 9 H and 10 H out. J H and 10 C on Q C. Q S out. *Three vacancies.* Place K D to 5 C on 6 H. *Four vacancies.* 10 C out, J H out. *Q H* out. 6 D from WH in vacant space. Sequence 5 S to Q C on 6 D. *9 H* in vacant space. *3 S* over *2* D. *2 C* on WH. *J C* and Q C out. *10 H* on J S, *9 C* on 10 H. *4 H* over 3 S, *6 D, A D, 6 S* on WH. *10 S* and *J D* arrange over 9 H. *A S, 3 D, 3 S* on WH. *8 H* out. *Q C* on K H. J D to 9 H on Q C. *4 S* in vacant space. *Q D* out, *7 S* out. *3* D on 4 S, *8* D on 7. *9 D, K S, K H, 8 C* out to foundations from top line. 9 H, 9 C, 10 H, A S, K D out. *6 C* on WH. *10 C* out. *4 S* on WH. *J H* out. *9 S* on WH. *8 S* out. 9, 10, J S, Q H, K C, A C, A H, 2 S all out. A C to J D on 2 D. 2 H out. 2 D on 3 C. 3 S, 3 H, 4 H out, 3 D on 4 C, 4 S out. *10* D out, J D out, *3 H* on WH. *Q S* out. *4* D and *4 C* (last card of stock) on WH.

REVERSE WH. *J C, Q D, Q C* and *K H, A, 2, 3* D out. *5 C* in vacant space, *5 H* out, 6 H from top line out. *5 D* in vacant space. *K S, K D* out. *2 H* on 3 C. *A H* and 2 H out, *K C, A C, 2 C, 3, 4, 5, 6* C out. *6 D* in vacant space, A and 2 D out. *6 S* in vacant space. *A S* out, 2 S from top line, 3 D out, *3 S* out, *6 C* in vacant space. *4 S* out. 3, 4, 5 H out, 2 C (from top row) out, 3 C, 4, 5, 6 D out. 5 S (from above) and 6 S out, 4 D and 5 D, 4 C, 5 and 6 C, 5 and 6 S, 6 D, 6 H, all out.

APPENDIX X: GRANDFATHER'S CLOCK –
Solution

WITH diagram and pack as given.

Put 10 S, J H and 4 C on their respective foundations. *Deal 5 D* (cards dealt in italics) above Q S, *5 C* on 7 C, *6 H* on A H. Put 5 D on foundation. *3 D* from stock on Q S, 5 C on 4 C, 6 C on 5, 7 C on 6, 8 C on 7 (2 o'clock).

Deal both *8 H, 8 H, A S, 10 S* to vacant spaces in packets in proper order. Deal second *A S* from stock on K S (foundation), *Q H* on J H (foundation), *2 S* on foundation, *6 S* on 5 S (foundation). Pack 10 C at 5 o'clock on J C at 10 o'clock, 3 H on 2 H (foundation), *4 S* and *7 H* on 7 D, 7 and 8 H out on 6 H (foundation). *2 D* on 8 H. *9 D* on 4 S. Put 9 D out on 8 D (foundation), *9 C* on 8; take 10 and J C. Deal *K H* on Q, *3 S* on 2 S (foundation), take 4 S on 3. Take A H on K. *2 D*, *10 D* on 7 D, *3 H* on 9 S, *J S* on 2 H. Take J S out on 10, take 2 and 3 H. Deal *8 C* on 9 S, *9 H* and *Q C* on A C. Take Q C out on J (6 o'clock), 10 D on 9, 8 C on 7. Deal *K D* on 2, *10 H* on 9 S, *7 S* on 9 H. Take out 7 S. Deal *5 H* on 9 H, 8 S goes on 7, *2 C* on 3 S, *6 D* out, take K D on Q (foundation). Pack 5 H on 6. Put 9 H and 10 H on foundation. Deal *Q C* on 2 D (5 o'clock), *9 D* on 9 S, *K C* on A C, *4 H* on K C. Take Q S on J, 4 H on 3 H, K and A C on Q C (6 o'clock). Deal *J D, J S, Q H* on vacant packet, *K D* on 9 H. Take 2 C from 12 o'clock on A C (foundation). Pack 2 S on 3 S. 9 C goes now on foundation and *10 C* (dealt) on him. Deal *6 S* and *5 H* on 2 C – take Q C (at 5 o'clock) out on J C (foundation) – *7 D* on 2 D. 7, 8, 9 D out on 6. 9 and 10 S out. Deal *K C* on Q (2 o'clock). Take A C,* 3 and 4 C out at 6 o'clock, 5 H on 4 H, A S on 2 S (at 12 o'clock), 4, 5, 6, 7 H out (N.B. on two foundations), 2 D (behind 3 o'clock) on 3 D (6 o'clock). 8 H out. Deal *5 D* on 6 S, *J H, 10 D* at 3 o'clock, *J D, Q D* on 8 S, *K S* on 2 D, *6 D* on 2 D (the first behind 5, the second behind 6 o'clock), *5 C, A D, 4 S* in vacant packet, *4 D* (last card in pack) at 8 o'clock.

* At 2 o'clock.

Pack Q D on K D.

Then J, Q, K D out at 3 o'clock. 10 D on 9 D (11 o'clock); J, Q H on 10 H; K, A, 2, 3 S out at 4 o'clock; 4 S on them. A to 7 D out at 7 o'clock; A, 2, 3 D out at 3 o'clock; 5 and 6 C out at 6 o'clock; J and Q S out at 12 o'clock; K and A H at 1 o'clock; 9 H at 9 o'clock; 5, 6, 7, 8 S at 8 o'clock; 2 C at 2 o'clock; J D at 11 o'clock.

APPENDIX XI: THE HARP – *Solution*

TAKE A S exposing 10 D, pack 9 S exposing 2 H, pack 8 C exposing 4 C, pack 3 H exposing Q S, pack Q S exposing J C, pack J C exposing 5 H. Build 2 S. Transfer K H, Q S to col. 9 exposing 3 C.

Deal *J D* on Q S, *A D* on foundation, pack 2 H. *Deal K D* to vacant col. 8. Deal (cards in italics are cards dealt) *J, 5, 3 H* to W H, *8 H* on 9 S, *A H* out on foundation. Build 2 and 3 from board. Pack 4 C on 5 H exposing A C which place on foundation, exposing K S. Deal *9 C* on W H, *7 C* on W H, *2 C* on foundation, build 3 C exposing 7 C which place on 8 H and put K S in col. 7 exposing 7 D, 4 C on foundation. Deal *K C, 3 C* on W H, *6 D* on 7 C. Pack 7 D on 8 C, exposing 3 S. Build this on 2 S (foundation) exposing Q D which build on K S exposing K C. Build J C on Q D, Q H on K C exposing 5 C. Pack and expose 8 D. Deal *7 H* on W H, *8 D, 7 S* on W H, *2 D* out, *7 H* on W H, *4 S* out, *J S* on Q H, *3 D* out, *7 D* on W H, *10 S* on J D, *4 C* on W H, *5 S* out, *J C* on W H, *4 D* out. Build 5 D exposing 2 D, build 6, 7 and 8 D exposing 9 H. Place this on 10 S exposing A D which place on foundation exposing 2 S; build 2 D exposing 4 D. Deal *9 S* on W H, *6 D* on 7 C, *6 S* on foundation, *J S* on W H, *10 D* on J S, *6 C* on foundation, *Q D* on W H, *A S* on foundation, 2 S out, *K H* (dealt) into vacant row (4), *5 D* on W H, *8 C* on W H. Put 8 C (from board) on 9 H. 9 D out exposing J H. Deal *10 C* on W H, *A H* on foundation, *Q S* on K H. Pack J H on Q S, 10 C from W H on J H, 10 H (exposed by packing J H) on J C, 3 D (exposed), build on 2 D (foundation) exposing 6 H, build 4 D exposing 10 H.

Deal *4 H* on foundation, take 5 and 6 H exposing respectively
8 S and 5 S, *3 S* out on foundation. Pack 5 S on 6 D exposing
6 S. Deal *Q H* on WH, *8 S* on WH, *9 C* on 10 H (in col. 7),
7 S on 6 (foundation). Take 8 S (from col. 1) exposing 6 C.
Deal *A C* on foundation, *9 D* on 10 C, *9 H* on WH, *2 H* out
on foundation, *4 S* on foundation. Take 5 and 6 S, leaving
col. 3 blank. Place *K D* there (from stock), *4 H* on WH,
5 C on 6 D, pack 4 H from WH, *2 C* out on foundation, *6 H*
on WH, *8 H* on 9 C.

END OF PACK. REVERSE WH.

J H, 5 H on WH. *3 H* out; take 4 H from col. 5 and 5 H from
WH. Take 10 D from col. 2 on foundation. Transfer 10 H
from col. 6 to J S. Put J H from WH in vacant place. *Deal
9 C* on 10 H, *7 C* on 8 H, *K C* on WH, *3 C* out, *7 H* on *8 C*,
6 C on 7 H exposing 10 C. Take 10 C on J H exposing Q C,
place on K D exposing J D, place on Q C. Put K C in vacant
row. Deal *8 D* on 9 C, *7 S* on 6 (foundation), *7 H* on foundation, *7 D* on WH, *4 C* on foundation. Take 5, 6, 7 C. Deal
J C on WH, *9 S* on foundation, *J S* on WH, *Q D* on K C, take
J S from WH, *5 D* on foundation. Take 6 D, 7 C, 8 H (all from
col. 5), *8 C* (dealt) on foundation. Put 8 D (col. 2) on *9 S.*
Take 9, 10, J C (from WH), 7 D (from WH), 8 D from col. 5,
9 D from col. 4, 9 S from col. 5 on 10 H (col. 2), 10 D out
exposing 10 S. Take this on 9 S exposing Q C, put on K D
exposing K S. Deal *Q H* on K S, *8 S* out, *9 H* out. *9 H* out,
6 H out. *8 H* last card. *Rest out.*

APPENDIX XII: THE HAT – *Solution*

TAKE figure and arrangement of pack as given in the text.
Take out for foundations K H, K D, A D. Put Q C in vacant
side depot: take A C for foundation and 2 C. *Deal* to brim
depots: 9 C, J S, 4 S, *A S* (top-cards in italics); K S, 2 C, 10 C,
Q D; 7, J, 6 C, *2 D*; 7 D, 10 H, 10 D, *A H*; 5 H̲, 5 H, 7 S,
9 S; 5, 7, 2 S, *Q D.*

Take A H and A S for foundations, 2 S from side depot,

2 D out, Q D (over 10 C), J D from side, 10 D. Risk 10 C in one vacant side depot.

Deal A H, K D, K C, *9 D*; 8 H, K H, 3 C, *8 C*; 9 D, J S, A and *5 C*; 2 and Q H, 3 C, *6 D*; 5 D, 7 H, 4 C, *K S*; 3 and 4 H, 7 D, *8 H*.

Take 9 D, K C, Q, J, 10, 9 C (all from side), 8 C, K S, 3, 4, 5 C (ascending). Take to side depot 6 D and 3 C, then out to foundations Q and 2 H. Take to side depot 10 H. (You have still two vacancies.)

Deal Q S, 2 H, 5 D, *10 S*; A, 6, 8, *3 S*; K C, 2 D, 3 D, *Q S*; Q, 10, 5, *6 C*; A D, 4 H, 6 D, *J H*; 8 D, 6, 3 and *9 H*. (All pack now on table.)

Take 3 S, Q S, 3 D, 4 D (from side), J H, 10 H (from side), 9 H, 3 H, 6 C. Put 10 S on side depot; then 5 D, 6 D (from brim), 4 H out. Put 6 H to side depot; then 8 D and 8 H out (descending), 7 D, 6 D (from side) descending. Put A D on side; then 7 H, 6 H (from side) descending. 5 D (descending); 2 D, K C

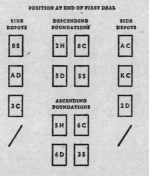

POSITION AT END OF FIRST DEAL

SIDE DEPOTS	DESCENDING FOUNDATIONS		SIDE DEPOTS
8 S	2 H	8 C	A C
A D	5 D	5 S	K C
3 C	ASCENDING FOUNDATIONS		2 D
	5 H	6 C	
	6 D	3 S	

and A C to side places; then J S, 10 S (from side), 9 S, 8 S (side), 7 S out descending. Put 8 S on side depot; then 6 and 5 S (from side) out descending; 5, 4, 3, 2 H descending, 5 H ascending. *Pick up brim depots and shuffle.*

Second deal. (To Brim Depots.) 10 C, 4 and 7 S, *8 H*; J and 6 S, Q D, *7 C*; J C, 3 D, A H, *2 S*; 6 C, J H, 8 C, *6 H*; *K S,* 4 D, 9 S, *Q H*; Q C, 2 C, A S, *10 H*. Take 6 H and 7 C (ascending). *Deal* 5 S, 8 D, 7 H, *4 C*; Q S, 9 D, 3 S, *J D*; K H, 7 D, 5 C, *9 C*; 10 S, 9 H, 7 C, *4 S,* K and *10 D.*

Transfer 7 and 6 C to descending sequence. Put 9 C in side place. Then 5, 4, 3 C (from side) out. Take 7 H, 7 D, 8 D, 4 S, 5 S, 8 H. Put 7 C to side. Take 9 H, 10 H. Put A S to side. Take 2 and A C. *Pick up brim depots and shuffle.*

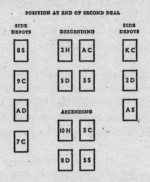

POSITION AT END OF SECOND DEAL

In brim depots from left to right twenty-six cards thus:

7 S, 4 S, 10 C; *J D,* 3 S, 9 D, Q S, Q D, 6 and J S; *K H,* 2 S, A H; 3 D, J C; 6 C, J H, 8 C, *10 S*; K S, 4 D, 9 S, Q H, K D, *10 D*; *Q C.*

Third deal: J S, 8 C, 2 S, *J C*; 10 C, J D, 10 S, *Q C*; 6 and 9 S, K S, *6 C*; J H, Q S, 3 D, *7 S*; Q D, 9 D, 4 S, *K D*; A H, 3 S, K H, *10 D.*

Take 6 and 7 C (from side); K S on side; 9 S to side. Take out 6, 7, 8, 9 S. Deal last two cards (Q H, *4 D*). Out 4, 3, 2 D. Put Q C to side, 10 S out. Put K D to side, 4 S out; 9, 10, J, Q D out, K D from side. Put Q S to side. J, Q, K H out; 3 S and A H. Put J C to side, 2 and A S out. *All out.*

APPENDIX XIII: HEAP – *Solution*

USE the lay-out given in the text: then
Take 8 D over (1), 9 C on (2), 10 D on (3), J S on (4), Q D on

(5), K C on (6), A D on (7), 2 C on (8), 3 D on (9), 4 C on (10), 5 D on (11), 7 S on (13), 6 S on (12).

Take 8 H on (13), Q S on (4), 7 S on (12), 2 H (over 10 H) on (7), A S on (6), J D on (3), 6 H on (11), 5 C on (10), 4 H on (9), 3 S on (8), K D on (5), 10 S on (2), 9 D on (1).

Take 9 S on (13), 8 C (over 7 H) on (12), 7 H (over 4 C) on (11), J C on (2), 10 D on (1), 4 C on (8). K C on (4), Q H on (3), 3 H and 4 D on (7), A H on (5), 5 H (over Q C) on (9), 2 S on (6), 6 C on (10).

Take 2 H on (5), J H on (1), Q C (over 6 C) on (2), 10 H (over 6 D) and J S on (13), 6 D on (9), K H, A D and 2 D on (3), 5 D on (7), 9 C on (12), 7 C and 8 C on (10), 5 S on (8), 10 C (over K S) on (12), 7 D on (9), 6 S on (8), 6 D and 7 H on (7). *Turn down* 7 H.

Take 3 C on (6), A and 2 C on (4), 8 D and 9 H on (11), 3 D on (3), Q H on (13), K S (over J H) on (13). *Turn down.* 3 H, 4 D, 5 H on (5). *Turn down.* 3 S and 4 S (over A) on (4). *Turn down.* 4 S, 5 C, 6 C, on (6). *Turn down.* 7 C and 8 S on (8). *Turn down.* 9 S, 10 C on (10). *Turn down.* 8 H and 9 D on (9). *Turn down.* 10 H and J H on (11). *Turn down.* K, A and 2 S on (2). *Turn down.* Q D, K D and A H on (1), J and Q C on (12).

APPENDIX XIV: KC – *Solution*

PACKETS (cards in italics are top-cards).

3 D, 4 D, 10 H, 8 S; *9 D*, A and 6 S, 6 C; *K S*, 10 S, 3 C, 10 H; *Q S*, 2, 5 and 8 H; *K D*, 8 H, 2 and 7 S; *8 C*, A C, J S, K H; *6 D*, 4 H, 2 D, 8 D; *4 H*, Q C, 3 S, Q H; *Q S*, 7 S, 9 C, 6 H; *8 S*, K D, K H, 6 H; *4 C*, J H, 10 D, 3 S; *2 S*, 7 D, 9 and 5 C.

Deal (cards in italics are cards dealt) on WH. *2 C, Q H, Q D, K S, 5* and *10 S*. 2 D on 3 D, *3 H* on 4 H. On WH. *9 H, 9 S, 5 S, 3 H, J C, 8 D, K C, 4 S.* *5 D* on 6 D, *4 D* on 5 D. *9 H* on WH. *7 C* on 8 C, *7 H* on WH, *2 H* on 3 H, *3 C* on 4, *9 D* on WH (seventeen cards on WH!) *A H* at last for foundation. Take out *2, 3, 4 H. J C* on Q C, *3 D* on 4. Deal *10 C* on J C, *2 C* on 3, *5 H* on foundation, *J D* on WH, *A S* on foundation. Take out 2 S. *7 D* on WH, *6 D* on 7 D (in lay-out). *Q D* on K. *7 C, K C, 5 C* on WH. *J D* on Q, *4 S, 9 S* on WH (twenty-four on WH!). *A D* and *A H* on foundation. *Take out 2 to 6 D* (*packets 1 and 7*). 7 H on WH. *J S* on *Q* (packet 9), *6 S, 4 C, 10 C* on WH. *A C* on foundation. *Take 2, 3, 4 C out, 10 D* on J, 9 D* on 10. A S (exposed) from packet to foundation. Transfer Q S (packet 4) to K S. 2 H out. *J H, Q C* on WH. Transfer 4 H to 5 (packet 4). *5 D* on 6 D. *A D* out. *Take out 2, 3, 4, 5, 6, 7 D.* Transfer 9 C on 10. Take 5 C to foundation. *6 C* (dealt), 7, 8 C to J C (from packets) out, Q C *from W H by rule*. Take A C (exposed). Put 8 D on 9. Put Q S in one vacant space, K S, then Q on K, J S (packet 6) on Q, 10 S (from packet 3). Q C in packet 8 on vacant space (say No. 12), 3 S out, Q on K H, J H on Q, 10 H on J. Still a vacant space. Take out 8 to K D. Deal *8 C* (last card in stock) to WH, leaving a vacant space. A S (exposed) to foundation. *Turn W H.*

Second deal. *2 C* out, take 3, *Q H* on WH. *Q D* in vacant space, *K S* on WH. *5 S* on 6 S, *10 S* on J, *9 H* on 10 (packet 6). Take 8 H on 9, 2 S out, put 7 S on 8 (packet 10), *9 S* on 10, take 8 S (packet 1) on 9. Put K S from WH in one vacancy (packet 1), *5 S* on WH. *3 H* out, take 4, 5 H. *J C* on Q, *8 D* on WH, *K C* on foundation, *4 S* on foundation. Take *5 S* to *K S.* *9 H* on 10, 8 H (singleton) on 9. *7 H* on 8. Put 10 D into vacant space. Take 3 S. *9 D* on 10 D, 8 D from WH on 9, *J D* on Q, *7 D* on foundation. *8—Q D out.* *7 C* and *K C* in vacant spaces, 6 C on 7, *5 C* on 6, *4 S* out, 5 S from WH. *9 S* on 10, 8 S on 9, K D out, K H in vacant space, Q H on him from WH. *7 H* on WH. *6 S* on foundation, *4 C* on foundation, 5–7 C out 6 H, 7 from WH, 8 H to K H out. Put 8, 9, 10, J, Q S in vacancies exposing 7 S. Take out 7 S to K S, *10 C* on J. Take 9 C (exposed under 7 S). *J H* on Q. *8 C,* last card in WH, to K C out. All Hearts out.

* Packet 2.

WITH lay-out and order of pack as given in the text:

Take for foundation A, 2, 3 D.

Deal on W H (cards in italics are cards dealt) K D, 7 H, 2 H, *Q* H, *3* S, *8* C, *2* D, K H, *4* S, *Q* D, K H, J D. Deal *10* S on J S, *2* S on W H. *10* C, 7 and *6* H, Q and *8* S, *9* H, *6* C, 7 D, *8* D, *3* D, *7* C, J D, *6* H, *5* S – *4* H all on W H (where now twenty-eight!). *A* S as foundation, take 2 S. *A* H as foundation, take 2, 3 H, 3 S. Take 4 H from W H. Deal *4* S, take it out, 5 from W H and 6 from lay-out, 4 D from lay-out. *One vacancy.*

Deal *K* S on W H, *K* C to vacancy, take on him Q C. *5* D out on foundation, 6 and 7 D from lay-out. *A* C for foundation, *5* H out, *A* C (second) on foundation, *9* C on 10 (in lay-out), J S, *K* S on W H. *A* S on foundation, *8* S and *9* D on W H. *3* C on 4 (col. 4), *3* H on 4 H (col. 8), *2* C out, 3 and 4 C out. 7 S out (from lay-out to foundation), *Q* C, J H on W H. *A* H out, *8* H, *9* S on W H, *2* C out, *10* H on J, *K* C, J C, *5* D on W H, *A* D out, *Q* S, *6* S on W H (forty cards in W H!). *6* C on 7 C, *5* H on W H, *5* S on W H, *5* C out; 6 to 10 C out. 3, 4, 5 C out. J, Q, K C out, 8 and 9 D out, 10 D out, *9* H on 10 (col. 1). *10* S on W H, *8* H in vacant space (last card).

Turn over waste-heap and take the four 'grace' cards: K D, 7 H, 2 H, Q H. 2 H out, followed by 3 and 4, 7 H on 8. G(race) C(ards) *3* S, *8* C. 8 C on 9. GC *2* D out. GC*K* *H* put in vacant space, and take on him Q. GC *4* S and *Q* D. Now put K D (GC) in vacant space and Q on him. GC *K* H and J D. Take out J and Q D (over 10). GC *2* S. Out with 3 and 4. GC *10* C, *7* H, *6* H. Take out 6 H (GC), 7 H and 8 H from lay-out, 9 and 10 from table *Q* S (GC) in vacant space. *8* S dealt out. 8 S to Q S out. *9* H in vacant space, *6* C out, *7* D in vacant space, 6 D on him. *8* D in vacant space. *3* D out, 4 D also, *7* C out. 8, 9, 10 C out. *J* D vacant space, 10 D on him. *6* H, *K* S ('grace' cards). Put 7 H in vacant space, 6 H on him. K S out. *J*, *K* and *8* S. Put 8 up, 7 S on him. *9* D up in vacancy, 8 on him. *Q* C up, *J* H out, Q, K H out. *8* H on 9. *9* S up. *K* C up. Q C on him. *J* C out, Q and K C out. *5* D out; all Diamonds out to K. *Q* S up, *6* S up in vacancies. *5* H out

(last card of WH). Hearts to Jack out. *5 S* out. 6–9 S out.
10 S out. All Spades out. K D, Q H, K H out.

APPENDIX XVI: MISS MILLIGAN – *Solution and Example*

   1st eight: 8 and A C, 10 S, 9 D, K S, 3 H, A S, 4 D.
Aces out, 9 D and 8 C on 10 S.
   2nd eight: 6 D, K S, 9 C, J S, 10 H, 2 D, 5 H, Q H.
Q, J, 10, 9 on K S in space (2).
   3rd eight: 7 C, 2 S, K and 4 C, 6 and 7 D, A H, 6 C.
A H and 2 S out, 6 C on 7 D, 5 H on 6 C, 4 C on 5 H. K C
in vacant space (No. 4). Sequence 7–4 on 8 C. 6 D on 7 C.
   4th eight: A C, 8 H, 5 S, 8 C, A H, 8 D, 3 D, 7 H.
Aces out, 5 S on 6 D, 7 C–5 S on 8 H, 7 H on 8 C, 4 D on
5 S, 3 D on 4 C.
   5th eight: J H, 8 S, Q H, J D, 6 H, 2 H, 5 C, 10 D.
2 H out, 5 C on 6 H.
   6th eight: 3 C, J S, 3 S, 5 S, 3 C, K C, A D, 9 S.
A out, 3 S out. Q H, J S, 10 D, 9 S, on K C into 7th place.
8 D on 9 S. 2 D, 3 H, 3 D out.
   7th eight: 10 and 6 S, 7 and 4 D, 9 S, 2 C, 9 H, 5 D.
2 C out, 4 and 5 D out, 6 S on 7 D, 8 S on 9 H, 7 D and 6 S
on 8 S.
   8th eight: K D, 4 S, 9 C, J C, Q S, 8 D, 4 H, A S.
A out, 4 S, 4 H out, 8 D on 9 C. K D and Q S in vacant
space.
   9th eight: 10 C, 2 H, 2 D, 8 H, 2 C, J D, 10 D, 7 C.
2 H and 2 C out, J D on Q S, 10 C on J D, 9 S and 8 H on
10 D, 3 C out. 7 C, 6 H, 5 C on 8 H (from cols. 8 and 5), 4 D
on 5 C, 5 S and 6 D out.
   10th eight: 7 S, Q S, Q D, 5 H, 6 H, 4 C, 5 C, 3 D.
5 and 6 H out, 4 C out, 5 C out. Q D on K S.
   11th eight: K D, 6 S, 4 H, J and 3 H, A D, Q D, 2 S.
2 S, 3 and 4 H, A, 2 and 3 D, 6 S out. Q S on K D, J H on
Q S, K D to J H on vacant space, 7 S out, 10 S on J H, 3 C out,
J C on Q D (col. 5).

12th eight: 8 and 4 S, 9 H, 6 C, 7 H, Q C, 5 D, 3 S. 3, 4 and 8 S, 7 H, 6 C, 5 S, 7 C, 8 and 9 H out.

13th eight: K H, 9 D, 10 H, Q, J, 10 C, 7 S, K H.

Q C on K H (col. 8), 10 H on J C, 9 D on 10 C, 9 C and 8 D on 10 H, 4 C and 5 H out. 7 S on 8 D, 5 D on 6 C (col. 3), J D on Q C, 8 C and 7 H (col. 4) on 9 D (col. 6). Q D (col. 7) on K C (col. 4).

Take 10 C to 7 H (col. 6) on J D (col. 8). Q C on K H. J C to 7 S on Q D (col. 4). 10 D with sequence to 4 D (col. 7) on J C (col. 5).

4 and 5 D, 5 and 6 C, 6 and 7 S, 6 and 7 H, 7 D and 8 C (from col. 3), 8 and 9 D, 7, 8 and both 9 C, 8 H, 9 S, 10 S *all out*. K H and Q C (col. 1) to vacant column (3). 10 H, J H, 6 D out. K H, 9 D (in col. 8) to vacant space (col. 1). 7 D, 8 S, 9 H out. *Rest out.*

APPENDIX XVII: PERSIAN – *Solution*

REMOVE A S, A and 7 C, A and 7 H. Move Q H on K S, 8 D on 9 S, 10 H on J S, J C on Q H. *8 C out.* Move 10 D on J C. *7 and 8 S out.* Move J D on Q S, 9 D on 10 C. *9 C out.* Move Q C on K H. Take out A D. 7, 8, 9, 10, J and Q D (*over K H*), 9 S, 10 C, J, Q and K C all out. Move 10 H to space. J S on Q H. *10, J, Q* and *K S, K D, A and 7 S out.* Move 9 C on 10 H, 10 D on J S, 9 C on 10 D. *8 H out.* K H (over J H) to space. J H on Q S. Take out *9, 10, J, Q, K H (over A C), A C, A D, 7 D.*

Move K S to space, Q C on K H, Q S on K D, Q H on K S, J D on Q C. Take out *8 D, 9 D, A H.* Move J C on Q H, 10 H on J C, 9 C on 10 H. Take out *8 S, 7 C, 10, J, Q D, 9, 10, J* and *Q S, K D.* Move K C and J H to vacant spaces. Take out *7, 8, 9, H, 8, 9, 10 C* and the rest.

APPENDIX XVIII: RIGHT AND LEFT – *Solution*

WITH cards and lay-out as given in the text.

From the L(ay) O(ut) take A S and A H, 2 H. Doing at

present no packing, deal (cards dealt in italics). *K H, 10 H, J S, J C, 8 S, 8 C* all on WH, *2 C* pack on *3 C, 4 C* on WH. Pack 5 D on 6 S (RH square), 4 C from WH on 5 D, 3 C (from LO) on 4 C, 7 H (LO) on 8 H, 2 D (LO) on 3 C, A D out to foundation, 2 D out, 6 S on 7 H. *J D* (dealt) on Q H, 10 D on J D, 9 C on 10 D. *Vacant space,* keep for a K. *7 D* on WH. *8 H* on 9 C. Take 7 D from WH on 8 H. *5 S* on 6 S, 4 H on 5 S. A C out on foundation. 2, 3, 4 C out (3 and 4 from RH square). *K D* in vacant space. Q D on him. A D out to foundation. 3 D out on 2 D. *Vacant space.* 3 C on 4 H, J H on Q D. *10 H* on J. 9 D from LO on 10. *A S* on foundation. *9 C* and *10 C* on WH. *3 H* out on foundation, *Q H* on K S, 6 H on 7 D. Put 8 S on 9 D in LO. *Two vacant spaces.* 5 D on 6 H, *7 H* on 8 S, 6 S on 7 H, *6 D* on 7 C, *5 H* on 6 D, *A H* out. 7 S and 5 H on WH. *2 S* on foundation, *4 D* on foundation, take 5 D, 5 H from LO on 6 H, 6 D from LO on foundation. *6 C* on WH, *4 S* on 5 H, *8 D* on 9 H, 7 C on 8 D, *5 C* out. *J D* on Q H, *8 D* on 9 S. *K S* in vacant space. *2 D* out on foundation. *Q D* on K S. *3 D* out, *3 S* out on foundation, take 4 S. 6 C from WH, 7 C from LO on foundation. *5 D* on WH. *A C* out, *2 C* out. 3 C, 4 H, 5 and 6 S out, 5 H, 6 H, 7 D, 8 D, 7 H and 8 H (from top) out, K C in vacant space. 10 S on J D, 9 S on 10 S, 8 D on 9 S, 9 H out. J S on Q D. *Three vacant spaces. J H* on WH, *4 D* and *2 S* out, *5 S* on 6 S, *K D* in vacant space. *7 C* on 8 H, *3 H* on WH. *2 H* on foundation with 3 H, *10 S* on J S. *4 S* on *5*, 7 S on *8 D, 8 C* out. *Q S* on K C, J H from WH, 5 D out from WH. *9 S* on 10 S. *Q C* on K D, *10 D* on J H, *3 S* out, *10 C* on WH. *K H* in vacant space, *9 H* on 10 D, *J C* on Q C, 10 C from WH on him, *4 C, 6 D, 7 D* out. *6 C* on *7 C, 6 H* on 7 S. 5 H from WH. 7 S out from WH. *K C* in vacant place. *4 H* out, 5 H, 6 H, 4 S, 5 S, 6 S, 7 H, 7, 8, 9, 10, J S all out from lay-out, 8 D, 9 D out, 10 H out. *Do not* take J, but put 10 C from WH on him, then 9 C and 8 C from WH. 8 S out, *9 D* out, *Q S* out, *5 C* out. The last card being the *Q C. All out.*

POSITION AT END OF STOCK

K H (alone)...............K C (alone).

Q D, K S...................K D, Q D, J H, 10, 9, 8 C.

9 S, 10 S, J D, Q H, K S...............K D, Q, J, 10 C.

9 H, 10 D, J H, Q S, K C..............Q H, J D, 10 D, 9 C, 8 H, 7 and 6 C.

In *WH* (from top): J C, J S, 10 H, K H.

In *stock:* Q C.

Bases:

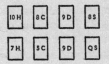

APPENDIX XIX: RUSSIAN – *Solution*

TAKE Q H and Q S. Put 8 D on 7 (col. 1), then J, 10, 9 H (col. 12) out. 9 C on 10 C, 7 D on 6. J and 10 S out (10 S col. 4), 2 S, 3 C, 2, 3, and 4 H out. 7 C on 6, 10 S on J, 9 and 10 C on 8, 2 D out, 3 H on 4, 8 C on 7, Q and J D out, 7 and 6 D on 8 (col. 1), 6 C on 5, A C on 2 (col. 11), K C on A; 5, 6, 7, 8, 9 H out (ascending), 3 S out. 10 C on J, 8 C on 9, 7 C on 8, 6 C (col. 12) on 7, 5 C on 6 (col. 4) – 6, 7, 8 back again, 9 and 8 on 10 C, 10 H and J H out (ascending). Q C on K C. A H on K H. 5 D on 4 D, 8 H and 7 out (descending), 4 S and 5 out (ascending); 8, 9, 10 C on 7 C (cols. 8–12), Q, J, 10 C out (descending), 10 C (col. 10) on 9 C, Q C on K C. 3 H in *vacant space,* 4 H on it; 6, 7, 8, 7, 8 D on col. (2) on the 4 and 5 D. 3 D out. 5 H and 6 H on 4. 6 H, 5, 4, 3 out (descending). *Vacant space.* A H and K H in it. A S on 2, 3 S on 4, 8 D on 9, 6 D on 7. 6 S out, 2 H out. *Vacant space.* 6, 7, 8, 7, 6, 5, 4 D in it. 4, 5, 6, 7, 8 out (ascending). 7 S out. Q D on K D, J D on Q. 8 S out, 8 D and 9 on 7 D (col. 1). J C on Q C. *Vacant space.* A S in it, 2, 3, 4 S on it. 9, 10, J S ascending out. A D on 2 D, Q S, 4 C, K S out. 9 D (col. 9), 10, J, Q, K out,

Q and K H, A H (descending) out, 8 C, 7, 6, 5 on 9 (col. 8).
Take out this lot and 10 C from col. (12), J C, Q C, K C from
col. (11) and 9 C, 8, 7, 6, 5 C descending. Put 5 S on 4, 4 C on 3;
A D in vacant space, 2 D, 3, 4, 5 on him, 7 S, 8 and 9 on 6 S,
A C in vacant space. *All out.*

APPENDIX XX: THE SNAKE – *Solution*

WITH diagram and stock as given in text.

Put 3 H from snake on 4 S, 2 S on 3 H, 9 D on 10 D (col. 6),
8 C on 9 D. Deal (cards dealt are in italics) from stock *7 H* on
8 C. 6 C (col. 2) on 7 H. J S from snake on Q H, 2 C out from
snake on foundation. 10 S on J S, 9 H and 8 S on 10 S. 2 D
and 3 D out on foundation, 5 C on 6. Q D on K C. 3 C out.
10 D on J H, 6 H out. 7 C from snake on 8 S, 6 H on 7 C, 5 S
on 6 H. Sequence J H to 5 C on Q D (col. 7). A C out to
foundation. 9 H (col. 8) on 10 D. Sequence 4 S to 2 S on 5 C.
6 D on 7 C (snake), 8 H on 9, 4 C out, 7 H and 8 H out, 8 D on
9 H. Sequence Q H to 5 S on K S (col. 8). J C and 10 H on
Q S (col. 5). Sequence K to 10 H in vacant space (col. 6),
7 C and 6 D from col. (1) on 8 D (col. 4), 5 D on 6 D. 2 C,
2 H out on foundation. 4 H and 3 S (col. 1) to col. (8), 8 C
in vacant col. (5), 9 D on 10 H, 8 C and 7 D on him. Sequence
J H to 5 D on Q C (col. 1), 6 S on 7 D. K D, Q H, J C (col. 4),
10 C (col. 2) to vacant col. (5). 9 S on 10 C. K C to 2 S (sequence)
to col. (2), 5 H on 6 S, Q D in vacant space, 8 D on 9 S. Still a
vacant space. *Start snake again* at 5 D by dealing *6 C, 3 C* out
on foundation, *9 C* on 10 C (col. 3), *7 D* out with 8 D, *4 C* out
on foundation, *9 C* in vacant space, *7 S* on snake, *5 C* out,
K D on snake, *A S* out. 2 and 3 S; 3, 4, 5 H; 4, 5, 6 S; 5, 6 C;
6 H, 7 C, 7 H, 8, 9, 10 C; 8, 9 S; 9 and 10 H, 9 and 10 D, J H,
10 and J S, Q and K H all out.

K D from snake to vacant space, Q D on him. 7 S and 6 C
out from snake, 9 C on 10 C (in lay-out). Sequence Q C to 5 D
on K S, *K C* and *Q C* dealt on vacant space, *Q S*, *J D* out, *10 S*
and *J D* on Q C, *8 S* out, *4 D* out, *8 H* out, J S on Q D, *9 S*
and *K S* out. Rest clear.

WITH position at end of stock as given in diagram:

Put 7 D on top left-hand corner 6 D; 4 D and 7 H, out; 6 D on 7, 4 H on 5, Q H out, J, 10 D out, J H, J S, 9 D, 8 D out. 8 C on bottom right-hand 7, the other 7 C on the 8. 8 H, 10 C out, 2 C on A C. 3 C on 2. 4 C and 9 C out, 4 D on 3, 8 C and 5 C out, 9 S on 8 S, 6 C out. 7 C and 8 out ascending, 7 C (descending), A D into one of the two vacant spaces. 5 D out, 7 S on 6. 10, 9, 8, 7, 6 S out descending, 6 D (ascending), 7, 6, 5, 4, 3 D out descending, 5 S (descending), 2 and A D out. 9 H (ascending) out. Q H on J H, 4 C on 3, Q S on K S, 5 C on 4, 6 S on 7 S. K C in vacant space. Q C on him. 9 C and 4 S out (ascending), J D on Q D, Q and J H on K, 9 S and 8S on 10. 6 C out descending, rest of descending Clubs out. 3 H on 4 H. 5 to 10 S out ascending. Position now:

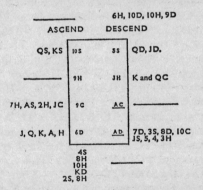

	6H, 10D, 10H, 9D
ASCEND	DESCEND

QS, KS	10S	5S	QD, JD.	
———	9H	JH	K and QC	
7H, AS, 2H, JC	9C	A C	———	
J, Q, K, A, H	6D	A D	7D, 3S, 8D, 10C	JS, 5, 4, 3H

4S
8H
10H
KD
2S, 8H

Gather up depots, beginning with Q, K S and deal – when in whatever order the packets are picked up the game will come out.

But picking up in the order dealt one by one and starting each packet with its outer (or exposed) card, at the second deal.

1st round: 10 H and 10 C (both ascending) *out.*
2nd round: J S (ascending) 10 H, 9 H descending.
3rd round: (incomplete).

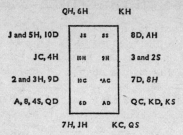

J, Q, K H and J C ascending out. Place 2 H on A: descending Hearts out: Q and K S out. A S in vacant place, 2 S on him. Descending Spades out: then ascending Diamonds and Clubs.

APPENDIX XXII: THE SULTAN – *Solution*

WITH lay-out and order of stock as given in text.

9 H and Q C on WH, A C out with 2, 2 D on WH, A D out. Take 2, 3, 4 D. 10 S on WH. A H out. 3 C and 4 C out. *Four vacancies.* J D on WH. 9 H in vacancy. J S, 8 H on WH. 2 D in vacancy. 7 H in vacancy. Q D, 8, 9, Q C on WH, 2 H out on top A. 7 S, 2 C WH, 4 H *vacancy.* 8 S, 7 D on WH, 5 C out, 3 H out. Take 4, 5, 6, 7, 8, 9 H. Take 7 D, 8 S, 2 C from WH to vacancies, leaving 7 S top-card. 8 S, 9 D on WH. 3 C in vacancy. Q S WH. 5 D, A S out, 9 D WH to side, 6 D, A S out, 7 D out from side, take 9 D from WH. Q H on WH. 7 C on side. 5 D, 6 S on WH, 2 S and 3 S out, 6 S in vacancy. J C on WH. 4 S, 10 H, 6 C out. 7 C out, 10 C, J S on WH, 2 S out, Q D on WH. 5 S out, 6 S out, A D out, 2 D out, Q D in vacancy. 7 C on WH, 3 S, 8 C, 7 S out, 8 S out, 3 H in vacancy, 5 H on WH, 2 H, 3 H out. 5 S and 5 H to sides. 6 D, 7 H on WH. 9 C out. A C, 2 C, 3 C out. J H out. Take out 7 H, 6 D, 7 C, J S from WH to sides, then 10 C, J C on foundation. 6 C, 10 S on WH. 8 D, 3 D, 9 D out. Q S in vacant space. 10 D out, Q H out, 9 S out, 10 from WH, J and Q from sides. 4 S out, 5 from side, 6 S out. J D out. Q from side, 4 H out, 5 from side. Fill up spaces from WH, 6 C, 5 D, Q H, Q S, 9 D (leaving 8 S top-card). 4 D out,

5 and 6 from side. 8 S from W H to side. 7 S and 8 out. Q C out from WH, 7 D out. 6 H out, take 7. Put 9 and 8 C from WH on sides, Q D on side, 8 H out. J H, 10 C on WH. 8 D out, take 9. 10 H on side, 5 C on WH. 10 D out. 4 C out, take 5, 6, 7, 8, 9, 10 C. J H, J S on sides. J D out. 10 S and Q C in vacancies. Hearts out. Last two cards 9 S, J C. *All out.*

Part Three

PATIENCE PROBLEMS AND PUZZLES

PATIENCE PROBLEMS

BATTALION
PROBLEM I

With lay-out:

5 H	2 H	9 S	7 C	2 C	8 S	Q D	9 C	7 S	7 C	4 C	4 C
9 H	3 S	2 H	4 D	K C	8 C	8 H	4 S	10 D	6 C	9 S	10 H
10 S	K H	A H	7 H	5 D	6 D	8 D	J H	A S	J S	Q S	2 C
3 H	K C	6 D	6 C	3 C	4 H	7 S	6 H	6 S	3 H	J H	9 D
9 C	4 H	J C	2 S	6 H	K S	K S	A C	K D	A C	5 S	5 S
J D	Q H	7 D	8 S	5 C	10 C	3 D	2 D	8 H	8 D	Q H	5 D
2 S	A S	Q C	Q S	5 C	10 S	6 S	J D	5 H	10 C	A H	8 C
9 H	3 D	3 C	J S	4 D	4 S	10 H	9 D	7 D	K H	2 D	Q C
3 S	Q D	A D	J C	7 H	10 D						

And foundations: A D, K D (the only ones obtained in dealing).

To win Patience without redeal.

PROBLEM II

With lay-out:

6 C	5 C	2 S	Q S	9 S	J S	J D	8 H	J D	4 C	8 H	9 C
5 H	K H	4 D	7 D	10 S	8 C	3 H	A D	9 H	4 S	K H	J H
J H	2 S	2 C	3 C	6 H	Q S	10 H	A H	6 S	8 S	A D	10 C
Q D	9 D	4 H	10 S	2 D	Q C	6 D	K D	4 H	K D	5 S	2 H
3 D	10 D	9 S	7 D	10 D	6 H	9 C	J C	K C	5 D	10 C	8 D
8 D	A H	4 C	2 H	3 S	K S	7 H	4 S	7 H	3 S	7 S	2 D
6 C	Q D	10 H	7 C	7 C	J S	5 H	2 C	5 S	8 S	A C	8 C
7 S	A S	Q H	A S	Q H	5 C	3 H	6 D	5 D	4 D	Q C	9 D
6 S	9 H	3 C	J C	3 D	A C						

And foundations: K C, K S.

To win Patience without second deal.

BISLEY

Problem I

To solve in Descending Order without building on the Aces.
Lay-out:

AH	AS	AD	AC	KS	2H	KC	KD	2S	JH	2C	KH	2D
4D	3S	8C	6D	4S	QC	7D	5S	4H	8S	9C	QD	3H
10S	7H	5H	9S	JS	3C	5C	8H	7S	QH	5D	10C	JD
10D	9D	9H	6C	6S	6H	8D	3D	10H	7C	QS	4C	JC

Problem II

With the same lay-out, transposing only the Knave and Queen
of Hearts, to solve in Ascending Order without building on
the Kings.

THE BRITISH BLOCKADE

Problem I

With Pack arranged thus:

A C (top card), 4 C, 5 C, K D, A S, A C, 5 C, Q D, 6 S,
K C, J C, Q C, 6 H, 5 H, 4 D, 7 H, 2 H, 5 D, 8 H, 6 D, 8 C,
10 S, 3 C, J C, Q H, 8 S, A H, 7 S, J D, 6 S, 3 H, 10 C, 4 S,
7 C, 5 S, 9 D, J S, J H, 5 H, K S, A H, 6 C, 5 S, 7 C, 2 H, 4 H,
J S, 8 H, 3 D, 9 H, 3 S, 3 H, J D, K H, 7 D, 10 D, 4 H, 9 C,
9 D, 4 D, 4 C, K D, 7 D, 10 C, J H, 7 S, 2 S, 2 D, A D, 9 S,
10 S, 9 C, 7 H, 8 C, 3 S, 4 S, Q S, 8 S, 3 C, 2 C, Q H, 8 D, 10 D,
2 D, 10 H, A S, A D, 6 D, 10 H, Q D, Q S, K H, K C, 8 D,
2 S, Q C, 5 D, 9 S, 6 H, 3 D, 6 C, K S, 9 H, 2 C (end card).

To solve with one 'merci'.

Problem II

With Pack in this order:

A D (top card), Q H, K D, 9 D, 8 H, 2 D, 8 S, A C, 8 H, 7 S,
J H, K S, 7 H, 2 H, 6 C, 7 C, 10 D, J S, 10 S, K H, 6 D, K C,
10 C, A H, Q D, 4 S, 10 C, 2 C, Q H, 7 H, 8 C, J D, K S, 5 C,
9 S, Q S, K H, 6 H, 2 H, 5 S, 5 D, J S, 7 C, 4 C, A C, 6 S, Q D,
2 S, A D, J H, J D, 7 D, 5 H, K C, 6 H, 9 C, 3 C, 8 D, 6 D,
2 D, 5 H, 4 C, 10 H, 3 C, 8 C, 8 S, K D, 10 D, 9 C, 9 D, A S,

6 S, 4 S, Q S, Q C, 5 C, 3 D, 4 D, 9 H, 3 H, 4 H, 10 S, 8 D,
3 S, 2 C, 5 S, 2 S, J C, 9 S, 9 H, 10 H, Q C, 7 S, 7 D, J C, 5 D,
4 H, 3 D, 3 H, 6 C, A H, 3 S, 4 D, A S (last card).

To solve Patience without a 'merci'.

THE EMPEROR

PROBLEM I

Columns. Forty-three cards (*three sealed*):

1.   2.   3.   4.   5.   6.   7.   8.   9.   10.

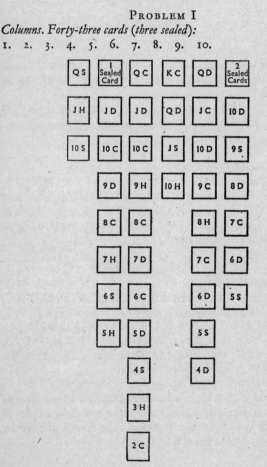

Foundation packets. Twenty-five cards:

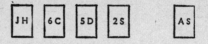

K C (top card), K S, 8 and J S, K D, 2 H, K H, 9 D, K H,
6 H, Q and 3 C, Q H, 8 D.
Waste-heap. Fourteen cards:
Stock. Twenty-two cards:

J C, 6, 3, 8, 3, K S, K D, 4 C, 3 D, 5, 9 C, A H, 10, Q, 7, 4, 9,
2 S, A D, A C, 7 D, 2 D (last card).

Seeing 101 cards you know the three sealed must be Q H
and 4; 7 S. Actually the Q and 4 are together (Queen on top)
at head of col. 10; the 7 S in col. 4.

PROBLEM II

With sealed packets:

(1) *9 C*, K H, 3 S. (2) *5 H*, 2 S, 9 C. (3) *6 D*, 4 S, 6 C. (4)
Q C, 5 S. (5) *8 H*, K S, 4 D. (6) *7 D*, K S, 3 C. (7) *K H*, A C,
2 H. (8) *K C*, 10 H, Q H. (9) *6 S*, 3 H, 5 D. (10) *2 D*, 9 H, 7 S.
(Cards in italics top of packets.)

With single row:

5 C, 2 D, 2 C, J D, 4 H, 2 C, 7 S, 9 D, 6 H, 7 C.

And Packs in this order:

7 H, 3 D, 3 S, A D, A S, 4 S, J C, 6 C, 3 C, A D, Q D, 8 C,
Q S, Q S, A C, 9 S, J H, 3 D, 2 S, A H, 7 C, 10 S, 4 H, A S,
A H, K D, 8 S, 8 C, 10 S, 9 S, 8 S, 5 C, 9 H, Q D, K D, 4 C,
10 D, 10 C, 7 H, 10 C, 6 S, 4 D, 8 D, J S, 8 H, 3 H, J C, J S,
J H, 10 H, 10 D, 8 D, 4 C, 6 H, Q C, 6 D, J D, 5 H, Q H,
K C, 2 H, 9 D, 7 D, 5 D (bottom card).

To win Patience *without turning the waste-heap.*

A knowledge of cards in a sealed packet may be assumed as
soon as the first card of it is taken, and the pack may be played
face upwards so as to see the next card to be dealt, but its order
is not supposed to be known further.

THE GENERAL

PROBLEM I

With first thirteen:

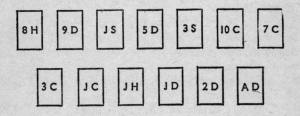

Three candidates for base card:

Other seven cards as heads of column:

And Packs in this order:

7 S, 10 S, Q D, 10 D, 9 S, 5 C, 6 C, Q C, 9 H, 9 C, 8 C, 6 S,
10 D, 3 S, 2 H, 10 H, 4 S, A C, Q C, K D, 5 S, K H, Q S, A H,
7 C, 3 C, A D, 2 D, K C, 2 C, J D, 4 C, 6 H, 6 D, 5 D, 5 C,
2 S, K S, 7 D, 8 D, A S, 4 D, 7 S, 10 S, K S, 6 H, 7 D, 5 S,
4 S, Q S, A S, 5 H, 8 H, 8 S, 3 H, 9 C, 3 D, J S, 2 H, 2 S, 4 H,

K H, K D, K C, A C, Q H, 5 H, 8 C, 6 S, 6 C, 7 H, 4 D, 6 D,
9 S, Q H, 9 H, 7 H, A H, J H, 2 C, 9 D (last card).

To win Patience without turning waste-heap.

PROBLEM II

With first thirteen:

    J D, 7 C, 4 H, 5 S, 6 H, 7 C, Q D, 6 C, 6 H, 6 C, 4 D, 10 D,
4 S.

Base card chosen: 4 H.

Heads of columns:

    7 S, A C (discarded bases), K S, Q C, 3 H, A S, 2 C, 8 S, K H.

Pack in this order:

    J S, Q H, 3 H, A H, 7 D, 4 S, 7 D, 10 C, 4 C, K D, J H, 6 S,
A C, 3 C, 8 C, 9 S, K S, 2 D, 7 H, 7 H, 2 D, 8 D, 3 S, 5 H, 3 S,
8 H, 10 D, 9 H, 8 C, J H, 5 H, 2 H, 4 D, K H, 8 H, 9 S, Q S,
K C, 6 S, 10 S, J S, 2 S, 7 S, 10 C, Q H, 6 D, 5 C, 3 D, 10 H,
A S, 9 D, 8 D, K D, 9 C, Q S, A D, A H, 10 H, J C, 5 D, Q D,
3 C, Q C, 10 S, 3 D, 2 H, 5 S, K C, 6 D, J D 8 S, J C, 5 D, 2 C,
4 C, 2 S, 9 C, 9 H, 9 D, A D, 5 C (last card).

To solve without turning waste-heap.

GRANDFATHER'S CLOCK

PROBLEM

FROM the original lay-out with 5 S for 12 o'clock, 6 H for
one o'clock, 7 C for two, 8 D for three, 9 S for four, and so on;
with 10 H, J C, Q D, K S, 2 H, 3 C, 4 D, the game has reached
the point shown in diagram on p. 175.

    This accounts for ninety-one cards (fifty-five on foundations,
thirty-six in side-packets, whose top cards are underlined):
remain thirteen cards in stock in this order: Q S, K C, 2 D,
Q C, 6 D, A H, 8 H, 5 H, 10 S, A C, J H, 8 C, 3 C.

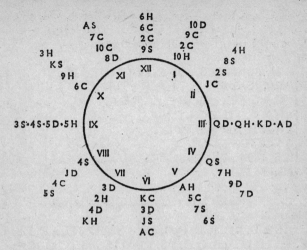

GRANDMAMMA'S

Problem

Original lay-out:

Foundations descending:

(3 H.)   (3 S.)

A. D. 9 D. 5 S. 10 D. 2 C. 7 S. Q. H. Q. S. K. H. 8 H. Q.D.
6 C. 6 H. K. H. 7 D. J. H. 2 D. J.D. 5 C. 9 D. 8 H. J. C.

Foundations ascending: (6 H), i.e. 4, 5, 6 H.

Pack in this order:

K C, 3 D, A D, Q H, 10 S, 8 S, 6 S, 4 S, 10 C, 7 C, 4 C, A S,
J D, 8 S, 5 D, 2 S, Q C, 9 C, 6 D, 3 C, 7 S, A S, 8 C, 2 H, 9 H,
3 C, 10 C, 4 D, K D, A H, 10 S, 2 H, K C, 6 S, Q S, 5 H, J H,
4 C, 10 H, 3 S, 9 S, 2 S, 8 D, A C, 7 C, 8 D, K S, 4 H, 8 C, Q C,
3 H, 7 D, J S, 2 D, 6 D, K S, 10 H, A C, 5 D, 5 S, 10 D, 2 C,
7 H, Q D, 9 S, K D, 4 S, 9 H, A H, 6 C, J C, 3 D, 4 D, J S,
9 C, 7 H, 5 C.

To solve without using grace cards, or covering more than
seven cards at any one time.

THE HARP

PROBLEM

With lay-out:

[A H, 4 C, 9 S, 8 S, 4 D, 2 D, 6 D, 3 S,] *3 D.*
[6 H, Q S, A S, Q C, 5 H, 5 S, 7 D,] *6 C.*
[3 C, 8 C, 8 H, 9 H, 10 C, A C,] *K S.*
[2 H, 6 C, J H, 2 C, 9 C,] *8 D.*
[J S, K H, 9 S, K D,] *9 D.*
[A D, 4 H, 6 S,] *5 H.*
[K S, 3 D,] *2 D.*
[7 S,] *10 H.*
8 C.

(Cards between brackets face down.)

And stock in this order:

7 H, A D, 8 D, K D, Q D, 9 C, J S, A C, 8 H, 4 D, 7 S, J C,
A H, 2 H, 4 C, 4 S, Q D, 8 S, 5 D, J D, 10 H, Q C, K H, 5 C,
6 D, 10 D, K C, 7 D, 4 S, 3 C, Q S, 5 S, 2 S, 2 C, 9 H, 5 D, 5 C,
Q H, 6 S, 2 S, 4 H, J C, 7 H, 3 H, 10 S, 10 D, J D, A S, Q H,
7 C, 10 C, 3 H, J H, 7 C, 6 H, 10 S, 3 S, 9 D, K C (bottom card).

To win Patience, turning waste-heap once only.

THE HAT

PROBLEM I

(*Adapted from Cavendish*)

END hand. Third deal. To be solved without 'merci'.

(Cards in italics are 'top' cards of the Brim Depots.)
In stock. Twenty cards:

9 S (top card), 10 D, 5 C, 7 S, 7 S, 6 C, 6 S, Q S, 3 C, 6 H,
5 S, A H, 2 S, A S, 7 C, 8 D, 4 C, 10 S, 6 D, 4 H (bottom card).

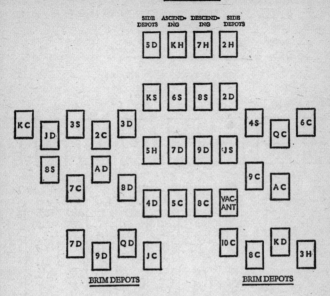

FOUNDATIONS

	SIDE DEPOTS	ASCENDING	DESCENDING	SIDE DEPOTS
	5 D	K H	7 H	2 H

PROBLEM II

Foundations

Side Depots			Side Depots
	Ascending	Descending	
4 D	4 H	7 H	5 D
2 D	9 S	8 S	Q H
6 C	7 D	9 D	2 C
3 H	9 C	J C	Vacant

Brim depots (cards printed slanting are top cards):

(1) *6 S*, 4 S, 8 H, 8 C. (2) *5 H*, J D, K C, 10 C.
(3) *7 H*, 4 H, Q C, K S. (4) *7 D*, 3 D, A H, 9 C.
(5) *5 C*, A D, 2 H, 6 H. (6) *8 D*, 6 H, J H, 3 C.

In stock. Twenty-three cards:

10 C (top card), 3 S, 2 S, 4 C; Q S, K H, 7 C, 10 H; J C, 6 D, 5 S, 7 S; J S, A S, 5 H, 10 S; A C, K D, Q D, 9 H, 10 D, 8 D, 9 D.

End game. After third deal.

To solve without 'merci'.

HEADS AND TAILS
PROBLEM

Heads:

| 5 S | 8 D | Q D | 10 H | 5 D | J D | 7 C | 6 S |

Packets:

Top cards.

	I	II	III	IV	V	VI	VII	VIII
	3 S	2 S	A H	9 D	K C	K D	3 H	K S
	5 C	4 C	7 S	10 H	2 S	A D	10 C	K S
	6 C	8 S	10 S	10 S	9 H	10 S	K C	5 C
	K H	9 S	5 H	K D	Q H	7 H	3 S	2 D
	8 S	Q C	2 C	9 H	K H	J C	10 D	2 D
	Q C	6 H	10 D	7 H	2 H	8 C	Q H	8 C
	J S	J H	A D	7 D	J C	4 D	A H	7 D
	3 C	8 H	A S	Q S	6 H	8 D	9 C	6 S
	Q D	6 D	9 C	2 C	A C	5 H	4 H	3 D
	4 H	9 D	5 S	8 H	J D	4 D	Q S	6 D
	6 C	A C	7 S	J H	3 D	4 C	4 S	5 D

Tails:

2 H   3 H   7 C   4 S   J S   A S   9 S   3 C.

To solve.

HEAP PATIENCE

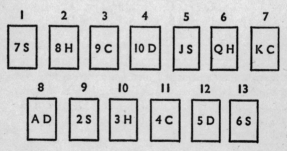

1	2	3	4	5	6	7
7 S	8 H	9 C	10 D	J S	Q H	K C

8	9	10	11	12	13
A D	2 S	3 H	4 C	5 D	6 S

Packets (from left to right):

2 H, J H, A C, *J D:*	6 D, K S, 9 D, *10 C:*	J C, 2 D, 5 C, *9 C:*
4 H, 6 H, 3 S, *7 S:*	J S, A H, 9 H, *K H:*	Q D, 7 D, 8 D, *K D:*
J C, 10 C, A D, *4 C:*	8 C, K H, 9 H, *7 H:*	2 S, 6 S, 10 S, *5 S:*
8 H, K D, 8 D, *2 D:*	7 D, Q D, K C, *A C:*	8 C, 4 D, 7 C, *10 H:*
6 H, A S, 10 S, *9 S:*	5 C, 2 C, 3 H, *10 H:*	2 C, 9 D, 3 D, *4 D:*
7 C, Q C, 3 D, *5 D:*	A S, J H, 3 S, *5 H:*	5 S, 8 S, Q S, *4 S:*
Q C, 3 C, 3 C, *6 C:*	6 C, 2 H, Q H, *5 H:*	7 H, 4 H, 4 S, *9 S:*
A H, 6 D, 10 D, *Q S:*	8 S, K S, *J D.*	

(Cards in italics exposed.)

To solve without second deal.

KING ALBERT

Problem I

Lay-out:

6 D, 8 S, K H, 5 S, 10 H, 6 H, 4 D, Q S, *J C.*
5 C, A C, 9 D, 3 H, 3 D, Q H, 4 S, *9 H.*
A H, Q C, 7 C, 2 C, 10 D, 4 H, *J H.*
5 H, A D, 10 S, K S, 6 S, *K C.*
8 C, 4 C, J D, 5 D, *2 S.*
A S, 8 D, 7 H, *J S.*
10 C, 3 C, *Q D.*
9 S, *2 H.*
7 S.

Reserves:

3 S; K, 7, 2 D; 9 and 6 C; 8 H.

To solve.

Problem II

Lay-out:

4 C, 7 S, J H, A D, Q C, 3 S, J S, K S, *6 S.*
5 S, Q S, 4 D, A C, 3 H, 5 H, 10 H, *8 S.*
K D, 5 C, 7 C, 8 D, 6 H, 9 H, *3 D.*
6 D, 2 D, 3 C, 2 H, 2 C, *K H.*
A S, 7 D, 8 C, 10 D, *10 C.*
4 S, 9 S, A H, *K C.*
8 H, 2 S, *9 D.*
5 D, *10 S.*
9 C.

Reserves:
  Hearts: Q, 7, 4. *Clubs:* J, 6. *Diamonds:* Q, J.
  To solve.

LIMITED

PROBLEM I

With lay-out:
9D QH 4C JH 4S AH 2H 9S 9S 4H 10D 2D
AD JH 7D 4C AS 10C 4H JD 5D 10D 5H QH
KD 3C 8H QS 6H 6S 5H 2C 3S JS AS 7S

And Pack in this order:
  2 S, 7 H, 4 S, K D, 6 C, 7 S, 10 H, 3 H, 2 S, 5 C, J C, A C,
5 D, 3 D, 2 C, 5 S, 10 S, 3 S, 10 C, 2 D, 8 H, Q C, 4 D, 8 D,
7 C, 6 D, 5 S, 6 S, 2 H, J D, 4 D, 3 H, K S, K H, K H, Q D,
K S, Q S, 9 D, 9 C, K C, 8 S, 6 D, 9 H, 3 D, 7 H, J S, Q D,
8 C, 6 C, K C, 3 C, J C, 10 S, Q C, 8 C, 7 C, 5 C, A C, 7 D, 8 S,
A D, 10 H, 8 D, 6 H, 9 H, A H, 9 C.
  To solve after turning waste-heap.

PROBLEM II

With lay-out:
JD JD 5H 9H JC 5C 4C 7H KD JH 9D AH
6C JS 9D 10D 3D 7D 6D 2D 2D QS 10S AD
AD 8S 6S JC 10C 3C 8H 8H QS 9S QH 3S

And Pack in this order:
  2 S, 6 S, 3 S, 5 S, 10 S, K S, 5 D, 4 D, 6 D, K D, A H, 5 H,
6 H, 7 C, A C, 8 C, 9 C, 7 C, J H, 3 H, 10 H, 2 H, Q D, 4 H,
2 H, 2 C, K H, 8 C, 9 C, 6 C, 4 D, 8 D, 3 D, 7 D, 10 D, 4 S,
A C, 2 S, K C, A S, 7 S, 8 S, J S, 5 D, 10 C, 5 C, 4 C, K C, 3 H,
6 H, A S, 5 S, 4 S, 4 H, 7 S, 9 H, 10 H, Q C, K S, 8 D, Q D,
Q C, 7 H, 2 C, Q H, 9 S, 3 C, K H (sixty-eight cards).
  To solve after turning the waste-heap.

MILTON

PROBLEM

At end of first deal:

Index row:

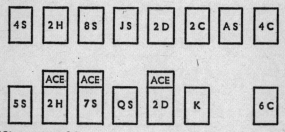

(Sixty-one cards.)

On waste-heap. Forty-three cards, in this order for dealing:

A C, 5 H, 10 C, 7 S, 9 C, K S, 6 S, K D, 9 D, 3 D, K H, A H, 9 S, 3 H, 7 D, 8 D, 4 D, A D, Q D, 5 D, 2 C, 8 H, Q H, K C, A C, 7 C, J H, 3 S, Q C, J D, 9 H, 8 S, 4 H, 8 C, 7 H, 2 S, J C, 6 H, 6 D, 3 C, 10 S, 10 H, 10 D.

To solve on third deal.

MISS MILLIGAN

PROBLEM I

To solve without 'waiving'.

Position at the end of a deal with 24 cards yet undealt:

Col. 1	2	3	4	5	6	7	8
J D	K H	K S	J C	10 D	K H	6 C	K D
10 C	Q S	Q D	10 H	9 S	Q S	5 D	Q C
9 H	5 H	J S	9 S	8 D	J D	7 S	J H
5 S		10 H	8 D	8 C	10 S	6 H	10 C
4 H		9 C	7 C	7 H	J H	5 S	9 D
7 S		9 C	3 D	6 S		4 D	8 C
10 D			7 D	Q D		3 S	7 D
Q H			6 C	J C		2 D	6 H
			5 D	6 D		8 S	5 C
			9 H	K C			4 H
							8 H

Foundations (built to):

2 H, 3 H, A C, 5 C, 4 D, 3 S. (The second A D and that of Spades not yet turned up.)

Eighty cards accounted for (18 on foundations).

Stock (24 cards) in this order:

10 S (top card), 4 S, J S, 5 H, 7 C, 6 D, 8 H, Q C, K S, 2 C, 3 H, Q H, 6 S, A S, 2 S, 7 H, 8 S, 3 C, 9 D, K D, K C, 4 S, A D, 4 C (bottom card).

PROBLEM II

Board before last eight cards dealt:

Col. 1	2	3	4	5	6	7	8
J C	5 S	8 D	5 D	K H	K C	K H	K C
		K D					
8 C	8 D	J D	4 S	6 H	Q H	Q C	Q D
		10 S					
7 D	K D	9 D	J C	5 S	J H	J H	J S
		6 S					
6 C	Q S	5 D		2 H		10 C	10 H
		4 C					
5 H	10 D	K S		9 H		9 D	9 C
		Q H					
4 S	9 S	J S		8 S		8 C	8 H
		10 D					

Col. 1	2	3	4	5	6	7	8
10 C	7 C	9 S		7 H		7 H	7 C
		Q S					
		J D		6 C		Q D	6 D
		10 S					
		9 H		5 H			5 C
		8 S					
		7 S		4 C			4 D
		6 D					
		5 C		3 H			3 C
		4 H					
		3 S		3 D			10 H
		2 D					
		9 C		2 C			
		8 H					
		7 S					
		6 H (28 cards.)					

Foundations:	A H	3 H	A D	4 D
	A S	2 S	—	3 C

Last eight cards in this order: 2 S, 6 S, 7 D, Q C, A C, K S, 3 S, 4 H.

To solve with one card 'waived'.

PERSIAN

PROBLEM I

With lay-out:

1	2	3	4	5	6	7	8
9 S	K C	10 D	A D	10 H	8 H	A S	9 D
J H	K S	10 H	9 C	10 D	Q H	7 H	J C
K H	J S	9 H	7 S	10 C	7 D	10 S	8 D
K C	A D	J D	K S	K H	10 S	Q C	Q S
Q D	J D	A S	9 C	K D	8 D	Q D	8 S
8 S	A C	7 S	9 H	10 C	Q S	8 C	A H
8 C	7 C	9 D	7 H	J S	K D	8 H	7 D
9 S	A H	7 C	Q C	Q H	J C	J H	A C

To solve Patience without a second deal.

PROBLEM II

End hand. Patience to be won.

Arrange the Depot cards as under:

1	2	3	4	5	6	7	8
K S	J D	K S	J C	9 S	K H	10 S	*Vacant*
Q C	9 D	A D	J H	J H	Q D	10 D	
Q D	9 S	K H	Q H	J S	J S	Q S	
10 C	A S	8 D	K D	K D	10 H	8 D	
	K C	Q C	9 D	8 S		J D	
	Q H		8 C	10 S		8 S	
	J C		K C	7 D		Q S	
	10 D		9 H			7 S	
	9 C						

On foundations:

> A H to 10 (top), A C to 10 (top),
> A D to 7 (top), A S to 7 (top),
> A H to 8 (top), A C, 7 C (top).

RUSSIAN

Problem I

To solve in one deal from given *lay-out*.

Lay-out:

Col I	II	III	IV	V	VI	VII	VIII	IX	X	XI	XII
6H	10H	3D	6D	5S	7D	9H	AS	5C	10S	3H	6C
7C	JH	6S	JC	2C	QD	9D	6D	3C	4S	8C	8H
7S	2D	7C	5S	QH	2H	10C	7H	5H	6C	KH	10H
4S	9C	QC	7H	JD	5D	10C	KC	JH	7S	2S	10S
8D	4H	AH	3D	9S	9D	4C	JS	9S	6H	5C	AC
5H	4D	QS	9C	QS	8S	4C	5D	KD	8C	8H	6S
3S	7D	2D	8D	JS	JC	AD	9H	8S	10D	4H	4D
KS											

Foundations:

Descending: Q H   Q C   *Ascending:*   3 H   3 C
            10 D   K S   A D   3 S

Problem II

To solve without a second deal from the given *lay-out*.

Lay-out:

1	2	3	4	5	6	7	8	9	10	11	12
6D	4S	7S	5H	9S	JS	8C	KC	9C	AS	6H	5H
AC	3D	8H	8H	7C	9S	2D	5S	5C	6D	9D	2C
7D	10C	3D	2S	QS	4C	10H	3H	JD	JH	8C	10S
7H	8S	5C	4D	10S	10D	3C	4H	8D	AH	2S	6S
7S	7C	5D	8D	JD	4C	9C	6C	10C	9D	QC	4D
KD	3S	9H	QH	KH	4H	6S	5S	5D	3S	4S	10D
KS	6C	8S	7D	2D	2H		10H	JS	JC	7H	AD
6H	9H	QD									

(Card under 6 S in Row 7 taken for foundation.)

Foundations:

Ascending: 3 H   3 C   *Descending:*   J H   J C
            A D   A S   Q D   Q S

'S' PATIENCE

PROBLEM

On foundations of a Sequence of Diamonds:

7, 8, 9, 10, J, Q, K, A, 2, 3, 4, 5, 6.

Following a rotation of suits:

Diamonds, Spades, Hearts, Clubs.

And assuming at the end of the first deal the foundations built to:
9 H, J C, K D, A D, K H, A H, 2 H, 4 C, 4 H, 6 C, 7 C, 8 C,
9 C (forty-nine cards out, thus in packet [1] 7 D, 8 S, 9 H; in
packet [3] 9 D, 10 S, J H, Q C, K D; in packet [13] 6 D, 7 S,
8 H, 9 C, and so on).

To solve the Patience *without a third deal,* showing finally a
Sequence from Ace to King of Clubs, the fifty-five cards in the
waste-heaps being, after shuffling, in the following order in
rows from left to right:

9S	9C	3C	10C	3D	KC	AC	Q.S	7S	8H	3S
8D	2C	4D	7H	7D	8S	AH	10H	3C	JD	5C
10C	7C	AS	5H	4H	5D	QD	4C	QH	4S	AC
KS	2H	JS	2S	3H	9H	QC	5S	6D	6S	JH
6C	5C	10D	6H	9D	JC	10S	2D	2C	8C	KH

(last card.)

SENIOR WRANGLER

PROBLEM I

To win the Patience with *lay-out:*

(1)	(2)	(3)	(4)	(5)	(6)	(7)	(8)
2 H	3 C	4 D	5 S	6 H	7 C	8 D	9 S

Packets under:

(1) *J C* (top card), 7 D, K H, 10 S, Q H, 8 S, 2 C, 6 D, J S,
6 S, K D, K S.

(2) *Q S* (top card), 8 H, 4 S, A S, 9 H, J H, 10 C, K C, 9 D, 5 C, 6 C, 5 D.

(3) *4 S* (top card), 9 C, 3 S, K H, Q H, 10 H, 3 D, 7 S, Q C, 4 C, Q S, J S.

(4) *A D* (top card), 9 S, 5 S, 4 H, 4 D, 8 D, 10 C, 3 H, A C, 10 S, 2 S, Q D.

(5) *7 C* (top card), 5 D, A C, 3 S, K S, 7 H, 10 H, 6 S, 9 D, 10 D, J D, A S.

(6) *9 H* (top card), J H, 2 C, A H, 7 H, Q D, 4 C, 6 H, 5 H, A H, 7 D, K D.

(7) *6 D* (top card), 8 H, 9 C, 5 C, Q C, 3 D, 8 C, 2 S, A D, 2 D, 5 H, 10 D.

(8) *2 H* (top card), 3 C, 2 D, 7 S, 6 C, 8 S, K C, 3 H, J D, J C, 4 H, 8 C.

PROBLEM II

The game has reached this position:

Columns:

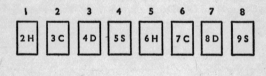

1	2	3	4	5	6	7	8
2 H	3 C	4 D	5 S	6 H	7 C	8 D	9 S

Packets:

K D	A D	8 C	Vacant	3 S	5 C	2 C	10 S

If the designated cards are used, the suit of those in the sequences is immaterial: any 4 or K will serve.

Sequences:

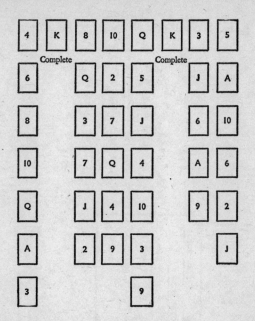

The packets contain:

(1) *K D* (top card), K S. (2) *A D* (top card), 9 H, 7 D, Q D,
K S. (3) *8 C* (top card), A S, 4 S, 2 D, 3 H. (4) Vacant. (5) *3 S*
(top card), Q C, K C, 6 C. (6) *5 C*, 7 H, 6 H, A H, 7 H, J S,
K H, 8 C. (7) *2 C* (top card), 10 D, K D, 7 S, 9 D. (8) *10 S*
(top card), 5 H, 5 S, J C, 4 H, 8 H.

Packets 1 to 6 having been picked up and dealt round
according to rules.

To solve Patience *without dealing* round another packet.

SPIDER

Problem I

END hand. Second deal. Patience to be won.

6H, 6H, 9S, 3C
4S, 3S, 5H, 4H, 10C, 7S, AH
9C, 8C, 3H, 7C, 9S, KS
QS, 2D, 10H, 9D, 4D, 2C, 5D, 5C

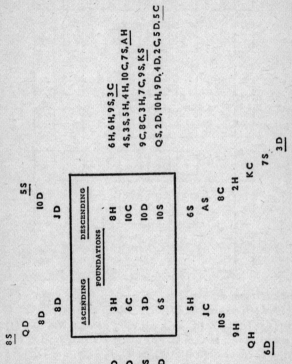

| | FOUNDATIONS | |
ASCENDING		DESCENDING
3H		8H
6C		10C
3D		10D
6S		10S

5S
10D
JD

8S
QD
8D

6S
AS
8C
2H
KC
7S
3D

5H
JC
10S
9H
QH
6D

AD, 7C, 6C, QC, 9D
7H, 8H, 4D, 4C, KH, 6D
JH, JS, 4H, 9C, 7D, 5D, 7H, 2S
7D, AC, 8S, KD

PROBLEM II

END game. Second deal. Patience to be won. Eighty-one cards in depots.

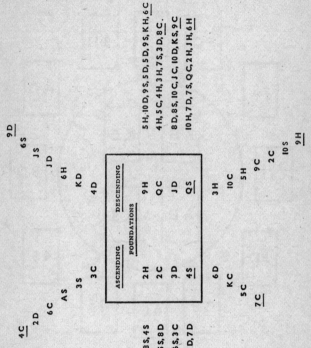

5H,10D,9S,5D,5D,9S,KH,6C
4H,5C,4H,3H,7S,3D,8C.
8D,8S,10C,JC,10D,KS,9C
10H,7D,7S,QC,2H,JH,6H

9D
6S
JS
JD
6H
KD
4D
3C
AS
3S
6C
2D
4C

FOUNDATIONS	
ASCENDING	DESCENDING
2H	9H
2C	QC
3D	JD
4S	QS

3H
10C
5H
9C
2C
10S
9H

6D
KC
5C
7C

7H4C,QD,8S,4S
10S,AC,8H,4D,QS,5S,8D
2S,9D,6D,7H,AH,6S,3C
8C,QH,JC,7C,8H,JS,AD,7D

SQUARING THE CIRCLE

PROBLEM

With this lay-out (after deal):

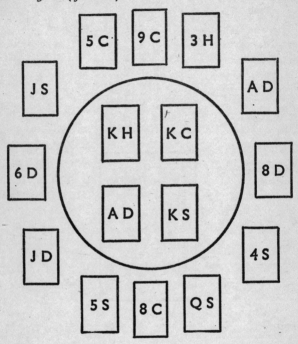

And cards in the following order, reading in rows from left to right:

2D	2H	AS	7S	4H	JS	JC	8D	6S	10D	4C	10C
6C	10S	7D	9C	8S	4H	10D	7C	KD	KS	6D	5D
10H	6H	JH	4S	5S	QH	6H	5H	JC	8S	6S	3S7C
10C	3D	7S	2S	KH	3C	8H	6C	8C	2C	10S	QC
7H	9S	2S	QS	4C	QD	9D	QH	AC	9H	QD	KD
JD	5C	5D	QC	4D	8H	10H	AH	7D	3C	5H	3S
3H	KC	7H	3D	9H	4D	9D	JH	2C	9S	2H	2D

(bottom card.)

To win Patience without a second deal.

SUPERIOR DEMON

PROBLEM I

Stock (all exposed):
  3 D (top card), 8 H, 5 H, K H, A S, 2 C, 8 S, J D, 3 S, A C, 4 S, 8 D, 3 H.
  Heads of columns: Q S, 10 D, Q D, 3 C.
  Base: 6 D.
Reserve (in this order):
  2 S, 8 C, *9 H*; 5 D, 10 H, *4 C*; 6 H, 9 C, *4 D*; 7 D, K C, *9 D*; 4 H, K D, *5 S*; 10 S, Q C, *6 C*; K S, 6 S, *Q H*; 7 C, A D, *J S*; 9 S, 2 H, *J C*; 10 C, J H, *5 C*; 7 S, 2 D, *7 H*; *A H*.
  To solve.

PROBLEM II

KINGS have been *foundations.*

Bases built to Columns:

Stock in this order:
  6 D, 5 C, 7 C, 4 C, 6 C, 9 H, Q S, J D, 10 S, 10 C, 8 C (last card).

8 H	3 C	5 D	6 S

Q H	9 D	Q D	Q C

J C	8 S	J S	J H

10 D	7 D	10 H

9 S		9 C

8 D

7 S

To solve.

BATTALION

Problem I.   Solution

Take K H, Q D on foundations. *Do not* take 2 or 3 D out, but put on A D (col. 3). *A S and A H out.* J C on Q C, 10 C on J, 8 D on 7, 9 D on 8. Then *J D, 10, 9, 9, 7 out, 2 D and 3 out* (2 D from col. 8). *A C (col. 8) out, Q H (col. 11) out.* 6 H on 7 H, J H on 10 [*do not* take J out], Q H on J, 5 H on 6, 4 H on 5, 5 S on 4 (col. 6), 4 S (col. 8) on 5. 10 C, J, Q on 9 C. *K C out. Descending Clubs to 8 out.* K H on Q H (col. 7). 4 S, 5, 4, 3 S (col. 2) on 3 S (col. 1). *2 H, J H out.* Two vacant spaces. Place Hearts from K to 10 in one (col. 2), A C in the other. *3 H, 4, 5, 6, 7 out, 4 D, 5 out.* Q S on J (col. 4), J S on Q. 6 C on 5; then *7, 6, 5 C out descending.* J S, Q S, J S, Q S on 10, 8 S on 9, 3 S, 4, 5 on 2 S. 5 S, 4, 3 on 6 S (col. 7), then *2 S, 3, 4, 5* and *6 S* (last from col. 7) *out.* 2 D on 3. A D in vacant space. 2 D, 3 on him. 6 C on 5, 7 H on 8, 4 D on 3, 6 C and 5 on 7, 7 H and 8 on 6, 4 S and 3 on 5. 9 H, 8, 7, 6 on 10 H. K S on Q. *7, 8, 9 S* out. 4 C on 5. 3 C (col. 5) on 4, 5 D on 4. K C in vacant space. *2 C to 7 out.* 3 S, 4, 5 on 2, 9 D on 8, 2 C on A, 3 C on 2. *10 H, 4 C, 3, 2, A out.* Q C on K. K S, Q and J in vacant space, Q S and J on first J. *10, J, Q out ascending.* K D in vacant space. 6 S on 5, A S in vacant space, 10 D on 9, 6 S to 2 on 7, then on A S. 10 D and 9 on J, 8 D on 7. 9, 10, J on 8. *8 H out.* Q D to 7 on K. J C on Q, 10 C on J, 6 D on 7. *K S to foundation.* A H to vacant space, 2 H on him, 9 C on 10, 3 H and 4 on 2. 6 D (col. 6) on 5, 8 C on 9, 8 S, 9, 10, J, Q on 7. *9 H and K S out.* 5 H, 6, 7, 8 on 4.

Hearts ascending and descending, Diamonds ascending and descending, ascending Clubs and descending Spades *all out.*

Problem II. Solution

Take Q C (col. 11). Do *not* take A C (col. 6), but *A C* (col. 11),
J C out. 4 D and 5 on 3 D. 6 D on 5. *2 C and 3 out.* 8 S on 7,
4 S on 3. 5 S, 6, 7, 8, 7 on 4. J C on 10. *K D, A H, A D out.*
8 H and 9 on 7. *A S (col. 2), Q D out.* A H in vacant space.
10 D and 9 on 9 D (col. 12). *2 S and K H out, Q H out.* 10 H
on 9, 5 C on 4. A S in vacant place. 6 C and 7 on 5. *2 H and
3 H out.* Put 9 D, 10, 9 on 8, 8 C on 7, *2 D out,* 6 D, 5, 4, 3 on
7; then *3 D to 8 D (col. 12) out.* *9 D, 10 from col. (1).* 2 H on
A. 10 C on J. Then *J, 10, 9, 8, 7 H out; 10 C, 9, 8, 7, 6, 5 out
descending.* *4 C ascending.* A C in vacant space. *5 C out ascending,*
10 S and J on 9. K S on A. *6 H and 5 out descending.* K C, Q,
J, 10 on A; Q S, J, 10, 9 on K. *4 H descending, 4 H ascending out.*
Spades 7, 8, 7, 6, 5, 4, 3 on 6 S. *3 S, 4, 5 out ascending.* Second
5 S on 6. 2 C on 3. 5 D on 4. A D on K D. K H on Q. 8 H
on 7. A D in vacant space. K D on him. 8 S on 9 S. 5 S, 6, 7,
8, 7, 6 on 4 S. *6 S, 7, 8 out ascending.* 8 S to Q from col. (2) on 7;
then *descending Spades out to 4.* *4 C out descending.* K H and Q in
vacant space. 8 H and 7 H on 9. 9 C, 8, 7 on 10 C. *3 S out
descending.* 9 D on 10, 8 on 9, 5 D on 6, 4 D on 5, 3 D on 4,
Q D on K, J H on Q. *5 H out ascending.* *Ascending Clubs 6–K out.*
2 C on A. *Descending Clubs out.* 8 D, 9, 10 on 7 D; 3 D, 4, 5, 6
on 2 D, 10 H on J. *Descending Hearts out, descending Diamonds
out to 2 from J.* *Ascending Hearts out from 6.* *Ascending Diamonds
and A D out.* 10 S on J. *Ascending Spades out, 2 S and Ace out.*

BISLEY

Problem I. Solution

9 D on 10, 8 D on 9, 5 C on 4, 6 C on 5, 7 C on 6. 6 H on 7.
9 H on 10. 5 H on 6, 7 C to 4 on 8, 3 C on 4, 7 D on 8. *K C,*

Q, J, 10 out. Q D on J; *K and Q H out,* 9 S on 8. 7 D to 10 on 6. 10 S on 9. 3 D on 4. 9 H, and 10 on 8. 6 S on 7. J S to 8 on Q S. *J, 10, 9, 8 H out.* 6 S on 5, then 7 S, 6, 5, 4 on 8 S. 5 H, 6, 7 on 4. 4 S to Q on 3 S. K D, K S ready for foundations. Then *Hearts out to 4, Spades to 2, Diamonds to 5.* 9 C, 3 H and 2 *out.* 3 D on 2, 3 C to 7 on 2. *Both Diamonds and Clubs out as required.*

Or 6 C on 7, 9 D on 8, 10 D on 9, 10 S on 9, 3 D on 4, 9 H on 10, 6 H on 5, 7 H on 6, 8, 9, 10 H on 7. 6 S on 7. J S on 10. 4 S on 3; 5, 6, 7 S on 4, 4 C on 3. J C on 10; 10, 9, 8 D on J; 5 C, 4, 3 on 6. K S being already exposed. Q S, J, 10, 9 on K. 7 D, 8, 9, 10, J on 6 D. K C being exposed, Q, J, 10 on him. Q, J, 10 to 5 D on K. 9 C on 10, 3 C–7 C on 2. Q H on K; 8 S, 7 S–3 on 9 S. J H, 10 H–5, 4, 3, 2 H on Q. 8 C, 7 C–2 C on 9 C. 2 S on 3, 3 D on 2. 4 D, 3, 2 on 5.

PROBLEM II. SOLUTION

With same lay-out, transposing only the Queen and Knave of Hearts to solve in *ascending* order, building only on the Aces.

6 C on 7, 9 D on 8, 10 D on 9, 10 S on 9, 3 D on 4, 9 H on 10, 6 H on 5, 7 H on 6, 8, 9, 10 H on 7, 6 S, 7 on 5 S, 3 C on 4, J S on Q, J C on Q C, 10 D, 9, 8 on J; 6 C, 7 on 5 C. J H on 10, 8 S on 7. J H, 10–4 H on Q. 10 S, 9, 8, 7, 6, 5 on J. 3 S on 4; then Spades out. 5 D on 6, 8 C on 7, 9 C on 8, 3 C and 4 on 2, 10 C–3 on J. 8 D to J on 7 D. 3 H on 4. J to 7 D on Q, then Diamonds, Clubs, and Hearts out in ascending order as required.

THE BRITISH BLOCKADE

PROBLEM I. SOLUTION

Deal 1st row from left to right:

A, 4, 5 C, K D, A S, A C, 5 C, Q D, 6 S, K C. Take A C, deal Knave C. Take K D, deal Q C. Take A S, deal 6 H. Take Q D, deal 5 H. Take K C, deal 4 D. Take Q C, deal 7 H. Take J C, deal 2 H.

Deal 2nd row:

5 D, 8 H, 6 D, 8 C, 10 S, 3 C, J C, Q H, 8 S, A H. Take A H, deal 7 S. Take 2 H, deal J D.

Deal 3rd row:

6 S, 3 H, 10 C, 4 S, 7 C, 5 S, 9 D, J S, J H, 5 H. Take 3 H. Deal and take K S. Deal A H. Take J D, deal 6 C.

Deal 4th row:

5 S, 7 C, 2 H, 4 H, J S, 8 H, 3 D, 9 H, 3 S, 3 H. Take Hearts 4, 5 (top row), 6, 7, 8, 9. Fill up in due order with J D, K H, 7 D, 10 D, 4 H, 9 C. Take K H, deal 9 D. Take 10 D, deal 4 D.

Deal 5th row:

4 C, K D, 7 D, 10 C, J H, 7 S, 2 S, 2 D, A D, 9 S. Take A and 2 D, 2 S and 3 S, 3 D, 10 and 9 C (descending), 9 D (in third row) descending, 4 D (in fourth row), 4 S, 8 C.

Fill up vacancies in due order 10 S (in second row, next to 10 S), 9 C, 7 H (third row). 8 C, 3 S, 4 S, Q S in fourth row, 8 S, 3 C, 2 C, Q H in bottom row.

Take Q and J H; Q and J S, 2, 3, 4 C (from bottom row), 5 S and 6 (from top row), 7, 8, 9 S. 5 C (the one nearer left hand), 6, 7 C. 5 D, 6, 7 (below), 10 S (the one under 9 D) descending.

Transfer 9 S from ascending sequence and take 8 S. Take 8, 9, 10 C ascending.

Fill vacancies 8, 10, 2 D in top row. 10 H, A S, A D, 6 D in second row. 10 H, Q D, Q S in third row. K H, K C, 8 D, 2 S in fourth row. Q C, 5 D, 9 S, 6 H, 3 D, 6 C, K S, 9 H, 2 C (last card in Pack) in fifth row.

Take 8 D (ascending), 10 H, 9 (descending). Transfer 9–Q D to ascending sequence. Take K D from bottom row. Take 7, 6, 5, 4 C (descending), J, Q C, 9 S and K C (ascending), Q D, J, 10, 9 (descending), 8 H, 7, 6 (descending), 8 D and 7.

Take 6 D as 'merci'. Then descending Diamonds out. 7 S and 6 out. Descending and ascending Hearts, ascending and descending Spades, descending Clubs *all out*.

PROBLEM II.   SOLUTION

Deal 1st row:

A D, Q H, K D, 9 D, 8 H, 2 D, 8 S, A C, 8 H, 7 S. Take A D,
A C, K D, 2 D. Deal to vacant places J H, K S, 7 H, 2 H.
Take K S, deal 6 C.

Deal 2nd row:

7 C, 10 D, J S, 10 S, K H, 6 D, K C, 10 C, A H, Q D. Take
K H, K C, A H, Q and J H, Q D, 2 H. Deal in vacant spaces
4 S, 10 C, 2 C, Q H, 7 H, 8 C, J D. Take J, 10, 9 D and 2 C;
places filled with K S, 5 C, 9 S, Q S. Take Q, J, 10, 9, 8, 7 S.
Vacancies K H, 6 H, 2 H, 5 S, 5 D, J S.

Deal 3rd row:

7 C, 4 C, A C, 6 S, Q D, 2 S, A D, J H, J D, 7 D. Take 6 S,
replace with 5 H.

Deal 4th row:

K C, 6 H, 9 C, 3 C, 8 D, 6 D, 2 D, 5 H, 4 C, 10 H. Take 3 C,
4, 5, 6. 5 S and 4. 7 C, 8 D, 10 H, 7 D and 6. Into vacancies
3 C, 8 C, 8 S, K D, 10 D, 9 C, 9 D, A S, 6 S, 4 S, Q S. Take
A S, fill with Q C. Take 8, 9, 10 C, fill with 5 C, 3 D, 4 D.
Take 3 and 4 D, fill with 9 and 3 H. Take 9 H, fill with 4 H.
Take 3, 4, 5, 6 (over J S), 7 H ascending, 8 H (over 8 C) descending. Fill spaces with 10 S, 8 D, 3 S, 2 C, 5 S, 2 S. Take 2 S,
3 S ascending.

Transfer 4 to J S from descending to ascending. Take Q and
K from lay-out, 5 D (descending). Transfer 7 H from ascending
to descending. Take 6 and 5 H from lay-out.

Fill vacancies with J C, 9 S, 9 H, 10 H, Q C, 7 S, 7 D. Transfer
5 D and 6 descending to ascending. Take from lay-out 7 D,
8, 9, Q C (col. 2), J C descending. Transfer 10 C from ascending
to descending. 9 C (descending) from lay-out. J S, 10, 9, 8 out.
10 C (ascending). 8 C (descending). 7 S, 6, 5, 4. 10 D and J,
6 D out.

Fill vacancies with J C, 5 D, 4 H, 3 D, 3 H, 6 C, A H, 3 S,
4 D. A S, last card. Then J, Q, K C and 7 C out: then Clubs out,
6 to A; Hearts out, 4 to A; Diamonds, 5 to A; Spades, 3 to A.
Hearts out, 7 to K. Q and K D out.

THE EMPEROR

PROBLEM I.   SOLUTION

TRANSFER sequence 9 C to 4 D from col. (9) to col. (8) on
10 H. Take K C from W H, and put Q D to 10 D on him; then
back to (9). Transfer sequence 9 S to 5 S from 10 D (col. 10)
to 10 D (col. 9). Take 10 D (col. 10) to vacant col. (4), unsealing
Q H. Put K S from W H in col. (3). Q H on him, 4 H exposed
on 5 S (col. 9). Put K S and Q H back in (10) col. Deal J C on
Q H, 10 D on J C.

*Deal *6 S* on W H, *3 S* out, *8 S* on W H, *3 S* on 4 H, *K S* on
W H, *K D*. Work to top of col. (5), *4 C* on 5 H, *3 D* on 4 C,
5 C on W H, *9 C* on 10 D. *A H* out, *10 S* and *Q S* on W H.
7 S in col. (4). 4 D to 6 D on him. 7 C out to foundation,
7 S on 8 H (col. 8), 6 D to 4 D back with 7 S. *4 S* out, *9 S* on
W H. *2 S* out. *A D, A C* out for foundations, *7 D,* W H, *2 D*
(last card) out. 3, 4 D, 2 C, 3 S out. 3 H on 4 C, 4 and 5 S out.
5 D and 6, 7 D from W H out. 3 H, 4 C, 5 H (col. 6) on 6 C
(col. 7). 6 and 7 S out. 7 C–4 H (col. 9) on 8 H (col. 8). 8 D
out, 7 H in vacancy, col. 4. C 8 and 9, 9 D and 10, 10 C and J.
J D out. 7 S (last sealed card) exposed.

Reverse W H. Deal in threes *8 D, Q H,* 3 C–Q H out, 3 C out,
8 D on 9 S, 7 S on 8 D. Deal *Q C, 6 H, K H,* 6 H on 7 S, K H
and Q C on foundation. Deal *9 D, K H, 2 H.* 2 H out, 9 D on
10 S. Deal *K D and J S.* J S on Q H. Deal *8 S* on 9 D, 7 H on
8 S. Deal *6 S* on 7 H, *8 S* out. Deal *K S,* filling up the three
grace cards allowed.

Pack from lay-out: 3, 4 H, 4 C, 5, 6 H, 5, 6, 7 S, 7 H and
8 S, 6 C in vacant space. 6, 7, 8, 9 D out; 9, 10, J S, 10 D out;
J C on Q H, Q D out; K D from grace cards; K C out. Deal
5 C, 5, 6, 7, 8 C out; 8 and 9 H, 9, 10, J C; 10, J, Q H, Q and
K S; J D, Q C out from columns. K H from grace cards.
Deal *10 S, Q S.* Q S on K D. Deal *9 S. All out.*

---

* With cards printed in italic, thus, *K S, K D*, understand 'deal'.

Problem II. Solution

6 H on 7 C, expose 6 S. 5 C on 6 H, expose 9 C. 4 H on 5 C,
expose 8 H. Place this on 9 C, expose K S. 7 S on 8 H, expose
K H.

Deal 7 H. *3 D* on WH. *3 S* on 4 H. *A D* out. 2 D from
col. 2, expose 5 H, place on 6 S, expose 2 S. 3 D out from WH.
A S out, take 2 S, expose 9 C. 3 S from col. 10. *4 S* not out,
but on 5 H. *Worry back 3 D.* Put on 2 C from col. 3, expose 6 D,
which place on 7 S, exposing 4 S, which goes out, exposing
6 C. J C, 6 C on WH. *3 C* on 4 H. *A D* out. *Q D* on K S,
8 C on 9 D. *Q S,* second *Q S,* both on WH. *A C* out. 2 C
(col. 6) out, exposing 7 D, 3 C from col. 10, 7 D on 8 C, 6 C on
7 D. K S exposed in col. 6. K H (col. 7) to vacant space
(col. 3), exposing A C, which out with 2 C. 3 D out. 2 H
(exposed) on col. 7. *Worry back 3 C,* put 2 H on. Q S from WH
on K H. J D on Q S (col. 3), exposing Q C. K S in vacant
space, exposing 3 C. This out on 2 C. *9 S,* WH. J H on Q C.
3 D and *2 S* out on 4 S (col. 9). *A H* out. 2 H out. *7 C* on WH.
10 S on J D. *4 H* on WH. *A S, A H* out. 2 S, 3 C out. Q D
on K S (col. 7), other K S in col. 6, exposing 4 D, out on
foundation.

K D, 8 S, 8 C, 10 S, 9 S, 8 S on WH. *5 C* on 6 D (col. 1).
9 H on 10 S, take 8 S from WH. *Q D* on K S. *K D* on WH.
4 C out (*13 cards in WH*). 10 D in vacant space, 9 C on him.
10 C on J H, 7 H on 8 S. *10 C* on WH. *6 S* on 7 H, *4 D* on
5 C, *8 D* on WH. *J S* on Q D (col. 6), 9 C from col. (5) to (2).
10 D on J S, 9 C on 10 D. 8 D from WH on 9 C.

Two vacant spaces, cols. 2 and 5.

Get 7 C to 4 H from col. (10) on 8 D (col. 6), exposing 2 D,
which out on A, exposing 9 H, which out on 10 C, exposing
7 S.

Get 5 H–3 D (col. 9) on 6 S (col. 3). 3 D and 4 D. 5 C and
6 C out. 6 S on 7 D, exposing 3 H, which out, expose 5 D,
which out with 6 D. 6 H–4 H (col. 6) on vacant spaces (of
which three), 7 C out. 7 S from col. (10) on 8 D. 6 H, 5 C, 4 H
back on 7 S. Get Q C, J H, 10 C, 9 H to col. 2, exposing 5 S,

which out. Take out 6 and 7 S, 7 D and 8 C. 4 H on 5 S. 5 C,
6 H, 7 S on vacant space. 8 D and 9 out, exposing K C. 8 H on
9 C (under 10 D, col. 6). 7 S, 6 H, 5 C back on him. 9 C out
(col. 1), exposing K H. Put in vacant space, exposing 3 S,
which out. 4 S out, 4 H and 5 H, 5 and 6 S out. Q C–9 H on
K H. 10 C out from WH. Close up ranks so that cols. 1–5 are
vacant. Call col. (6) K H, Q C–9 H. (7) K H, Q S–7 H. (8)
K S, Q D–5 C. (9) K S, Q D. (10) Last two sealed cards. K C.

FOUNDATIONS. – 5 H, 10 C, 9 D, 7 S, A H, 3 C, 4 D, 6 S.

WH (13 cards): K D (top), 9 and 10 S, 8 C, 8 S, K D, 4 H,
7 C, 9 S, Q S, 6 C, J C, 7 H.

PACK. – 8 H (top). Twenty cards.

Put K C in left-hand row, exposes 10 H. Put 5 C in vacant
row. Take out 6, 7, 8 (pack), 9, 10 H exposing Q H, which
place on K C. K D in vacant space from WH. 7, 8, 9, 10 (last
two from WH) out on 6 S. 8 C from WH on 9 H. 8 S out from
WH on 7. K D from WH in vacant space. 4 H from WH on
5 C. 7 C from WH on 8 H. 9 S from WH out. Q S from WH
on K D. *Deal* 3 H on WH. *J* C on Q H. *J* S on Q D, *J* H on
Q S, *10* H on J C, *10* D on J S. *Worry back 9 S on 10 D.* 8 D
on 9 S. 4 C out. 6 H on 7 C, *Q* C on K D. *Worry back 9 D on
10 C, 8 S on 9 D, 7 S on 8 D.* *Deal 6 D on 7* S. Put 5 C and 4 D
on 6 D. Deal *J* D on Q C.

Deal *5 H* to vacant space. *Q H* to WH. *K C* in vacant space.
Q H from WH on him. *2 H* out, take 3 from WH, 4, 5, 6 H
from lay-out. 5 C out from lay-out. 6 from WH. J C from
WH on Q H. *9 D* out. *7 D* on 8 C, *5 D* (last card) out. 7 H
(last card in WH) out. Rest out.

THE GENERAL

PROBLEM I.   SOLUTION

TAKE 10 C for foundation (*not* J, or you block the second
Club sequence). 3 D on 4 C. Do not pack J C on Q D. Deal
7 *S* on 8 D, *10 S* out. *Q D* on WH. *10 D* out. *9 S* in vacant
col. (4). Put 7 S in vacancy, 8 D on 9 S, 7 S on 8 D, *5 C* on top of

4 H, *6 C* on WH, *Q C* on WH, *9 H* on top of 8 S, *9 C, 8 C,*
6 S on WH, *10 D* out, *3 S* on 4 H, *2 H* on 3 S, *10 H* out, *4 S*
top of 3 H, *A C* on 2 H, *Q C* on WH. *K D* on A C, Q C from
WH on K D, *5 S* on WH, *K H* in col. (2), *Q S* on K H. *A H* on
WH. *7 C, 3 C, A D, 2 D* on WH. *K C* top of Q D, *2 C* on 3 H,
J D out, Q D from col. 3 out, Q C from col. (8) to vacant col.
(9). K D out. *A D from top line and 2 D, J D, J H and J C from*
top line. Q, K, A, 2 C out from columns. *3 C from top line.*
3 D and 4 C out from columns. 2 D (WH) to vacant col. (3).
A D (WH) to vacant col. (5), 3 C (WH) on 2 D, *4 C* on WH.
6 H on 7 S, *6 D* (WH), *5 D* (WH), *5 C* out. *2 S* on 3 H. A D
on 2 S. *K S* on A D. Transfer 5 C to 2 H on to 6 H. Having
three vacancies, put 2 S to K S in one; take 5 D from WH, 3 H
to last vacancy; then 4 S, 3 H on 5 D. 2 S to K S, back on 3 H.
7 D on 8 S, *8 D* on WH. *A S* on 2 H, K H, Q S on A. *4 D* out.
Having *four* vacancies, transfer 3 H to KS to one, 4 S to another;
take out 5 D and put 3 H to K S back on 4 S. 8 D from WH to
vacant space; then 6, 7, 8 D out. 4 C (WH) to vacant column.
7 C (WH) to vacant column, *7 S* to WH. *10 S* out, *K S* to WH.
6 H on *7 C.* *7 D* on 8 S. *5 S* on 6 H, *4 S, Q S* on WH. *A S*
on 2 D, *5 H* top of 4 C. 5 S and 6 H to vacant place. *8 H* to
vacant place. 7 C, then 6 H, 5 S on it. *8 S* WH. *3 H* on 4 C,
9 C WH, *3 D* WH, *J S* out. Q, K, A out. *2 H* on WH.
2 S out. *4 H* on 5 S, 3 C and 2 D on 4 H. *K H, K D* on WH
(eighteen cards in WH). *K C* on A D, *A C* on 2 D. K D from
WH on A C, *Q H not out,* but on K C. J C on Q H. Transfer
2 S to J C on to 3 H (under 4 C, col. 4). *5 H* on top of 4 S, *8 C*
on WH, *6 S* on 7 D, 5 H to 3 H on 6 S. 8 C from WH to vacant
space. *6 C* out, *7 C from top line.* 8 C (singleton) out. *10 C out*
from top line. J C, Q and K H out. K H (WH) on A S. 2 H and
3 D from WH to vacant spaces, 9 C out from WH. 8 S (WH)
to vacant place. Q S (WH) on K H. 4 S (WH) in vacant space.
3 D on him. K S (WH) on vacant space, 7 S (WH) in in last
vacant space. A H (WH) and 2, 3 H out. *7 H* on 8 S. *4 D* in
vacant place. *6 D* on 7 S. 5 S (WH) on 6 D, 4 D on 5 S. 6 S
(WH) on 7 H. *3 S out from top line.* 3 D on 4 S (under 5 H).
4 S out. With *two* vacant spaces, transfer K D to 3 C on to 4 D,

4 H and 5 S out and 6 S. 8 and 9 C from W H to vacant spaces.
Q C out. K C out, 6 C from W H on 7 H. Q D (last card in
W H) out with K and A. A C and 2, 3 D out. Deal *9 S* on W H.
Q H on K S, *9 H* on W H, *7 H* on 8 C, *A H* on 2 S. *J H* out
with Q. *2 C* out with *3 C* (from col. 9). 4 D from col. *5 D,
J S, 9 D from top line.*

REST OUT THUS: Q S and K, K H, A, A S, 2; 2 H and 3, 3 S,
4, 5. 4 H, 5; 4 C, 5, 6; 5 H, 6, 7, 6 H, 7, 8 from top line, 9 from
W H. 6 S, 7, 8, 9 (the last from W H), 7 C, 8, 9. 6 D, 7, 8, 9.
8 H, 9. *9 D* (last card of stock). *All out.*

PROBLEM II. SOLUTION

Transfer the 6 H and 4 H nearer the left (cards 3 and 5).

Take 4 S from top row. Pack 2 C on 3 H, K H on A S,
Q C on K H.

Deal J S to vacant place. *Q H* on K S, J S on Q H, *3 H* to
vacant space.

Place J S in one vacant space, Q H in the other, then J S on
Q H. Deal A H on 2 C, K S on him, Q H and J S on K (via
vacant space), 7 D on 8 S, *4 S* to base, 7 D to vacant column;
10 C to vacant column, *4 C* to base, K D on A C. *J H* on Q C,
10 C on J H. *6 S* on 7 D (the singleton), *A C* to W H, *3 C* to
W H. *8 C* to vacant space, 6 S to vacant space. 7 D (over 6 S)
on 8 C, 6 S back on 7 D. *3 C* from W H to vacant space, *9 S,
K S* to W H, *2 D* on 3 C, A C and K D on 2 D, *7 H* to vacant
column. *7 H* (second one) to W H. *2 D* to W H. *8 D* to vacant
column. 7 S on it. *3 S* to vacant column. 2 D on it from W H.
5 H out, *3 S* on W H; *8 H* on W H. *10 D* on J S, *9 H* on 10 C,
8 C on 9 H, 7 H on 8 C, *J H* on W H, *5 H* on 6 S, *2 H* on W H,
4 D out for foundation, *K H* on W H, *8 H* in vacant space,
9 S on 10 D, 8 H on 9 S, *Q S* on K D, *K C* on W H, *6 S* on 7 H,
10 S, J S on W H, *2 S* on 3 H, *7 S* on 8 H, *10 C* and *Q H* on W H,
6 D on 7 S (in col. 5), *5 C* out, *3 D, 10 H* on W H, *A S* on 2 D,
9 D, 8 D on W H. *K D* on A S, *9 C* in vacant space. *Q S* on
K D, *A D* on 2 S. *A H, 10 H, J C* on W H, *5 D* out, 6 D and
7 out. *Q D, 3 C* on W H. *Q C, 10 S, 3 D. 2 H* on W H (twenty-
seven cards on W H). *5 S* out with 6, 7 (under 8 D), 8 S, 8 D

out. 8 H and 7 S (col. 5) to vacant space. 9 S out, 9 C on 10 D,
8 H and 7 S back to 9 C. 2 H, 3 D from WH to vacant cols.
(2 and 3). 10 S out from WH. *K C* on A D, *6 D on* 7 S, *J D* on
Q S (col. 1), *8 S, J C, 5 D* on WH, *2 C* on 3 D, 4 C to foundation.
2 S, 9 C, 9 H on WH. *9 D out. 10 D,* 4 D, *6 C* and 6 H, *from
top row* to foundations. *A D* on 2 C, *5 C* (last card of stock)
out. *6 C from top row.* J D and 7 H out from columns. *Q D,
7 C, 4 H, 5 S from top row,* 5 H from columns, *6 H and 7 C from
top row*. 6 S and 8 C from columns. 8 C and 7 D on to 9 H.
9 H (top card of WH) in vacant space, 9 C (WH) out, 2 S
(WH) to vacant space, 5 D (WH) out, 6 D and 7 from columns;
7 S, 8 H and 9 (the singleton), 8 C and 9 out from columns,
10 D (col. 5) into vacant space. J and Q S (col. 1), K and A D
out. Q H on K C. K S and A; 2 D; 2 and 3 S out. J C (WH)
on Q H, 10 D back on J C. 8 S (WH) out, Q C (WH) to
vacant space – call it col. (7). 3 C (WH) on col. (8), 2 H on 3 C.
Q D (WH) to space (2), J C on her, 10 H out, A H on 2 C.
8 D and 9 out from WH, 10 D from col. (4). 10 H (WH) on
J C (col. 4). 3 D (WH) out. *J D out from top row*. Q H (WH)
to col. (1), 10 C (WH) out, J C, Q and Q D out. J S (WH) on
Q H, 10 S (WH) to col. (7), K C on A H (col. 2), Q H and J S
on him. K H (WH) to col. (1). 10 H to J S, 9 H to 10 S.
10 C and J out; J H, Q, K, A, 2 (from WH) out. J H (WH)
on Q S. 10 S and 9 H on J H. 8 H (WH) in vacant row.
3 S in vacant row. 7 H out with 8, 9, 10. K C out, K S (WH)
on A D, 9 S out. 10, J S, J H, Q S, K S; Q H; Q, K C; A C
(last card of WH), 2 C; K, A D; K, A, 2, 3 H; A S, 2, 3; A C,
2, 3; 2 D and 3. 3 H, 3 C. *All out.*

GRANDFATHER'S CLOCK

PROBLEM.   SOLUTION

PUT A C on K. Deal *Q S* to Clockmaker. (She would have to
go over the Knave of Spades and thereby block the 12 o'clock
foundation unless you were lucky enough to work her off on
the K S at 10 o'clock.) *K C* on J S. Put 5 S on 4. *Deal 2 D* over

4 C. Put A D on 2. Place K D, A and 2 on Q D (foundation).
Q C on J, with K C. Put 3 H (from 10 o'clock) on 4 H at
2 o'clock. K S and A out, 6 and 7 S, 7 C and 6 H out. Deal *6 D*
on Q H. *A H* to Clockmaker (if placed would block the
10 o'clock foundation). *8 H* on 6 D, *5 H* and *10 S* on 5 C,
A C on J S, *J H* on 4 C, *8 C* and *3 C* on 9 H.

A C out, also 10, J S, 3 D, J H. Put 3 C on 4. 8 C out.
8 H on 9, 6 D on 7. Q H, K H. A H (from Clockmaker) out.
4 D at 7 o'clock. 2 H, 3, 4, 5 at 5 o'clock. 8 S at 8 o'clock.
2 S, 3, 4, at 4 o'clock; 5 D, 6, 7 at 7 o'clock; 9 D and 10 at
11 o'clock; 9 C and 10 at 10 o'clock; 2 C, 3, 4, 5, 6 at 6 o'clock;
7 H, 8, 9 at 9 o'clock; 2 C at 2, J D at 11 o'clock. Q S from
Clockmaker at 12 o'clock. Q E F.

GRANDMAMMA'S

Problem. Solution

Put *K C* on J C. *3 D* out, 2 D on it. *A D* on it. *Q H* in vacant
space. *10 S* on Q H, *8 S* on K H, *6 S* on 7 D. *4 S* out, 5 S, 6,
7, 8 out. *10 C, 7 C* in vacant spaces. *4 C* out, 5 C out from
lay-out. *A S* in vacant space. *J D* on J D. *8 S* on K H, *5 D*
on 7 D. *2 S* out with A. *Q C* in vacant space. *9 C* on 10 C.
Take 6 C, 7 from lay-out. *6 D* in vacant space. *3 C* out.
Take 2 C. 7 S and A S in vacant spaces. *8 C* out, take 9 and 10.
2 H out. *9 H* in vacant place. *3 C* on A S. *10 C* on 6 H. *4 D*
out, 5, 6, 7 D out, *K D* out, Q, J, 10, 9. *A H* out, with K,
Q, J. Fill vacant spaces. *10 S, 2 H, K C, 6 S, Q S, 5 H, J H,
4 C. 10 H* out, 9, 8 H out. *3 S* in vacant space. *9 S* out, 10 S
(the one covering Q H), *2 S* in vacancy. *8 D* out, ascending
take 9. *A C* out. Take K C (the one covering J), Q C, J C,
10 C descend.

7 C, 8 D, K S in vacant places. 8 D out (descend). *4 H* in
vacant place. K and Q S out. *8 C* and *Q C* in vacant places.
3 H on 4 H. *7 D* out. *J S* out (descend) with 10. *2 D* in vacant
place. *6 D* out (descend). *K S* on K C. *10 H* on J H. *A C* on
A D. *5 D* out. *5 S* on 3 S. *10 D* out, ascend with J. *2 C* on

vacancy. *7 H* out (descend) with 6 and 5. *Q D* out, ascend.
9 S out with 8, 7, 6, 5. *K D* and *4 S* out. Fill vacancies with *9 H*,
A H, 6 C, J C. J C and Q C out, ascend. *3 D* in vacant space.
4 D out. *J S* out with Q, K. K C, A, 2, 3 out; A S, 2, 3 out.
A D, 2, 3 out. *9 C* out with 8, 7, 6. *7 H* out with 8 H to 3
(ascending). *5 C* out with 4 C and 4 H. *All out.*

THE HARP

Problem.   Solution

PACK 8 C on 9 D, exposing 7 S; 7 S on 8 D, exposing K S.
Deal *7 H* on 8 C, 6 C on 7 H, exposing 3 S. 2 D on 3 S, exposing
6 S. 5 H on 6 C, exposing K D. Deal *A D,* 2 D and 3 out.
K D to vacant space, exposing 2 C, *8 D, K D* to WH, *Q D* on
K S (col. 1). *9 C* on WH. *J S* on Q D, 10 H on J S, exposing
3 D, 9 C from WH on 10 H. 2 C on 3 D, exposing 9 H. *A C*
out, 2 C out. *8 H* on 9 C, *4 D* out, *7 S* on 8 H, *J C* on WH.
A H out, *2 H* out, *4 C* on 5 H, 3 D on 4 C, exposing 4 H, 3 S
on 4 H. K S with sequence to 7 S in vacant space, exposing
A D. This out, exposing J S. *4 S* on WH. *Q D* on K S. J S on
Q D, exposing 2 H, 2 H on 3 S, exposing 3 C, which out,
exposing 6 H. 6 H on 7 S (col. 8), exposing A H, which out.
Put K S–J S in vacant space, exposing 7 D. 2 H out. *8 S* on
9 H. 7 D on 8, exposing 6 D. (Do *not* take this out yet or
build.) 6 S on 7 D, exposing 9 S. *5 D* on 6 S (not out). 4 S
from WH on 5 D. 3 D on 4 S. 4 C out. *J D* on WH. *10 H*
on J S. 9 S on 10 H, exposing J H. *Q C* on K D. J H on Q C,
exposing 8 H. 8 H on 9 S, exposing A S. A S out, exposing
9 S. 7 S on 8 H. 8 D on 9 S, exposing A C. A C out, exposing
5 S. 5 S on 6 H, exposing 2 D. 2 and 3 D out. *K H* top card
of pack in vacant space. 4 S on 5 H. 5 D out. (Do *not* yet take
6 D.) *5 C* out. *6 D* (dealt) on 7 S. *10 D* on WH. *K C* top card
of stock; so take singleton 6 D, K C in vacant place. *7 D* out,
8 D out. *4 S, 3 C,* WH. *Q S* on K H, *5 S* on *6 D, 2 S* out, 3 S,
4, 5 (col. 8) out. 5 H on 6 S. 6 C out. *2 C* out, 3 from WH.
4 S from WH on 5 H. *9 H, 5 D* on WH. *5 C* on 6 H. 4 H on

5 C, exposing K H. *Q H* on K C. *6 S* out. *2 S* on W H. *4 H*
on 5 S. *J C* on Q H. *7 H* on W H. *3 H* out. 4 H from col. (8).
10 S on J H. *10 D* on J C, *J D* on Q S, 9 S on 10 D. K H in
vacant space, exposing 6 C. 6 C on 7 H, exposing 8 C. *A S* out.
Q H on W H, *7 C* out. 8 C out, exposing Q S. Q S on K H,
exposing 4 C. Take out with 5 C and 6. *10 C* on J D. *3 H* out
with 4. *J H* on Q S. *7 C* out. *6 H* in vacant space (first card
from stock available). *10 S* on J H. *3 S* on W H. *9 D* on 10 C.
K C (last card) on W H.

  Reverse W H (twelve in it).

  8 D on 9 S. *K D, J C, J D, 10 D* on W H. Take out 9, 10,
J D, last two from W H. *9 H* on 10 S col. (3). *5 D* on W H.
2 S out. *7 H, Q H* on W H. *3 S* out, 4 and 5 S out. 5 H, 6
(col. 8), 7 H out. 6 S and 7. 8 H and 9. 8 C, 9, 10 out. 9 D on
10 S (col. 9), exposing 9 C. 9 C out, exposing 10 C. 10 C out,
exposing 5 H. 5 H out, exposing 4 D. 9 D on 10 S (col. 9 to
col. 3). 10 S on J D (col. 9 to col. 6). 10 H, J H, Q H (from W H)
out. 6 H out. *K C* (last card) in vacancy. 7 H (W H) out. 4 D,
5 (from W H), 6, 7, 8, 9 D out. 7 S, 8, 9, 10; 8 H, 9 out, exposing
Q C. 10 D out, J C, Q C out, exposing 8 S. 8 S, 9, 10, J out.
10 H, J out. J C from W H. J D, J S out. *All out.*

THE HAT

Problem I.   Solution

Deal to Brim Depots, from left to right, thus:

9 S (top card)	10 D	5 C	7 S (bottom card)
7 S ,, ,,	6 C	6 S	Q S ,, ,,
3 C ,, ,,	6 H	5 S	A H ,, ,,
2 S ,, ,,	A S	7 C	8 D ,, ,,
4 C ,, ,,	10 S	6 D	4 H ,, ,,

  If the 6 C (over Q C) had been taken before dealing, the
solution would be impossible without a 'merci'.

  Take 7 S (ascending); 6 C (over 6 S).

  Move 8 S from descending foundation on 7 S (ascending);
4 C to side depot.

Take 9 S (from depot), 10 S, J S.

Move 6 S to side depot.

Take Q S, K S, 8 S, 7 C (descending), 6 C (from depot).

Move A D to side depot; take 8 D (descending). Move 7 D (from ascending foundation) on 8 D (descending).

Take 6 D (from depot), 5 D, 4 D.

Move 10 D to side depot; Q C to side depot.

Take 5 C (descending); 4 C; 3 C; 6 H; 5 H; 4 H; 7 S; 6 S; 5 S; 4 S.

Move K C to side depot; J D to side depot; A H to side depot.

Take 3 S, 2 S, A S and the remainder.

Problem II. Solution

Take 8 D (descending).

Transfer 7 D, 6 D from ascending to descending.

Take 5 D, 4 D (both from side depots).

Put 7 D from brim to side depot.

Take 3 D from brim, 2 D from side depot.

Put 5 C from brim to side depot. A D out.

Put 2 H from brim to side depot. 6 H (over J H) and 5 H out (descending).

Put 7 H from brim to side; then 4, 3, 2, A H out.

Put J D from brim to side. K C ditto.

Then 10 C out descending. Transfer 9, 8, 7 C from ascending; then take 6 C and 5 C out from side.

6 H brim to side. Deal two more 'fours' to brim depots Nos. 2 and 5; thus:

10 C, 3 S, 2 S, *4 C (outside card).*

Q S, K H, 7 C, *10 H (outside card).*

4 C out (descending). Place 6 S in vacant side depot.

Deal. (1) J C, 6 D, 5 S, *7 S (outside card).*

(2) J S, A S, 5 H, *10 S (outside card).*

(3) A C, K D, Q D, *9 H (outside card).*

(4) 10 D, 8 D, 9 D.

7 S out (descending). 6 S (from side). 5 S, 6 D, 7 D (from

side). Place 9 D in side depot. 8 D, 9, 10, J D (side depot) out.
10 S, 5 H, 6, 7 out (last two from side). Put J C to side depot.
4 S, 8 H, 9, 10, J, Q out. Q and K D. 7 C, 8, 9. (*Rest clear.*)

HEADS AND TAILS

PROBLEM. SOLUTION

TAKE A S for foundation. K D comes down and out for
foundation – (hereafter abbreviated to fdn). A D down and
out for fdn. 10 S down, 7 H exposed. Place 10 S on 9 S. 7 H
down. Place J S on 10. K C down and out for fdn. 2 S
(exposed) out on A. 9 H down. Place 2 H on 3 H. 3 S down
and out to fdn. 5 C down. 4 S out; 9 D down. 5 S out. 6 C up,
6 S out. K S up and out for fdn. Second K S up. Q D out.
A H out for fdn. 7 S out. 10 C up. J D out (J C) up. Place
6 C on 7 (tail). K H out for fdn. 8 S up and to fdn. Q and J C
to fdn. J S and 8 C up. 10 C out, 5 H up. Place 9 D on 8
(heads), 10 H down, 6 C and 7 on 5 C. 2 C down and on 3.
10 D down and out to fdn. A D down. 9 H on 10 (tail). Q H
down and to fdn. K H down. 8 C on 7 C (tail). 4 D up. 9 D
and 8 out to fdn. 2 S up. Place 5 D on 4, 2 H up and to fdn.
J C up. 7 C on 8. 3 H exposed and out. 10 C up. Place J C on
10. 6 H up, place 6 H on 7. A C up and out for fdn. J D up.
2 C and 3 out. 5 C down. Place 5 H on 6. Place A S on K.
2 S on A. 4 C and 9 C up and out to fdns. 8 S and 5 S up.
5 C out, 2 D down and out to fdn. Second 2 D down and on
A. 8 C down. 7 C on 8 (from left-hand tail). 8 C and 7 C
(left-hand tail) out to fdn. 6 C out, ascending with 7 and 8 C.
7 D down and out. 6 S down.

Put 5 S on 6. 7 S up, place on 8. By rules 9 S goes into vacant
head-place and so out to fdn. Q C from packet 2 to vacant
place. Place 10 H on 9 H. 10 S up and out to fdn. K D to
head-place. J S (tail one) out. 10 S and 9 on J S (head 1).
K C down. Q, J, 10 on him. 6 H and 3 S up. 3 S on 2. 10 D
up. Place on J D. 6 H on 5. J H up from packet 2. J H on 10
(tail); 8 H (from packet 2) up.

Take J, 10, 9, 8 H out descending. 6 D up. Q H on K. A H up, 2 H and 3 H on him. 9 D down. 6, 5, 4 D out to fdn. A C up and 8 D. Place 9 D on 8 D. 3 C down from packet 1. 10, J D on 9. 3 D up and out. 9 H up, place on 10. 7 H up and out with 6 and 5 from tail. 7 D up. Transfer 3 D ascending to 4 D descending: then 2, A D (tails) out. Q D down from packet 1. Place on K. 4 H down and out with all descending Hearts. 9 C up and out. 4 H up and out. Q S up and out. 4 S up and on 3 S (head 8). Supply 5 H from packet 6 – out. 6 C from packet 1 down to tail 3. 4 D up. Transfer J, 10, 9, 8, 7 D to Q D (head 4); Q S and 4 C up. Take out ascending Clubs (10–K), 2 C supplied from packet (4). Place 5 and 6 S on 4. 3 D down and out. 6 D down, place on 7 D. 5 D down; place 4 D on. 8 H up from packet 4. All ascending Diamonds out. J H up. All ascending Hearts out. Transfer 7, 8, 9, 10, J S to head 8. All descending Spades out. Descending Clubs and Q, K S out.

HEAP PATIENCE

Problem.   Solution

PLACE J D (over K S) on 4, K H on 6, 9 H on 2, 2 D on 8, Q and K S on 5, A C on 7, 4 D on 10, 5 D on 10, 7 H on 13, 8 S on 1, 9 C on 1, 10 D on 2, 6 D on 10, 5 S on 11, 6 C on 11, 3 C on 9. 4 S on 9, 10 C on 3, 7 S on 11, A H on 6, J and Q S on 3. 8 S and 9 D on 13, 10 S and J D on 13, 5 and 6 S on 9, 2 and 3 S on 7, K C on 3, Q D on 4, 6 H and 7 D on 12, K D on 4, 8 D (over 7 D) on 12, 7 and 8 D on 10, 3 D (over 9 D) on 8, 9 H on 12, A C on 5. 10 H (over 7 C) on 12, 7 C on 9, 4 D on 8, 5 H (over Q H) on 8, J, Q and K H on 2, the two 8 C on 11 and 9, the two 9 S on them. *Turn down* No. 9. 9 D on 10, 10 H on 10, 2 H (over 6 C) and 3 H (over 2 C) on 6, 4 S (over 4 H) on 7, 4 H (over 7 H) on 6, 2 C (over 5 C) on 5, 3 C and 4 C on 5, A D on 4. *Turn down No. 10.*

10 S and 10 C on 1 and 11, 5 C (over 2 D) on 7, 5 H on 6, 2 and 3 D and 4 H on 4. *Turn down.* J C and Q C (over 7 C) on 1,

second Q C and K D on 13. *Turn down.* A S, 2 C, 3 S on 3. *Turn down.* J H and Q D on 12. *Turn down.* J C on 11. *Turn down.* K and A S on 1. *Turn down.* 5 C on 5. *Turn down.* 6 H on 6; 6 and 7 C on 7; 6 D, 7 and 8 H on 8; A and 2 H on 2. *Solution complete.*

KING ALBERT

PROBLEM I. SOLUTION

Q D on K C, J C on Q D, *vacant space,* 2 S in it. 6 S on 7 H, 10 D on J C, 2 S (from ninth col.) on 3 D, 7 S in vacant space. 9 S on 10 D, 8 H* on 9 S, 7 S on 8 H. 9 H in vacant space. J H on Q S, 10 C on J H, 9 H on 10 C. *Vacant space.* A S out first. 8 C on 9 H, 7 H and 6 S on 8 C via vacant space. 5 H on 6 S. A H out, 4 S on 5 H, 2 S and 2 H out. 3 D on 4 S. Still a vacant space. 5 C to vacant space. 6 D on 7 S. 5 C on 6 D. 4 D on 5 C. 3 C on 4 D. *Three vacant spaces.* Put J S in one, 10 H on J S. 9 C* on 10 H. 8 D on 9 C, J D in vacant space, 10 S on J D. 7 C on 8 D, 9 D on 10 S, 4 C on 5 D, A D out, Q C on K H. A C out. Here two vacant spaces. Transfer J D–9 D on to Q C. 8 S on 9 D, 7 D* on 8 S, 6 C* on 7 D, 5 D and 4 C on 6 C, K S in vacant space, 2 C and 2 D* out, 3 H and 3 S* out. 3 and 4 C; 3, 4, 5 D, 5 and 6 C, 4 and 5 S, 6 and 7 D, 7 C, 8 D out. 8 H and 7 S on 9 C. Transfer sequence K C–9 S to vacant column. 4 H out. Q H on K S. 5 and 6 H out; rest clear.

PROBLEM II. SOLUTION

9 D on 10 S, *A H out,* 8 C on 9 D, 7 H* on 8 C, 6 S on 7 H, K C in vacancy. Q D*, J C* on K C, 10 D on J C. *2 H out.* 9 C on 10 D, 8 D on 9 C. *A C and A D out: vacant space.* 10 C in vacancy. *2 and 3 C out.* 7 C on 8 D, 6 H on 7 C, *3 H out.* Q C on K H, 6 S in vacant space. 7 H on 8 S. 6 S on 7 H (col. 8). 5 D on 6 S. 8 C and 9 D on 10 C via vacant space. 10 S in vacant space. 2 S on 3 D. 8 H on 9 S, 4 S on 5 D,

* Cards from Reserve.

A S out.   2 S out.   J D* on Q C.   10 S on J D, 3 D on 4 S.   8 H
and 9 S on 10 H.   7 D on 8 C.   *2 D, 3, 4 out.*   5 C on 6 D.   Q S
in vacant space.   J H on Q S.   7 S on 8 H.   6 D and 5 C on 7 S.
K D in vacant space.   Q S and J H on him.   5 S on 6 H.   4 C,
5, 6 out.*   10 S on J H.   *Three vacancies.*   K H, Q C, J D into one.
9 H on 10 S.   *4 H,* 5 H, 3 S out.   Rest clear.*

LIMITED

Problem I.   Solution

Take A S.   Deal *2 S,* out on foundation, with 3 S.   J S on Q.
2 C on 3.   10 D on J.   *7 H* on 8, 4 S out.   K D, *6 C, 7 S, 10 H,
3 H* on W H.   6 S on 7.   4 H on 5 (col. 11), 10 C in vacant space.
A H out.   5 H on 6.   4 H (col. 7) in vacant space.   2 H, 3 (W H),
4 (the singleton), 5, 6, 7, 8 H out.   A S out.   2 S out.   K D in
vacant space.   A D out.   *5 C* on W H.   *J C* in vacant space,
10 C on it.   *A C* out, 2, 3 on it.   7 D in vacant space.   4 C out
with 5 from W H.   10 H from W H on J.   *5 D, 3 D, 2 C* on W H.
5 S out, take 6 and 7.   *10 S* on W H.   *3 S* out, take 4.   Q H (col.
12) in vacant space.   2 D out.   Still two vacant columns: close
up the columns and call the vacancies cols. 11 and 12.   *10 C,
2 D, 8 H, Q C* on W H.   *4 D* on 5.   8 D in vacant column.
7 D on him, then back in col. 10.   *7 C,* 6 D on W H.   *5 S, 6 S* out,
2 H, J D, 4 D, 3 H, K S on W H.   K H in vacant space.   Q H on
him.   K H (second one) on W H.   *Q D* on K.   *K S, Q S, 9 D,
9 C, K C* on W H.   *8 S* out.   *6 D* on W H.   *9 H* out with 10,
J, Q, K.   *3 D* out with 4, 5, 6 from W H.   7, 8, 9, 10, J, Q, K D,
9 S out.   *Now seven vacancies.*   Take from W H.   K C, 9 C, 9 D,
Q and K S (arrange in one space).   K H (over Q H) second
K S, leaving *two* vacancies.   *7 H, J S, Q D* on W H.   *8 C* on 9.
6 C out, *K C, 3 C, J C* on W H.   *10 S* out with J, Q, K.   *Q C* on
K.   *8 C* on W H.   *7 C* out with 8, 9, 10, J, Q, K.   *5 C* in vacant
space.   4 on him.   *A C* out.   *7 D* in vacancy.   *8 S* on 9.   *A D* out.

* Cards from Reserve.

10 H on J. *8 D* in vacant space. *7* on him. *6 H* in vacant space. *9 H* on W H. *A H* out. *9 C* on W H.

End of first deal.

Position.

Foundations:

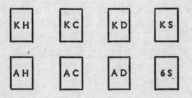

Lay-out:

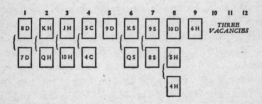

Waste-heap. Twenty-six cards:

9 C (top card before turning), 9 H, 8 C, J C, 3 C, K C, Q D, J S, 7 H, 3 H, 4 D, J D, 2 H, 6 D, 7 C, Q C, 8 H, 2 D, 10 C, 10 S, 2 C, 3 D, 5 D, 7 S, 6 C, K D.

Turning W H, the first four 'Grace Cards' will be *K D, 6 C, 7 S, 5 D.* 7 S out with 8, 9. *3 D* (grace card) to vacant space. *2 C* out, *10 S* out, *10 C.* Take 5 D to vacant space. *2 D* out with 3. *8 H.* Take 6 C to vacant space. *Q C.* Take 8 H to vacant space. *7 C* to vacant space, 6 C on it. *6 D* to vacant space, 5 D on him. *2 H* out. *J D* last vacant space. *4 D* out with 5, 6, 7, 8, 9. *3 H* out with 4, 5, 6. 10, J D out. *7 H* out with 8. *J S* out with Q, K. *Q D* out with K. *K C* in vacant space with Q C (grace card) on him. *3 C* out with 4, 5, 6, 7. *J C* in vacant space, with 10 on him. *8 C out. 9 H* out with rest of Hearts, *9 C* with rest of Clubs. *All out.*

Problem II. Solution

(Cards in italics dealt)

Play *2 S* on *3* S, *6 S* on WH. *3 S* on WH. *5 S* on 6, *8 S* on 9,
10 S on J, *K S, 5 D, 4 D, 6 D, K D* on WH. *A H* out. *5 H,
6 H, 7 C* on WH. *A C* out. *10 C* on J. *8, 9, 7 C* on WH. *J H*
on Q. *3 H, 10 H* on WH, *2 H* out, *Q D, 4 H, 2 H* on WH, *2 C*
out with *3*. *K H, 8, 9, 6 C* on WH. *4 D, 8, 3, 7, 10 D, 4 S* on
WH. *A C* out, *2 S, K C* on WH. *A S* out with *2, 3.* Both Aces
of D and A H out. 8 H (col. 7) in vacant col. (12). 6 D on 7,
4 C out, 8 H (col. 8) to vacant col. (7), 2 D out, 3 D out, 7 H on
8 (col. 7). *7 S, 8 S, J S* on WH. *5 D* in vacant column. *10 C*
on WH. *5 C* out with 6. *4 C, K C* on WH. *3 H* out. *6 H* on
WH. *A S* out. *5 S* on WH, *4 S* out with 5, 6 from lay-out.
4 H out. *7 S* out with 8, 9, 10, J, Q (col. 9). *2 D* out. *9 H, 10 H,
Q C* on WH. *K S* out. *8 D* on 9, *Q D* on K. *Q C* on WH.
7 H on 8 (col. 12). *2 C* out. *Q H, 9 S* on WH. *3 C* out. *K H*
on WH. Forty-five cards in WH at end of deal.

The board:

JD JD 5 H   9 H J C   5 C $\begin{cases}8 \\ 7\end{cases}$H 5 D $\begin{cases}K \\ Q\end{cases}$D J H   9 D $\begin{cases}8 \\ 7\end{cases}$H
    $\begin{cases}8 \\ 9\end{cases}$D $\begin{cases}10 D \\ J C \\ 10\end{cases}$ $\begin{cases}7 \\ 6\end{cases}$D   QS 10 S $\begin{cases}Q \\ J\end{cases}$H

Foundations:

A H, 4 H; 3 C, 6 C; 2 D, 3 D; A S, K S.

Reversing the WH:

First four *Grace cards:* 6 S, 3 S, K S, 5 D.

Fifth card *4 D* out with 5 from lay-out, 6, 7, 8, 9. 5 H out,
5 D into vacancy. G(race) C(ard) *6 D* into vacancy, put 5 D on it.
G C *K D* into vacancy. G C *5 H,* fifth card *6 H* out with 7, 8.
Put the G C K S to vacancy. Q S on him. G C *7 C* out. G C
8 C out. G C *9 C* out with 10, J C, 10 D out and J, Q and K.
9 H out. G C *7 C* in vacancy. G C *3 H* in vacancy. G C *10 H*
out with J, Q. *Q D* on K, *4 H* in vacancy, *3* on it. *2 H* out with
3, 4, 5 (from G C). *K H and 8 C.* K H out, 8 C in vacant space.

7 C on it. *9 C* in vacant space. *6 C* in vacancy, 5 C on it. *4 D*
vacant space. *8 D, 3 D* out with 4, 5, 6. *7 D* out with 8. *10 D*
on J. *4 S, 2 S* out with 3, 4, *K C* and *7 S*. 7 S in vacancy. 8 on
him. *J S, 10 C*. J S in vacancy. *10 S* on it. 10 C on J. 9 D, 10,
J, Q, K out. *4 C* out with 5, 6, 7, 8, 9, 10, J. *K C, 6 H*. 6 H out
with 7, 8. *5 S* out with 6, 7, 8. *9 H* out. *10 H* with J. *Q C* out
with K. *Q C* (the second) out with K; *Q H out*. *9 S* out and the
rest of Spades. *K H* out. *All out*.

MILTON

Problem. Solution

A C out, *5 H, 10 C, 7 S, 9 C* on WH, *K S* out – (*must not take
Ace*) – *6 S* out. *K D, 9 D* on WH. *3 D* out. *K H, A H, 9 S* on
WH. *3 H* out. *7 D, 8 D* on WH. *4 D* out. *A D, Q D* on WH,
5 D out, *2 C* out. *8 H, Q H, K C, A C* on WH. *7 C* out. *J H,
3 S* on WH. *Q C, J D, 9 H* on WH. *8 S* out. *4 H* out. *8 C* out.
7 H on WH. *2 S* on A. *J C* on WH. *6 H* on WH. *6 D* out.
3 C out with 4 C–8. 6 H from WH to vacant space. *10 S,
10 H, 10 D* on WH.

Reverse waste-heap (third deal):

  5 H out, 6 H on *10 C* in vacant space. *7 S* on 6. 8 S with
packet on 7 S. *9 C* out with 10. *K D, 9 D* to the two vacant
spaces. *K H, A H* to WH. *9 S, 7 D* out, *8 D* out, 9 out. A H
from WH to vacancy. 2 H plus packet to 6 below. *A D* in
vacancy. 2 D plus packet below. *Q D* in vacancy. *8 H* and
Q H on WH. *K C, A C, J H* on WH. *3 S* out. 4 S–9 below.
J H (WH) to vacancy. *Q C, J D, 9 H* on WH. *7 H* out, *J C*
out, *10 S* out. J, Q, K S out. 9 H (WH) to vacancy. *10 H* on 9.
10 D with J (WH), Q, K out. *Q C* (WH) out. *J H* (WH) on
10. *A C* (WH) in vacancy. 2 C with packet to Q below him.
K C (WH) on Q. Q H (WH) to vacancy. 8 H (WH) out with
rest of Hearts. *All out*.

MISS MILLIGAN

PROBLEM I.   SOLUTION

PLACE Q H on K C; 9 C on 10 D; 8 H on 9 C (col. 3); 8 S on
9 H. Then 4 and 5 H out to fdn. Transfer sequence 2 D–4 D
(col. 7) on 5 C (col. 8); sequence 5 S–7 S (col. 7) on 8 H (col. 3).
5 D and 6 C out. *Vacant col.* (7). Place K C and Q H therein.
Put J H on Q S (col. 2), 6 D out. J C on Q H. 10 D and 9 C
(col. 1) on J C. Transfer sequence 6 H to 2 D (col. 8) to 7 S
(col. 1). Transfer 9 H and 8 S (col. 4) to 10 S (col. 6). Then
7 D–5 D on 8 S. 7 D (col. 8) out.

DEAL: 10 S, 4 S, J S, 5 H, 7 C, 6 D, 8 H, Q C.

Put 8 H on 9 C, 7 C on 8 H, 6 D on 7 C, 4 S on 5 D, 10 S on
J H, J S on Q D, 4 S and 5 out. 6 H out. Transfer sequence
6 H–2 D (col. 1) on 7 S (col. 3). 6 D (col. 7) on 7 S (col. 1),
7 C out. 7 S and 6 D back on 8 H (col. 7). 4 H and 5 S (col. 1)
on 6 D (col. 7). 9 H on 10 S. J D and 10 C (col. 1) to Q C
(col. 8). *Vacant col.*

DEAL: K S, 2 C, 3 H, Q H, 6 S, A S, 2 S, 7 H.

A and 2 S out, 6 S, 2 C, 3 H, 7 H all out. Q D and J S in
hitherto vacant col. 1 on K S. 6 S–8 C (sequence col. 5) on 9 H
(col. 2). 10 D–8 D on J S. 4 H out. *Col. 5 vacant.*

DEAL: 8 S, 3 C, 9 D, K D, K C (in vacant col. 5), 4 S, A D, 4 C.

A D out for foundation. 3 and 4 C out. 9 D on 10 C (col. 8).
8 S on 9 D. 2 D and 3 S out. 8 D out. 7 H and 6 S (col. 2) on
8 S (col. 8). 8 C out. 4, 5, 6 S out. 8 S and 7 H (col. 8) to 9 H
(col. 2). 9 D out. 8 H–4 D (sequence col. 3) to 9 S (col. 1).
9 C out. 10 C out.

Sequence 9 S to 4 D (col. 1) to 10 H (col. 3). 10 and J D out.
10 D to 6 D (col. 7) on J S (col. 1). J, Q, K C out. J S to 6 D
(col. 1) to Q H (col. 7). Q and K D out. Q H (col. 4) on K S
(col. 1). REST CLEAR (as 5 H out, D 3, 4, 5, 6, etc.).

Problem II. Solution

Place 9 C–6 H on 10 H, J C on Q D. 10 H–6 H on J C. 10 C on J H. 3 D and 2 C on 4 S (col. 1). 3 H on 4 S (col. 4). 4 C out. 4 S and 3 H on 5 H. *5 D out.* 9 H to 3 H on 10 C. 2 D; *3 S*; 2 H; *3, 4, 5* J C; *4 S and 5*; 5 H and 6 (*last from col. 5*); *6 C, 7 H all out.* 7 D to 2 C (col. 1) on 8 S (col. 6). *8 C out, 6 D out.* 10 D, 9 S (col. 2) on J C. K D, Q S in vacant space. 8 D on 9 S, 5 S on 6 H (col. 7). 7 S (col. 8) on 8 D. Q S to 8 S (col. 3) on K H. K S to 9 S to vacant col. (2).

Deal last eight cards.

2 S, 6 S, 7 D, Q C, A C, K S, 3 S, 4 H.

A C; *2 S and 3*, *6 S*; *4 H out.* Do not take 7 D, but put on 8 S (col. 5); then on that 6 S to 4 C (from col. 9); then J D to 9 D on Q C. Q C to 9 D back on K D.

'Waive' K S at bottom of col. (6); and *all come out:* thus 2 C, 3, 4; 3 D, 4, 5; 4 S, 5, 6, 7; 7 D, 8, 9; 8 S, 9 (col. 1), 10 S, 10 D, J D out. Put 10 D, 9 S on J C. J S out, Q S out. J C to 9 S on Q H. K S (waived) in vacant col. 1. Q D to 6 H (col. 7) on him. As one sequence in Diamonds is built up the King goes and unblocks the 8 D.

PERSIAN

Problem I. Solution

A H, A C, 7 C (from col. 2), *A C out.* J D on Q C. *A D, 7 D, A H, 7 C out.* 8 S on 9 D, J H on Q S, 8 H on 9 S, *8 C out,* J S on Q H, Q D on K S, J C on Q D, Q C on K D, 10 S on J D; *7 H, A S out, 8 H out.* 8 S to vacant space, 9 D on 10 S, *7 S, 8, 9, A S, 8 C out.* J D on Q C. *9 H, 10, J out.* 10 D on J C. *Two vacant spaces.* Put 10 S, 9 D on J D (col. 6). Q C and J D in vacant col. (3), *7 H out.* 9 D and 10 S back on J D (col. 3). 8 S on 9 D, J S on Q D. *Q H out.* J S (col. 5) in vacant space. 8 S on 9 H, 9 D on 10 C. *10 S, J S (from col. 7, singleton), Q S out.* *8 D, 9, 10, J (col. 3) out.* 10 C on J D. 8 S in vacant place. 9 H on 10 C, 8 S on 9 H. *9 C out.* K D in vacant place

Q C on him (put for convenience in col. 3). *K H, 10 C, J C* (col. 2), *Q C, Q and K D out, K S* (col. 2), *K C* (col. 2) out. *Three vacancies.* 10 D on J S. 10 H on J C. *Four vacancies.*

Transfer K D to 8 S to one; K C to 10 D to another; K H to another. Put Q S and J H on him. 9 S on 10 D, 8 D on 9 S, 10 S on J H. K S in vacant space. *7 S and 8 S, 9 C, A D, 7 and 8 D out.* Q H on K S, 8 H, 9, 10 H out. J C on Q H.

9 D, 9 and 10 S, 10 C, 10 D and the rest. *All out.*

PROBLEM II. SOLUTION

9 and 10 H out. K C in vacant space. *8, 9, 10 C out.* Put J S on Q D (col. 1), Q D (col. 6) on K C, 10 D on J S, Q C on K H, 7 S on 8 D. *J and Q C out.* Q S on K H. *8 S out.* J D on Q S. *8 D and 9 out.* Do *not* take 10 D. Q S on K D. *10 D (col. 7), J and Q D out.* Do *not* take K C. Q H on K C (col. 8). *K C (col. 2) out. A S, 7 S out.* 9 S on 10 D. Do *not* take 9 S. 9 D on 10 S. J D on Q S. 9 D in vacant space. 10 S on J D. 9 D on 10 S. 8 D on 9 S. K H in vacant space (col. 2). *A D out. 7 D, 8, 9 out.* 10 S (col. 5) in vacant space. *8 S, 9, 10 S (from vacant space), 10 D, J S, Q S, K S, K D (col. 5) all out.* J S on Q H, J H, 9 S, 10, J S, J D, Q, K D, Q H (col. 4), J H, Q H, K H, J C, Q, K C, Q S, K S, K H. *All out.*

RUSSIAN

PROBLEM I. SOLUTION

4 H, J C out. A D on 2 D (!), *lower 4 C out,* 8 H on 9; higher 4 C on 5. *Lower 10 C out.* 8 D on 7, 10 C on 9. *9, 8, 7 D out.* 9 H on 8. *Vacant col. (7),* J S in vacant space. *Q S and J out descending.* 9 S on 8 S (col. 6), 8 S (col. 9) on 9 S, K D on A, 9 S on 8, *J H, 5 H out,* 3 C on 4, *5 C out. Two vacant cols. (7 and 9).*

10 D on J; 10 C in vacant col. 7; 9 C, 8 C on him; *6 H out,* 9 S in vacant col. 9; 8 S, 9, 8 and 7 S on him. *6 C, 4 S, 10 S out. Col. 10 vacant.* 7 S, 8, 9 into it, then out. 3 D on 4 (col. 12). *7 H and 5 S out.* 8 C, 9, 10 to vacant col. 10, J C on them.

6 D out. Two vacant cols. 4 and 7. Put K D in col. 7, A D in col. 4, then K on A. *2 D, 3 and 4 (col. 12). 6 S (descending) out.* 9 D on 10. *5 D and 4 out (descending).* Q S on K. 2 H on A H, Q D on K. 9, 10 D into vacant space, then J, 10, 9 D on Q D. Q H in vacant space, 2 C on 3, A C on 2, *5 S out descending.* 8 S in vacant col. (5), 9 S and 10 on it. *10 H out (descending), 8 H (ascending), 9, 8 H (descending), 9 H (ascending), 5 D (ascending) out.* J S on 10, Q and K on J. A C to vacant row (9), 2 C, 3, 4, 5 on him with 6 C from col. 12; 3 S on 2, 5 H on 4, 8 D on 9, 7 D on 8. *Row 12 vacant.* 4 S, 3, 2 out (descending). K H on Q H, K S in col. 12, Q S, J, 10, 9, 8 and 7 S on him. 7 C and 8 on 6. 5 H on 6 (col. 1), 4 H, 3, 2, A, K, Q on him. *Cols. now vacant: Nos. 5, 6, 7 and 11.* 9 C on 8 (col. 9), K C in vacant space. Q, J, 10, 9, 8 and 7 C on him, 6 S on 7. *3 D, 2 D, 7 H (descending), 6 D (ascending) out.* J and 10 H on Q H. *All out.*

Problem II.   Solution

Take to foundations J S, 10 H and 9, *but not 2 D,* on which place A D. 7 H on 6. 4 S on 5. J C on Q. 3 S on 4, 10 D on 9, 5 D on 4. J, Q C on 10, *2 to 6 S out.* 8 C on 9, 10 D on 9, 9 D on 10, 2 H on A, *4 H, 4 C out.* 9 D, 10, 9 back on 10 D. 6 H on 7. *Vacant col.* Q C, J, 10 in it. 8 D on 7. *J D out, 5 C out.* 9 C, 8, 9, on 10. *6 C out* (col. 8), 4 H in vacant space. 3 H on 2, 4 H on 3. Reverse Clubs into vacant space. Reverse 5 D and 4 into vacant place. 6 S on 5. *10 S out.* 2 C on 3, 5 H on 4. 6 S and 5 into vacant place. Clubs on K C. Reverse 4 D and 5 into vacant space. 6 H, 7, 6, 5, 4, 3, 2, A H into vacant space. 8 D, 7 on 9. J H on Q. 6 D on 5. A S on K. 7 D, 8, 9, 10, 9 on 6 D. *10 D and 9 out.* 2 C in vacant space. 3 C on 4, 2 C on 3. A D in vacant space. *2 D out.* J H on 10. K H, Q, J, 10 on A. *8 D out.* J D on 10 D, Q D on J. A D on 2. 2 C, 3, 4 in vacant space. 9 S on 8, 10 S on 9, J S on 10. A S in vacant space. K S, Q, J, 10, 9, 8 on him. 9 H on 10. K D on Q. A, 2 D on K. *7 C, 8, 9 out (ascending), 7 S, 8, 9 S (col. 5) out ascending. 9 S (descending),* 10 S, J, *Q, K (ascending).* 5 D on 4. 5 C, 6 on 4. *3 D out,* 5 D in vacant space. *4 D and 5 out (ascending).*

2 S and 3 on A. 7 C in vacant space, 8, 9, 10 C on him; *then 10 C–2 C out (descending).* 8 S, *10 C remaining ascending Clubs.* 8 H (col. 4), 7 *(descending),* 5 H *(ascending),* 7 D *(descending). A C and 6 D (descending) out.* 2 D and A on 3. K D–6 D in vacant space, then *out ascending.* A D, 2, 3, 4, 5 (last two by reversing in vacant space) in vacant space, *then out.* 8 H in vacant space. 5 S on 4; then *descending Spades out.* 9 H to A H on 8, 2 H to be reversed in vacancy. Ace to vacancy. K H to 7 on him. *All out.*

'S'

PROBLEM.   SOLUTION

(Cards in italic as dealt)

9 S WH (1), *9 C* WH (2), *3 C* on 2 H, *10 C* on 9 H, *3 D* WH (3), *K C* WH (2). *A C* on K H, *Q S* WH (1), *7 S* WH (1), *8 H* WH (2), *3 S* WH (1), *8 D* on 7 C, *2 C* on A H, 3 D from WH on 2 C, *4 D* on 3 C, *7 H* WH (2), *7 D* on 6 C, *8 S* on 7 D, *A H, 10 H* WH (2), *3 C* WH (3), *J D* on 10 C, *5 C* on 4 H, *10 C, 7 C* WH (3), *A S* on K D, *5 H* and *4 H* WH (2), *5 D* on 4 C, *Q D* on J C, *4 C* WH (3), *Q H* WH (4), *4 S* on 3 D, *A C* WH (3), *K S* on Q D, *2 H* on A S, *J S* on WH (1), *2 S* on A D, *3 H* on 2 S, *9 H* on 8 S, *Q C* on WH (3), *5 S* on 4 D, *6 D* on 5 C, *6 S* on 5 D, *J H* on WH (4), *6 C, 5 C* WH (3), *10 D* on 9 C. J S from WH on 10 D, *6 H* on 5 S, *9 D* on 8 C, *J C* WH (3), *10 S* on 9 D, J H from WH on 10 S, Q H from WH on J S. *2 D* on A C. 3 S (WH) on 2 D, 4 H (WH) on 3 S, 5 H (WH) on 4 S. 7 S (WH) on 6 D, Q S (WH) on J D. 9 S (WH) on 8 D, 10 H (WH) on 9 S, J C (WH) on 10 H, 5 C (WH) on 4 H, 6 C (WH) on 5 H, Q C (WH) on J H. A H (WH) on K S, 7 H (WH) on 6 S, 8 H (WH) on 7 S, K C (WH) on Q H, 9 C (WH) on 8 H, *2 C* on A H, *8 C* on 7 H. *K H* (last card in stock) on Q S. A C out from WH on K H. 4 C on 3 H, 7 C on 6 H, 10 C on 9 H, 3 C on 2 H. *All out.*

SENIOR WRANGLER

PROBLEM I. SOLUTION

PUT *4 S*, col. (1), exposing 9 C; *6 D* col. (2), exposing 8 H; *8 H* col. (3), exposing 9 C; *Q S* col. (5), exposing 8 H; *A D* col. (6), exposing 9 S; 9 C (col. 3) on 6 D, exposing 3 S, *3 S* on col. (7), exposing K H. *J C* on 3 S, exposing 7 D. Transfer Q S from col. (5) to 9 C (col. 2). *2 H* on Q S, exposing 3 C. *8 H* (packet 2) on A D. Transfer 2 H from col. (2) to 8 H (col. 6). *9 S* on 2 H, exposing 5 S; *5 S* on col. (8), exposing 4 H. Transfer *Q S* to 8 H (col. 3). Take *3 C* on Q S, 7 C on 3 S, exposing 5 D.

Take up and deal *first packet* – bad both face up or down, but on the whole prefer the latter, and start with K S (bottom card) in space of packet (1).

10 S col. (4), *Q H* col. (5), *6 D* col. (1), *8 S* col. (1). Transfer Q H to col. (2); *2 C* to col. (2), *5 D* to col. (2). *A C* to col. (8). *3 S* to col. (6) (exposing K S). *J S* col. (3), *2 D* col. (4), *7 D* col. (4), *6 S*, on col. (7). Transfer A C from col. (8) to col. (7). *9 C* on col. (7). *4 H* on col. (7).

Take up *Packet Two*, and deal face up.

10 C on col. (6). Transfer 4 H from col. (7) on to 10 C. *J H* on col. (6). *5 D* on col. (6). *A S* on col. (8).

Take up *Packet Three*, and deal face down.

Q H col. (5); *5 C* col. (5); *10 H* on col. (1); *Q C* col. (1). Transfer J S from (3) to (5). *4 C* on col. (5). Transfer *Q C* from col. (1) to 5 D (col. 6), 10 H (col. 1) to A S (col. 8), 8 S (col. 1) to 5 D (col. 2), 6 D (col. 1) to Q C (col. 6). *Take K S (packet 5) to crown this col.*

Take up *Packet Four*, and deal face up.

Q D col. (4); *4 D* on col. (4); *10 S* on 4 C. *3 D* on 10 S, *4 S* (packet 7) on 9 C. *Q S* on 4 S. *7 H* on Q, *2 S* on 7 H, *10 H* on 2 S. *6 S* on col. (1); *6 C* on 10 H (col. 8); *9 D* col. (5); *9 H* col. (4); *A C* on 9 H, *8 D* on col. (1), *10 D* on col. (1), J D on col. (2); *A S* on J D.

Take up *Packet Six* (Five being exhausted), and deal face down (starting with K D).

Q D on col. (1); *A H* col. (1). *4 C* col. (2), *3 H* col. (1), *2 C* col. (8), *7 D* col. (2), *J H* col. (8). *7 S* on J H. *5 C* on col. (7) Take K H (packet 3) to crown.

Transfer *3 H* from col. (1) to col. (8) on 7 S. *Q C* on col. (8,) *3 D* col. (1); *8 C* col. (8). *6 H* on col. (4). *10 C* on col. (2,) J S col. (3), *2 S* col. (3).

Transfer 6 H to 2 S (col. 4 to col. 3).

Transfer 10 C to 6 H (col. 2 to col. 3).

Take A D to col. (3), *2 D* to col. (5), *5 H, 7 H, 9 H* to col. (1). *5 H* to col. (3). *9 D* col. (3). *10 D* col. (2).

Take up *Packet Eight* (Seven being exhausted), and deal face up.

6 C on col. (4), *J D, 3 H, 8 S* on col. (4), *J C* col. (1), *8 C* col. (5), *4 H* col. (8), *A H* col. (5), *7 S* col. (5).

All remaining Kings now crown the cols. *QEF.*

Problem II.   Solution

Take *5 C* on col. (1), *7 H* on col. (1).

  Transfer 2 (col. 3) to 9 (col. 5).
  „   9 (col. 4) to 7 H (col. 1).
  „   J (col. 3) to (col. 1).
  „   7 (col. 3) to J (col. 8).
  „   3 (col. 3) to 7 (col. 8).

Take *8 C* on 2 (col. 5), *3 S* on Q.

Transfer 9 (col. 7) to 4 (col. 4).

Take *A D* on col. (4), *9 H* on col. (7), *3 S* on col. (3), *7 D* on col. (3), *A S* on 8 (col. 5), *4 S* on 9 (col. 7), *Q D* on 4 S.

Transfer J (col. 1) to 7 (col. 3). *2 D* on J, *6 H* on 2 D, *10 S* on 6 H, *A H* on 10 S (col. 3). *Q C* on 3 (col. 8), *7 H* on Q D (col. 7), *J S* on 9 (col. 1). *5 H* on A (col. 3), *K C* on J S (col. 1), *crowning it.*

6 C on A (col. 4), *2 C* on col. (7). *10 D* on 2 C. *5 S* on 10 D. *K D* (packet 7) on 5 S. *Crowning column.* *7 S* on A (col. 5), *9 D* on 5 H (col. 3), *J C* on 6 C (col. 4), *K H* on 9 D (col. 3), *3 H* on J C (col. 4). *8 C* on Q C (col. 8), *4 H* on 8 C (col. 8). *8 H* on 3. *Kings out.*

SPIDER

PROBLEM I.   SOLUTION

7 H on 8 (fdn).   6 D on 7.   Q H on J, 8 H on 9, *4 D out*, 4 C on
5.   K H on A.   Q and J H on him.   4 and 5 C on 3, 5 D on 6
(singleton).   6 and 7 D on him.   2 C on A, 4 D on 3, *9 D out*,
10 H on J, 2 D on A.   Q S on K.   8 H in vacant space.   9 on
10 H, 8 H on 9.   J S on Q.   *4 H* and 9 C out.   Upper 7 D in
vacant space, 6, 5, 4, 3, 2, A D on him.   *7 and 8 S out.   7 C out.*
5, 4, 3 C on 6 C.   9, 10, J, Q, K S ascending, 9 S descending.
3, 4, 5, 6 C on 2 C.   7 C on 6.   Q C on K.   J C on Q.   6 H on 5
(depot), other 6 *out* descending.   7 D on 6 (depot).   *5 D out.*
7 H on 8, 6 on 7.   *Ascending Hearts out to K.*   7 D in vacant
space (of which three available), *6 and 7 D out ascending.*   Q D
in vacant space, *8 D and 9 out ascending.   8 D out descending.*   5 S
in vacant space.   *10, J, Q out ascending D.*   A D in vacant space.
2 to 7 on him; then descending D out.   A H, 7 S in vacant
places.   10 C on J C.   4 H on 3.   *5 H, 4, 3 out.   8 C* and *9–K C out,*
2 and A H, 8 C, 7–A descending.   2 S on 3.   A S on 2.   Put A in
vacant space, 2 and 3 on him, then *Spades out and K D.*

Neater:

   7 H on *8 fdn*, 6 D on 7, Q H on J, 8 H on 9, *4 D out.*   4, 5 C
on 3 C, K H on A, Q, J H on him.   5 and 6 D (the one over 7 D)
out, 7 D on 6.   2 C on A, 4 D on 3, *9 D out.*   10 H on J, 2 D on
A, Q S on K.   8 H in vacant space.   9 H on 10, 8 H on 9, Q S
on J, K S in vacant space.   Q, J, 10, 9 S on him.   *7 D, 7 C, 4 H,*
9 C out.   8 S on 9, 7 D on 6, 4 and 3 D on 5.   *Ascending S out to*
K.   Q D in vacant space.   *Both 8 D out.*   3 to 5 D.   5 on 2 D.
Descending D out.   K C in vacant space.   2 H on 3.   *Descending*
Clubs out.   Q, J C on K.   *9, 8 S* (*descending*) *out.   6 H descending,*
5 H, 6, 7, 8–K H ascending.   A H in vacant space.   *7 S out,* 10 C
on J C.   2, 3, 4 H on A, *descending H out.*   A S in vacant space,
2, 3, 4 S on him.   *Descending Spades, ascending Clubs and Diamonds*
out.

Problem II. Solution

9 C on 8 (right hand), 6 H on 7, 8 C on 9, Q H on J, *J C out,*
7 C (over 5 C) on 8, 6 C on 7 C, RH, 7 C from LH on 6, *8 H
and J S out, 10 S out.* 4 C on 5, 2 D on A. 6 C on 7. A S on K,
2 S on A, 3 S on 2. *3, 4, 5, 6, 7 C out.* 6 and 7 C into vacant
space, *8 and 9 C out,* 8 C on 7. A C on K. 9 H on 8. K H on Q,
10 S on 9, 2 C on A, 9 C on 8, 5 H on 6. *10, 9, 8, 7, 6 C (descending), 3 H (ascending) out.* Two vacant spaces. 3 S in one, 2, A, K S
on it. *10 D out and 9* (over 6 D). *10 C and J C* out (ascending:
put J in vacant space first). 3 D on 2 D. 8 S on 7 S. *8 D out.*
9 H to vacant space, 8 H on it. *4 D out.* Q S on K S. *5 S out.*
5 H, 6 H into vacant space. 7 H on 8 (depot – *not out*), then
6 H and 5 back on 7. 3 D in vacant space, 2 and A on it.
7 D and 6 D out, 7 H *(descending).* A H on K. *6 S out.* 3 C on 2.
Two bottom left-hand spaces vacant. 10 S on vacant space, 9 and 8
on him. *7–10 S out ascending. Both 5 D, 9 S (descending).* 3, 2,
A, K C on 4 C, *6 D out (ascending),* 9 D on 10, 6 S on 5.

Ascending Spades out. A, K, Q, J H in vacant place, 3 H and
4 on 2. *5 C and 4 H out. 5 H to 9 H out ascending.* 4, 3, 2 H to
vacant space. *Q and K C out.* A, 2, 3 C to vacant space, then
descending Clubs out. J D on Q. *6 H out* (descending). K D in
vacant place. J D in vacant place. 9 D in vacant place. Q, J,
10, 9 D on K. *5 H and 4 D out.* A D in vacant place, 2, 3 D on
him. A S in vacant place, 2, 3 on him. *Descending Spades and
Diamonds out. Ascending Diamonds, ascending Hearts out.* 2 H, 3
and 4 on A. *Descending Hearts out.*

SQUARING THE CIRCLE

Problem. Solution*

(Cards in italics dealt)

2 D WH (1), *2 H* out on K, *A S* WH (2), *7 S* WH (3), *4 H*
WH (4), *J S* WH (4), *J C* WH (2), *8 D* WH (3), *6 S* WH (2),
10 D WH (4), *4 C* WH (2), *10 C* WH (3), *6 C* WH (4), *10 S*
WH (4), *7 D* WH (3), *9 C* WH (3), *8 S* WH (3), *4 H* WH (2),

* (·) = circle.

10 D WH (4), *7 C* WH (4). (*Nineteen cards in WH.*) *K D* out
on A, *2 D* from WH on K, *K S*, WH (1), *6 D, 5 D* WH (1),
10 H WH (3), *6* and *J H* WH (1), *4 S* WH (4), *5 S* WH (4).
[*Twenty-six cards in WH.*] *Q H* out, 3 H out from (·), J H out
from WH, 4 H from WH, 10 H from WH. *6 H* WH (2), *5 H*
out. 6 H from WH (2) to vacant place in (·), *J C* WH (2).
8 S WH (2), *6 S, 3 S* WH (2), *7 C, 10 C, 3 D* WH (3), *7 S* WH
(4). (*Thirty-one cards in WH.*) *2 S* out. Q S out from (·), 3 S
out from WH, J S out from (·), 4 S out from (·).

Fill up (·) with 6 S, 8 S, *3 D* from WH (2) and (3). *K H* WH
(1), *3 C* WH (1), *8 H* WH (4), *6* and *8 C* WH (4). *2 C* out.
10 S out, 5 S from (·), *Q C* out, 3 C, J C from WH. 4 C, 10 C
from WH. 5 C, 9 C from (·), 8 C from WH to (·), 6 C, 8, 7 out
from WH. Fill up (·) from WH with K H, 8 H, 7 S. *7 H* on
WH (3), *9 S* out on 5, 6 S from WH (2), 8 S from (·), 7 S from
(·), *2 S, Q S* WH (2), *4 C* WH (2). *Q D* out on 2. 3 D, J D
from (·). Take 5 S and 4 S to fill up (·) from WH (4). *7 C* out
from WH (4), 8 C from (·). 7 H and 8 S from WH (3) to (·),
also 10 D to (·). *9 D* WH (4), *Q H* on WH (4), *A C* WH (2).
9 H out. 6 H from WH. 8 H, 7 H from (·). Q H, 9 D from
WH to (·). *Q, K, J D* WH (1). *5 C* WH (1), *5 D* WH (1),
Q C WH (2), 4 D out. 10 D from (·), 5 D from WH. 9 D from
(·), 6 and 8 D from (·). 10 S from WH to (·), 6 C and 9 from
WH, 5 C from WH, 7 D from WH, 10 C from WH. Q C
and A C from WH to (·), 4 C out from WH. 8 D WH to (·),
7 S out from WH, 8 S from (·). *8 H* WH (4), *10 H* WH (1),
A H WH (3), *7 D* out, 8 D from (·). 6 S from (·). Q S and 2
from WH to (·), J C out from WH to fdn. *3 C* out, Q C from
(·), *5 H* WH (2), *3 S* to (·), *3 H* to (·), *K C* WH (3), *7 H* out, 8 H
from WH. *3 D* WH (3). 6 H from (·). *9 H* out. 5 H from WH.
10 H from WH, *4 D* WH (2). 10 D WH to (·), *9 D* WH (2),
J H WH (2), *2 C* WH (3), *9 S* out. 5 S, 10 S, 4 S out from (·),
J from WH. 3 S, Q S, 2 S out from (·). 4 H, J H from WH.
3 H, Q H from (·), *2 H* (dealt), K H out from (·). J, K, Q D
from WH to (·); 5 D, 6, 9 from WH to (·). 6 D, 9, 5, 10, 4
(last from WH) out. J D, 2 C, 3 D K C, J S from WH, 3 S,
2 S, Q S from (·). K S, Q D, *2 D* (dealt), K D and Aces *out*.

SUPERIOR DEMON

PROBLEM I.   SOLUTION

DEALING by threes, nothing doing till *6 C* goes to foundation, next *J S* on Q D, 10 D on J S. Do *not* fill blank column. *Reverse.* *4 D* out top of *3 C*, 9 C (exposed) on 10 D, 6 H (exposed) to fdn. *5 S* on top of *4 D*, K D (exposed) on Q S. *K S* on Q D, *7 C* out, *2 H* on *3 C*. J H and *10 C* on Q S. *A H* on K S. 7 H (exposed) out. *Reverse.* 9 H on 10 C, 8 C on 9 H. 2 S (exposed) top of A H. *3 D from stock on top of 2 S, 8 H from stock on 9 C. 4 C top of 3 D, 5 H from stock on top of 4 C.*

Take out 8 C, 8 H, 9 C, 9 H, 10 C, 10 H (exposed), J H. *Reverse.* Q H out. K *from stock.* 6 S (exposed) to fdn. J C out. 9 S (exposed) on 10 D. *A S from stock on 2 H.* K D, Q S on A S. *2 C (stock) to head* vacant column, *8 S for other* vacant column. *J D from stock* on Q S. *Reverse.* *10 S* on J D. *Reverse.* Q C out, *7 S, 8, 9,* 10 out. *3 S from stock* to vacant column. *2 D* (last card of reserve) on *3* S. *A C on 2 from stock. Reverse.* K C out. A C and 2. 7 D (exposed) out. *Reverse.*

4 H on *3* S, *4 S from stock* to vacant column. 8 D (stock), 9 D (exposed), 10, J out; J S, Q; Q D, K; K S, A; A H, 2; 3 H (last from stock). 2 S, 3 C out. 3 D on 4 S, 4 C and *5 C* out. A D (exposed) out. *Rest out.*

PROBLEM II.   SOLUTION

TAKE out *nothing*.

Pack 6 D on 7 S, 5 C on 6 D.

'Worry Back' 8 H on to 9 S.

Pack 7 C on 8 H.

Then 4 C, 5, 6, 7; 8 H, 9; 6 D, 7; 7 S, 8, 9; 8 D, 9, 10 out.

Transfer 9 C, 10 H to J C via vacant column.

Take Q S from stock to form new column.

J D out.   10 S out.   10 C on J H. *Rest out.*

TRICK AND PUZZLE PATIENCES

PATIENCE SQUARES*

I. THE SIXTEEN SQUARE

(Also called 'Court Puzzle')

Variation I:

TAKE the Aces, Kings, Queens and Knaves from a pack. Place them in four rows, each row of four cards, in such a way that the sequence King, Queen, Knave, Ace or Ace, Knave, Queen, King shall make up each side of your quadrilateral (horizontally and perpendicularly), and one of each denomination be found in the two middle rows.

Variation II:

Arrange the same cards so that there shall be an Ace, a King, a Queen and a Knave in each row (horizontal and perpendicular), *but not necessarily in the sequence given above*; on the other hand, one of each suit (a Spade, a Heart, a Diamond and a Club) is to appear in each row and each diagonal.

II. THE THIRTY-SIX SQUARE

AFTER removing the Aces, Kings, Queens and Knaves from the ordinary Whist pack, arrange the remaining thirty-six cards in a quadrilateral, so that:

(1) The pips of each row, both horizontal and perpendicular, amount to thirty-six:

(2) No two cards of the same value occur in any row or diagonal:

(3) Each row contains three *red* and three black cards:

* In these 'squares' the cards, though in reality oblong, are to be conventionally regarded as squares.

(4) One diagonal is composed entirely of black cards, the other of red.

(The '16' and the '36' square together, it will be noticed, include the complete pack of fifty-two cards.)

III.   THE SIXTY-FOUR SQUARE

WITH two Piquet Packs – i.e. Whist packs without sixes, fives, fours, three and twos – to arrange the sixty-four cards in a quadrilateral so that each row of eight cards, both perpendicular and horizontal, shall contain one card of each rank and two cards of each suit.

PIPS
(With complete Whist pack)

LET someone without your knowledge choose any card other than a picture card, and, placing it face upwards on the table, deal cards on it so as to complete an ascending sequence to the King. Thus, on a seven he would deal 8, 9, 10, J, Q, K. (Suit is of no importance.)

He then turns the packet over so that the chosen card comes to the top face downwards.

The process is repeated, a further thirteen cards – any he chooses – are to be separated from stock and the rest of the pack is handed over to the performer.

The performer is to tell the aggregate number of 'pips' of the chosen cards which lie face down on the top of the two turned packets.

All he has to do is to count the number of cards handed to him and subtract (mentally) eleven; the remainder will equal the number of pips.

Variation:

Three chosen cards can be similarly treated, only here the performer *adds* three to the remainder handed him. Thus, if 7, 8,

9 are chosen, twenty-one cards would be handed over. The total number of pips on the chosen cards is 24 (21+3).

If three Aces were chosen, no cards would be handed over. (13+13+13+13=52.) Ans. 0+3=3. (Cp. 'The Mysterious Deal'.)

THE MYSTERIOUS DEAL

(With one Whist pack)

THIS requires two persons – one to deal, the second to attempt to 'mystify' the company. Suppose you are the performer; ask someone to shuffle and deal the pack (ostentatiously turning your back the while!) in the following manner:

The dealer turns up any card and deals on it any number of cards up to twelve – that is, one card for each number counted. Thus, on a seven, five cards will be counted; on a nine, three; on an Ace, eleven. Court cards count ten, and have, therefore, two cards dealt on them. The packets should be dealt face downwards, with the selected cards at the bottom.

When twelve is reached the dealer should turn up the packet, so that the card from which the counting started comes uppermost. *Of course, he does not count aloud, or tell the performer what the cards are.*

When not enough cards are left to complete a packet according to the count, the dealer hands the cards over (if any) to the performer.

The latter, without looking, and only asking how many packets have been dealt, has to tell what the total number of pips on the top cards of the packets comes to. (Court cards counting ten each.)

He does it like this:

He counts the number of cards handed to him – the ones left over, that is – and asks the number of packets.

Whatever the number of packets be, he subtracts four – multiplies the result by thirteen, and adds the number of cards left over.

The result is the number of pips on the top cards of the packets.

Example:

Suppose first card is a 9; 3 cards are dealt on it.

	,,	second	,,	10;	2	,,	,,
	,,	third	,,	2;	10	,,	,,
	,,	fourth	,,	Q;	2	,,	,,
	,,	fifth	,,	Q;	2	,,	,,
	,,	sixth	,,	A;	11	,,	,,
	,,	seventh	,,	10;	2	,,	,,
	,,	eighth	,,	4;	8	,,	,,

The next card is a seven, say; and as (including it) there are only four cards undealt, the packet cannot be completed, and the four are handed to the performer.

On learning there are eight packets, he subtracts 4, multiplies by 13=52, adds 4 for remainder cards handed him; result 56 – which will be found to be the sum of the pips of the top cards.

SEQUENCES

THE ALTERNATE SEQUENCE

(To make a sequence of thirteen cards without regard to suit.)

ARRANGE the cards in a certain order given below, and, holding them face-downward, move the top card to the bottom. Before turning up second card, say 'Ace'.

Again move top card to bottom, and announce 'Two'; and so on, moving top card to bottom till the complete sequence appears, the last card (by your arrangement) being a King.

Arrange thus:

Seven; Ace; Queen; Two; Eight; Three; Knave; Four; Nine; Five; King; Six; Ten.

(Hold downward with the seven on top.)

THE OHIO CUT

PLAYED like the Alternate Sequence, but with the entire pack of fifty-two cards. The cards are to come out in Suits and Sequences, when moved and turned alternately.

Arrange thus in rows from left to right:

7 S	A H	A C	2 H	A S	3 H	2 C	4 H	Q S	5 H
3 C	6 H	2 S	7 H	4 C	8 H	8 S	9 H	5 C	10 H
3 S	J H	6 C	Q H	J S	K H	7 C	A D	4 S	2 D
8 C	3 D	9 S	4 D	9 C	5 D	5 S	6 D	10 C	7 D
K S	8 D	J C	9 D	6 S	10 D	Q C	J D	10 S	Q D
K C	K D	(Last card.)						

(Hold downwards with 7 S at the top; and move and turn as in the 'Alternate Sequence'. Arranged thus, the suits will come out in the order, Hearts, Diamonds, Clubs, Spades in ascending sequences from their respective Aces.

Of course, by altering the arrangement, e.g. putting Hearts for Spades, etc., any desired order of the suits can be obtained.)

THE SPELLING SEQUENCE

(To make a sequence of thirteen cards without regard to suit)

ARRANGE the cards in a certain order given below, and, holding them face downward, spell out the name of each card, and for each letter move one card from the top to the bottom.

Thus, 'A' – move one card, 'C' – move another, 'E' – move a third; and turn up next card – and so on.

Arrange thus:

Three; Eight; Seven; Ace; King; Six; Four; Two; Queen; Knave; Ten; Nine; Five.

(Hold downwards with the three at the top.)

THE FRENCH SPELLING SEQUENCE

PERFORMED just like the last; but arrange thus:

Trois; Dame; As; Cinq; Sept; Roi; Valet; Deux; Six; Quatre; Dix; Neuf; Huit.

(Hold downwards with the trois at the top.)

THE PIQUET POINT

(To make from a Piquet Pack two Sequences of eight cards each, each Sequence in suit)

PLACE the sixteen cards in a horizontal row.

Move any card over two cards, either to right or left, and place upon the third card.

Repeat eight times.

NB – (1) Only a card by itself can be moved.

(2) Two cards are to be jumped each time.

(3) That when a card has been placed on top of another, that packet counts as two cards.

(4) No packet is to have more than two cards.

The result will show two complete Piquet suits (seven to Ace) in sequence (one under the other).

Arrange thus:

1	2	3	4	5	6	7	8
K H	A S	K S	J H	Q S	A H	J S	Q H

9	10	11	12	13	14	15	16
9 H	10 S	7 H	9 S	10 H	8 S	7 S	8 H

Move No. 4 on 7; 6 on 2; 8 on 5; 1 on 3; 13 on 10; 11 on 15; 9 on 12; 16 on 14.

(Under the Heart sequence will appear one in Spades.)

(Cp. 'Ten to Five Puzzle'.)

TEN TO FIVE PUZZLE

LAY out the first ten cards (Ace to 10) of any suit in a row. The puzzle lies in placing them in such order that when you reduce them to doublets (packets of two) the top cards shall show a sequence of one to five; whilst, to bring them to doublets, each card, by the conditions of the puzzle, must jump over two others when moved, either two single cards or one doublet. The cards can be moved in either direction.

Solution:

Arrange thus:

(1) 2; 8; 4; 9; A; 10; 5; 7; 3; 6.

Place 5 on 6; A on 8; 4 on 7; 3 on 10; 2 on 9; the two last moving over doublets already formed.

Or,

(2) 2; 6; 4; 7; A; 8; 5; 9; 3; 10.

Place 5 on 10; A on 6; 4 on 9; 3 on 8; 2 on 7: the two last moving over doublets.

(Reprinted from *Games of Patience for a Single Pack.*)

SOLUTIONS TO THE SQUARES

THE SIXTEEN SQUARE.   SOLUTION

Variation I:

IMAGINE the two diagonals of your quadrilateral.

Put the Kings along one, the Aces along the other.

Two opposite corners will hold Aces; the other two Kings.

Next to the Kings must be Queens; next to the Aces, Knaves.

Thus:

THE SIXTEEN SQUARE.   SOLUTION – *continued*.

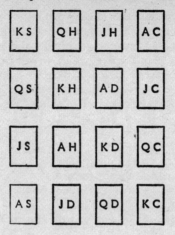

K S	Q H	J H	A C
Q S	K H	A D	J C
J S	A H	K D	Q C
A S	J D	Q D	K C

Variation II:

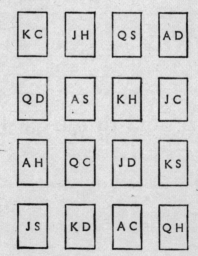

K C	J H	Q S	A D
Q D	A S	K H	J C
A H	Q C	J D	K S
J S	K D	A C	Q H

THE THIRTY-SIX SQUARE.   SOLUTION

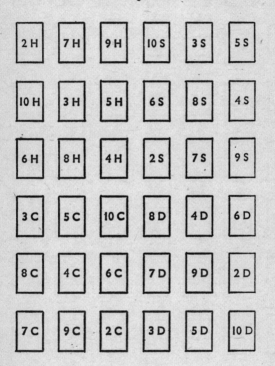

2 H	7 H	9 H	10 S	3 S	5 S
10 H	3 H	5 H	6 S	8 S	4 S
6 H	8 H	4 H	2 S	7 S	9 S
3 C	5 C	10 C	8 D	4 D	6 D
8 C	4 C	6 C	7 D	9 D	2 D
7 C	9 C	2 C	3 D	5 D	10 D

The Sixty-four Square. Solution

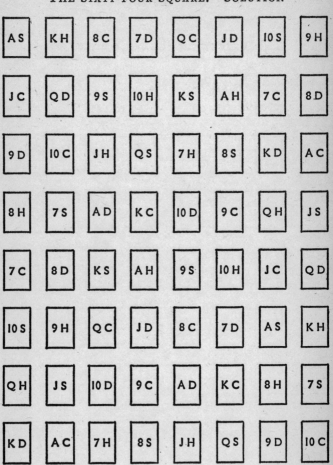

A S	K H	8 C	7 D	Q C	J D	10 S	9 H
J C	Q D	9 S	10 H	K S	A H	7 C	8 D
9 D	10 C	J H	Q S	7 H	8 S	K D	A C
8 H	7 S	A D	K C	10 D	9 C	Q H	J S
7 C	8 D	K S	A H	9 S	10 H	J C	Q D
10 S	9 H	Q C	J D	8 C	7 D	A S	K H
Q H	J S	10 D	9 C	A D	K C	8 H	7 S
K D	A C	7 H	8 S	J H	Q S	9 D	10 C

If you have enjoyed this Pan book,
you may like to choose your next book from
the titles listed on the following pages

How to Play a Good Game of Bridge 35p
Terence Reese and Albert Dormer

'This is the book for anyone who wants to make the transition from a pusher of pasteboard to a capable and intelligent player'
Sunday Times

'It will teach you the experts' approach'
Yorkshire Post

'A down-to-earth guide which will improve your game and help you to enjoy it more'
Financial Times

'Of high quality ... Particularly recommended for rubber bridge players. It simplifies the technical intricacies of both bidding and play and should convert most losing players into winners'
Sunday Telegraph

The Pan Book of Chess 40p
Gerald Abrahams

Starting – for the benefit of the complete tyro – with the basic moves and rules of chess, the author goes on to describe the subtle features of the game. The book initiates the beginner into methods of exploiting the 'fork', the 'pin', etc, demonstrates tactics and strategy, shows how battles are won – or lost – and examines and analyses openings and endgames.

Throughout, the author illustrates his lessons with examples from actual play, including many brilliant games by the masters.

'Offers much value for little money . . . The key chapter, nearly 100 pages long, contains much common sense on tactics, strategy and positional judgement, as well as copious examples from master practice, shrewdly selected for lapses no less than sparks of genius'
New Statesman

'Will be greatly enjoyed by anyone who likes to see the play of a highly intelligent and well-stocked mind over the chess scene'
Sunday Times

A Pan Original

Pan Craft Books

A useful new series of profusely illustrated (often in colour) and large-format books for the Age of Leisure.

Amongst this fast-growing series you will find:

Macramé 95p
Mary Walker Phillips

Macramé has been defined as the interknotting of yarns. It is, however, much more than that. The real wonder of Macramé is that anything as simple can produce such a variety of beautiful things and create such fun in making them – among the numerous projects the author has designed exclusively for the book are belts, sashes, hanging plant-holders, cushion covers, wall hangings, rugs, necklaces and bracelets.

Weaving 95p
Nell Znamierowski

Handweaving is an intriguing craft to most people but attempted by relatively few, probably because it seems more complex than it really is. Weaving can be defined simply as the interlacing of threads at right angles to form a web or fabric. And it is surprising the amount of excitement and satisfaction that can be had from the actual process of creating a fabric. This attractive book has been written both for the new weaver who has access to a floor or table loom and for the potential weaver who has not yet decided whether to invest in one. And for those who feel they can't afford to, there is advice on how to construct their own simple frame loom.

Pan Craft Books

Candlemaking 75p
Mary Carey

Making candles is a craft as old as man's rebellion against the tyranny of the night. From time-keeping to the act of worship, candles have always held a mystic charm of their own.

Now they have a whole new appeal for the thousands of people who derive interest and enjoyment from creating candles – in every conceivable colour and design – from simple moulds to unusual and inventive containers.

Many more titles available and in preparation.

You can buy these and other Pan books from booksellers and newsagents; or direct from the following address:

Pan Books Cavaye Place London SW10 9PG
Please send purchase price plus 10p postage

While every effort is made to keep prices low, it is sometimes necessary to increase prices at short notice. Pan Books reserve the right to show on covers new retail prices which may differ from those advertised in the text or elsewhere